Kathy Bu

SHLEP:

Finding Healing on Horseback in the Lower 48

a memoir
by
Kathy Burns

Author's note

SHLEP is a memoir and is factual to the best of my abilities and memory. Some names have been changed to protect those persons' privacy. A couple of personal insights and resolutions occurred later, but for the purposes of this book, I compressed the timeline.

Table of Contents

Chapter One

If at any point in my younger days you had told me I would end up living alone in a horse trailer, traveling around the country with my horses, dog and cat, trying to find myself, I would have told you that you were crazy. That just wasn't me. I'd been many things in my 59 years—a hippie, an artist, a marathoner, a New York City business woman, a suburban stay-at-home mom and an avid trail rider—but solo adventurer was not one of them.

Nevertheless, in September of 2013, I found myself preparing to do just that. My trip wasn't going to be about the thrill of an adventure; it was more about me running away from the mess my life, believing it was the only option I had left. I called my journey SHLEP, a Soul-searching, Home-seeking, Liberating, Equestrian Party. I figured it would take a year to complete, a week camping in the wilderness of each of the lower 48 states.

I had recently started hauling my horses with a small two-horse trailer that I pulled with a BMW X-5, a definite beginner's rig. Setting outrageous, unattainable goals can be a subconscious way of setting yourself up for failure, thus confirming your core belief that you indeed are a loser. But I wasn't self-aware enough at the time to have considered any of this. I was a basket case by then.

Nine years earlier, I'd bought my first horse, Dreamy, and learned to ride. She was a perfect first horse and never tried to hurt me. Dreamy was a thousand pounds of muscle, yet she let little old me mount her and direct her feet. When I got off balance, she'd shift her weight to get under me. When I said whoa, she stopped on a dime. She never bucked or reared with me in the saddle. She never spooked or ran off with me. As I got better at communicating with her, she began sharing her massive power with me. I found this transference of power physically exhilarating and psychologically healing. My husband, Bob, refused to support my new "hobby." He'd actually hadn't supported any of my hobbies and complained about them regularly. Fortunately, I had saved a nice nest egg before I'd retired to stay home with my three children. Horses quickly became my passion. As my marriage slowly rotted, riding became my life-line. When I was in the saddle, I was confident, brave and strong. The rest of the time I was pretty miserable. After a confrontation with Bob, I could be found in the backyard corral, crying into Dreamy's thick black mane. By 2012 my nest egg was almost gone and my Dad was paying for my horses' hay.

I'd joined our local trail council that summer and met Caroline at my first board meeting. She was in her 40's with bright, turquoise colored eyes and long, dirty-blonde hair. She sat at the long wood table next to me in my riding club's historic clubhouse. She wore a western style snap shirt, jeans and cowboy boots with super pointy toes. I noticed a slight tremor in her hands as she took notes. After the business part of the meeting was over, I invited Caroline to go riding with me. She said she had MS and hadn't ridden in years because of it. She'd never married and had to move in with her parents when she'd gotten sick. Her story touched me; a horse person needed to be around horses always, especially when that person wasn't well. I knew this was true for me and I couldn't stop thinking about how I could get her back in the saddle all week. By now I had two horses and I thought that trail riding on Dreamy would be safe for her, so I showed up at her house with Wildflower and Dreamy in my trailer and told Caroline to put on her boots. She was surprised and ecstatic. We rode a few times a week when it wasn't too hot; otherwise her MS symptoms would flare up. Caroline fell in love with Dreamy, which is what everyone does when they are around her.

In August, my Dad lent me ten thousand dollars for an attorney's retainer and I filed for divorce. Brian was the second attorney I'd consulted; the first one was back in Illinois over twelve years earlier. I don't know why I waited so long to go through with it; my mind was all mixed up.

In September, Caroline and I hauled to Malibu and Los Amigos with my mares. I felt so liberated; I was officially separated and could go on a trip with a girlfriend again. Even if I did have to return home when it was over, it was still so wonderful to have a good time for a little while. We slept in a wood floored teepee in the Malibu hills. We rode on a windy ridge overlooking the curving coastline of cliffs and sandy beaches with surfers dotting the waves. We then visited the resident trainer at an equestrian ranch with grass pastures, a rarity in parched southern California. They had a huge spread of rolling hills to ride through and round barns where all the stalls opened to a circular inner area and individual dirt paddocks to the outside.

While there, I got an email from Brian, my divorce attorney. The attachment was an "interrogatory," a list of some thirty-five questions in legal mumbo jumbo from Bob's attorney about my declared date of separation. I wondered what Bob was driving at; wasn't it automatically the day I signed the paper to file for divorce?

Caroline and I were in bunk beds in the trainer's guest room. I was jotting down my answers and trying not to cry. Reading the questions made me feel like I was talking directly to Bob, which usually tied my stomach up in knots. The questions were focused on the details of where and when and whom I had told that I was going to get a divorce. I racked my scrambled memory; I hadn't used that word to anyone. Had I used the D word to my therapist or doctor?

Some of the questions were so rambling I couldn't figure out what he was even asking. I wondered if something really was wrong with my mind that I couldn't figure them out. I heard Bob's voice in my head, "What's the matter with you?!!" Anxiety hit my stomach and twisted it; I froze. I stared at my notes, my handwriting looked like it was written by someone with Parkinson's Disease. *I'm not gonna survive this divorce; he's going to crush me like a bug!*

I took a calming breath and said, "I swear Caroline, I just want to run away from my life. I wanna load up my horses and leave California forever. I want to just head out and ride in every state until I find one I can afford to live in."

That got her attention. She put her phone down and with widened eyes said, "I've always dreamed of doing something like that!"

"Do you want to come with me?" I doubted she would, who in their right mind would want to share a trip of that magnitude with someone in the state that I was in?

"Really? You'd want me to come along?"

I wasn't expecting that; it sounded hopeful. I said, "Yes."

"I could do the cooking; I know you don't enjoy that much."

We both laughed, and I felt good for a second. She paused and asked, "Where would we sleep?"

That sounded like a yes and I wasn't going to miss my opportunity, "I'll have to get a bigger trailer, I guess, one with a living quarters."

I wondered how much they cost, I wondered if it would be cheaper than renting a place in La Canada, I wondered if I took the money out of my IRA before I was 59-1/2 how much the IRS penalty would be. I remembered Brian saying that all our assets were supposed to be frozen during the divorce procedure and wondered if that was really enforced. Maybe Dad would lend it to me until the divorce was over.

When I got back to Pasadena, I went to see Dr. Lydia Glass, my therapist for the last God-awful year. She was the fifth doctor in the last twenty-three years that had urged me to leave Bob, but she was the one I finally believed. Or maybe I had fantasized leaping from the third floor balcony a few times too many. Lydia told me that I was experiencing PTSD symptoms, and that I'd been emotionally abused. I'd done some horse therapy work with PTSD soldiers so I knew this was a diagnosis I shouldn't ignore. I wasn't so sure about the abused part. Even though I often felt like I'd been beaten up, Bob had never hit me. So how is that abuse?

I told Lydia what a great time I'd had up until I got that email from Brian and mentioned my fantasy trip idea, thinking that it sounded crazy as I said the words out loud.

Lydia's bare feet were curled up under her the way she always sat, in her armchair across from me. She perked up at my words, brushed back her long blonde curls and leaned in; her beautiful blue eyes focused hard on me. "I think you should do it!"

I paused; therapists usually make you figure things out for yourself, except for the one that told me Bob was going to kill me. Lydia was different; first of all, she was the first woman therapist I'd ever seen. She was so compassionate and she'd given me concrete advice on how to handle myself with Bob. She'd taught me coping skills for my anxiety that actually calmed me down.

I asked, "Don't you think it would be irresponsible and self-centered? I mean my kids are here; wouldn't I be *abandoning* them?"

Saying the word *abandoned* stabbed my gut. Junkies abandon their kids. I'd postponed cancer surgery to bear children and my primary mothering goal was to make them feel loved and cherished, the polar opposite of how I'd been mothered. But I think it backfired; they'd all turned out spoiled and had never held a job. Emily was in her senior year of high school and was looking at private colleges already; the boys, Brad and Teddy were both in college by the skin of their teeth. Teddy had OCD and type 1 Diabetes. None of them got along with their father either. I was sure that they still needed me around.

Lydia said, "No, I think it would be therapeutic. You

can't help your children until you are feeling better." She continued to hold eye contact. She was serious.

I'd been such a mess for years, crying most every day, cringing whenever I had to interact with Bob, I wasn't being the mother that I'd wanted to be. Not the one they deserved or needed. But even knowing that, I still felt intense guilt. It was a lose-lose situation.

But Lydia's endorsement was empowering. It was like she had opened a gate for me to pass through, the gateway to my new life. I craved emotional healing so badly and I thought maybe this could be a psychotherapy shortcut. I started to get excited. Maybe, I wasn't ruined for good. I had no idea how to actually facilitate this kind of a journey, but a seed was planted and from it sprung hope, something I hadn't felt in a very long time.

In November, I went to our support court date. That's what they called alimony now. Bob, his frumpy female attorney, my smartly dressed macho attorney, Brian, and I sat at a long table in front of the judge. The judge picked up our folder, which looked awfully fat for all that hadn't happened yet and said to no one in particular, "Who wrote Contentious on this?" No one answered. I wasn't sure what was going on, I'd never actually been in a court room before and asked Brian, "What's he talking about? Why is our file so fat?"

Brian told me to be quiet. Then the judge told us to go downstairs to Mediation. Panic seeped into my body. Wait, I thought a judge would decide all this stuff. I whispered to Brian, "Mediation? No one can negotiate with him! And I absolutely can't sit next to him!"

Brian said I could stay in a private meeting room while he went back and forth to meet Bob and his attorney with a Mediator.

Not having to face Bob for this process was a relief, but as I waited in the cubicle, I got depressed. I'd somehow been reduced to a wet washrag. I used to handle seven-figure dollar negotiations in NYC when I was in sales. Where had that part of me gone? Would I ever have it back? Why was I trusting this guy that I barely knew with such an important negotiation?

An hour later, Brian came back to the cubicle and said, "Bob has a copy of your prenup."

"He has it?! He must have taken it from my files. I'm not surprised. But, it has a twenty-year sunset clause anyway, I told you that, we've been married for twenty-three."

"He maintains that you were separated six years ago and all the assets are his."

Adrenaline shot into my bloodstream; my heart started racing. "That's bullshit! Why on earth would I have continued living with the asshole if we were separated?!"

Brian kept talking but I didn't hear him. My mind was wildly racing. Was I so mixed up that we were separated and I hadn't realized it? Did separate bedrooms count as being separated? When did he start sleeping in the guest room? Would anyone believe him? Oh my God, he's got so much more experience in legal battles than I do. I endured all these years of hell for nothing? I felt sick to my stomach; the floor dropped out from under me.

Sometime later, Brian stormed back into my cubicle punching at the air, "He's goin' down!"

Brian's bravado didn't impress me; he had no idea what he was up against. I was going down.

I said, ""I warned you."

"Oh, I've dealt with jerks like him before. Don't worry."

I didn't respond. Bob called 'The Art of War' his Bible; he'd been sued countless times and rarely lost as far as I knew. Bob would often ramble on about the never-ending battles that he seemed to thrive on; he probably just wore out his opponents, making them utterly crazy and eager to settle or drop it, just to get it over with.

Brian left and came back again, and said, "He refuses to move out of your house, suggesting instead that you both stay in the house until this is settled."

I was not prepared for this. Was he crazy? No, he knew I wouldn't agree to that. I blurted out, "I'd rather die!"

"He can't be forced out."

I wanted to scream, WHY NOT? HE ABUSED ME! But I heard different words come out of my mouth, "Then I'll move out." My whole body caved in on itself and my mind raced, What did I just say? I'll *abandon* my children? I'll leave them with *him*? I'm a bad mom! What's the matter with me? Oh, my God those were all Bob's words!

Brian left and came back again. We'd been there all day. My world was crashing in on me. We all filed back into the courtroom. Bill shot me a menacing look, I held my hands so they'd stop shaking. The judge asked him some questions, but I barely heard or understood anything. Then he said something about how Bob didn't have any of his last three year's tax returns or paystubs, so my support would be based on an income $120,000, since that's what he swore that he made.

I blurted out, "Our mortgage payment's $10,000 a month; that's an outright lie!"

Brian elbowed me, "SHHH!" Bob lunged down the table toward me and shouted, "What's the matter with you?!"

I froze. He'd never done this in front of anyone before. I was in a courtroom, there was a judge, an officer with a gun in his holster. This was a safe place. Did they see the hostility? Why was I so afraid?

The judge pounded his gavel and ordered *both* of us to be quiet. He then ordered a forensic accountant to analyze Bob's companies' cash availability and told Bob to produce a list of things that were long overdue. I whispered, "Good luck with that," and got elbowed again. I mumbled, "It's all probably in Switzerland by now anyway."

Another court date was scheduled and we were dismissed. I felt comatose.

Brian rode down the old escalators of LA Superior

Court with me. He was shorter than me and tan with white receding hair, I noticed his beautifully tailored suit. We rode the four flights in silence.

I was on my way to being legally free of my tormentor and that should have felt good, but my monthly support wasn't fair; none of it seemed fair. I had to move out and live on less than half of what I'd used for our household budget which hadn't included the mortgage, utilities, cars and cell phones, all the bills that Bob "took care of separately," which I had never understood and wasn't allowed to question. There was no way I could get a place big enough for my kids to stay with me.

Wait, what about the $30,000 balance on my Visa card? What about Emily's Prius lease that was in my name? What about three kids in private colleges, their tuition and housing bills that I'd been paying for out of my savings? How come all that hadn't been brought up?

I was relieved that my horses could stay at the house for free until it sold. But what then? Monthly board at my club was over $650 a month per horse! *I can't* get rid of them; they're my life line!

What if Bob convinced the judge of his cockeyed story, and I got nothing? Or worse, I had to give up half of my IRA, which Brian had warned me was a possibility. And I was too old and obviously messed up; who would hire me now?

I'd known that I might get nothing; Bob had threatened it often enough. I'd known that at the very least my lifestyle was going to drop significantly, but I'd signed the document in Brian's office anyway, rationalizing that my sanity was more important than money. But now faced with the reality of being alone and broke, I started to panic. What the fuck was I going to do?

Brian told me I had to pay taxes on my support and it would be reduced next year when Emily turned eighteen; we had joint custody of her until then. I tried to do the math in my head, but struggled with the numbers. Dad's rule of thumb was that housing should be less than 25% of your net income. Surely there'd be nothing in La Canada for $1,000 a month and I doubted there was a two-bedroom within 50 miles of there for that! And Teddy's and Emily's tuition was running what—$20,000 per kid per semester? I didn't just have to move out of the "family home" and out of town; I'd have to move out of California! I'd never see my kids! The boys might have to drop out of college! And do what, work for Bob?!

We arrived outside and on the steps of the courthouse I stopped and faced Brian, "What am I supposed to do?"

He said, "I suggest you just get on with your life. Where are you parked?"

Huh? Oh, you put him down, didn't you! My stomach was still clenched up in a knot from Bob yelling at me and my whole body was shaking. I felt broken, like a busted up doll that had once been treasured. Like a defrocked princess, as Bob had called his first wife and then me. I'd bailed him out when his company went under, I'd supported us for ten years, I'd followed that man to California! My breath came in tiny little puffs of air.

"I took the train; I can't afford the parking." The words "can't afford" stung my ears and I wondered how long it would take for me not be ashamed of saying it.

Brian paused and stared at me like I had cooties. "I'll give you a ride back." We walked to the garage and I got in his black BMW 735iL. It smelled luxuriously like leather and I slid into the familiar seat.

"I used to have one of these; it's a great car." I said. I gave it to Bob when I retired. I was such an idiot!

I quickly found a two bedroom apartment in Pasadena for $2,500 a month, more than double what I could afford, and my Dad helped me out with another loan. I moved out of our family home two weeks later and started having panic attacks. The first one hit me after an incident in Memorial Park where I walked my dog, Tucker. A homeless woman was sobbing in the bushes and I walked up to her and asked if she needed help.

"What should I do? What do I do?"

Over and over. My words! My heart started racing.

Her eyes pleaded with me. I asked if she had any children. Yes she did. I asked where were they? She said she went to the movies with them last week. I thought, well where are they now? Where are MY children? None had followed me to Pasadena!

I found a park employee and told him that there was a woman in the bushes that needed help now. I left a message for Lydia asking what I should do to help her. Sheer terror hit me like a tidal wave. The park worker told me that she had probably gone off her meds and he would get her back to the shelter where they could help her. I had a hard time catching my breath and rushed back to the safety of my apartment, where I fell to the floor and curled into a ball sobbing, my legs jerking around like I was having a fit. The fear was like nothing I'd ever experienced before, although I'd witnessed it in my son, Teddy, many years ago. I felt a deeper compassion for what he'd gone through now that I was the one panicking. Tucker, my Labrador, settled down next to me and I wrapped an arm around him, trying to hold on to reality. I wondered if Teddy had found comfort with any of our dogs. I'm crazy! I'm gonna be homeless! I'm gonna DIE! What should I do?! I want to die! I lay with Tucker as my tears soaked his velvety coat.

I remembered Lydia's words, "Keep your eyes open..."

I opened them and I looked around the room and named the colors I saw, "Brown, beige, black, red, taupe, sienna, red, white" over and over till I felt my breath and heartbeat slow down. It was now dark and I crawled into bed. How was I supposed to find a job in this wrecked state? How was I going to do anything at all when my day was being eaten up with this nightmare? I fell into a deep sleep, the only escape left that really worked.

The next morning, I woke as the sun came through the

window. I said, "Shit, I'm still alive."

When I told Lydia that I couldn't see her anymore because I couldn't afford to, she said, "I'm not going to let him get in the way of your happiness. I'll defer your payments until your divorce is settled."

"You know that could take years, right?"

A couple of weeks later Emily, showed up at my apartment with six large black trash bags. I had been waiting for her to come by, hoping she would comply with the joint custody thing. I'd started to think she wasn't going to and I couldn't bring myself to ask her about it. But here she was and I had to pull myself together.

"Oh, hi, honey. Is this half your stuff?" I asked, trying to sound cheerful and independent.

She didn't seem happy to see me. Or she didn't like what she saw. With a poker face, she said, "No, it's all of it, and I don't want to talk about it."

She looked a little like I had as a teenager, but not quite as sullen and angry. And way more confident too. That made me proud. Her eyes were black, her lips full and small, like a baby's. She was taller than me now but much smaller around the middle. I was thrilled that she wanted to live with me and thought of it as a personal victory or an affirmation of my sanity in leaving. Later, Teddy told me, "Dad was ordering her around to do stuff, like what you did, and he called her Kathy a couple of times too."

That hurt. My name was an insult. But I was relieved that she'd quickly recognized that leaving was in her best interests and had followed through with her conviction. She had something that apparently I'd lacked.

I continued trying to shape up and be a strong woman survivor role model for Emily, but I felt so insecure about every aspect of my life and she saw right through me. I think she was not only mad about me blowing up the family, but my weakness seemed to repulse her. When she was home, I felt like I was the new girl in high school again and she was the mean popular girl. I remembered how my mom's depression had annoyed me when I was Emily's age.

I felt so guilty, my baby needed coddling; she was just 17 and her home had fallen apart. I tried not to discuss Bob around her; I knew that was wrong to do. Unfortunately, I thought of little else, so I ended up not talking much. I missed how close she and I used to be. Emily spent most of her time in her room with the door shut or in front of the TV, texting friends and drawing. Her closed door hurt. Did she blame me for leaving him?! Didn't he drive her crazy too?

One afternoon she was shopping on line and asked for my credit card number. My shopping days had come to a grinding halt when I moved out.

I said, "Use your dad's card."

"Why does Dad have to pay for everything; why don't you just get a job? You're not even trying!"

I sighed and spoke as calmly as I could force myself to do. "Because I don't have any of our money; Dad has it all. Which, by the way, is considered community property and is legally half mine. And I have been trying to find a job, but it's not happening for me. I haven't worked for over 15 years and I'm 59, both of which are strikes against me."

"Well, you should keep trying."

I bit my tongue. I'd sent out countless resumes and had joined several job search websites. Rejection used to roll off my back when I was in sales, but not anymore. When I read the rejection letter from Trader Joe's, I cried. I had been a high-powered NYC executive earning six figures and now I couldn't get a job stuffing grocery bags. I wasn't getting any better at getting through the day without literally freezing in place from my anxiety. My mind was jumbled up, as if the wires in my brain had been tampered with. I'd spend an hour trying to write a grocery list and then I'd have to repeatedly backtrack the store aisles looking for items, as if I'd never been in the grocery store before.

One Sunday Emily asked me to come to church with her. I hadn't been to mass since I'd quit dragging the children to St Bede's years ago. Shortly after that Emily had started going to La Canada Presbyterian Church on her own and she was still very involved with their youth program. I knew very little about the church but, eager to spend time with her, I said yes.

I'd never been to a service like the one I attended that day. There was a live band that played Christian Rock, something I'd never heard before, and I found myself crying. As the pastor spoke, I had a slightly paranoid feeling that he was speaking directly to me, that someone had slipped him a cheat sheet of all my sins, pain and regrets in life and that God forgives everything. I wasn't sure about the forgiveness part, but thinking that I wasn't the only one that felt this bad somehow made me feel more normal. I started attending services regularly that summer. The band sang and spoke of a God that loved us, forgave us and gave us hope and joy, which was vastly different than the Catholic God that I was deathly afraid of and who would surely send me to Hell one day.

Bob didn't produce his companies' financial disclosures and eventually threw the forensic accountant out of his office, saying that he was too invasive. And apparently nothing could be done about it. Bob used to brag that his accountant was a magician when it came to hiding income from the IRS, so I knew the numbers weren't accurate anyway.

Around that time, a strange email address showed up in my inbox and I clicked on it.

I am not sure if I should send this or not but if I don't I will feel guilty. If you do not want this information or think it wrong please delete it and forget about it. This is confidential and it must be kept this way because I need my job for a little bit longer. Mr. Roettig is the most unethical and uncaring man that I have ever met. He treats his employees like dirt and takes advantage of anyone he can. This is why most people quit. He has no friends and is considered a jerk by all. He is laughed at behind his back. I heard him say that his wife will not be able to get his hands on his money in a divorce and this is wrong. You must look at the retirement plans in all his corporations, this is where they say he hides money so he does not pay retirement here. All of these small corporations are really related and a big scam. He also gets cash money for the sale of paper trash. He is a crook and a bad person who cares only for him. Good luck and sorry.

I wondered who'd sent it, a man or a woman, what department were they in, what color was their hair? I typed a reply:

Thank you.

He is an abusive man and that is why I left him. Whatever happens with the divorce settlement happens. I have a good lawyer but in the end it doesn't matter; he can no longer hurt me.

Thank you for caring.

God bless you.

I read it for typos. I couldn't believe how calm it sounded. "God bless you" was not something I said unless someone had sneezed. What was happening to me? I hit send.

I forwarded the email to Brian whose response was, "This isn't admissible evidence."

But to me it was, it was an affirmation, from someone who knew him well. *I wasn't making anything up; he was crazy, not me!*

Throughout that first year, I continued riding. Wildflower and Dreamy lived in the backyard corral at the *family home.* I was permitted access from Madison Street, which ran alongside the back of the property, during certain hours of the day. Setting foot onto the property made me feel like an intruder. I could often hear my sons' voices and laughter, or their loud arguments with Bob, and it broke my heart. I'd sometimes bump into Bob and feel terror, even though he didn't say anything mean to my face anymore. He spoke to me almost kindly now and it made me feel crazy that I still felt afraid of him. I'd slip in, take care of the horses and go riding on the trails in nearby Cherry Canyon. It was the only time I felt somewhat normal. Caroline was often with me, and we spent hours in the saddle talking about our "adventure of a life time," as she called it. We poured over weather histories for all the states, studied routes and horse camping facilities. We started staging horse supplies and gear in tubs on the terrace by the hay bales stacked in my old backyard.

The BMW I'd been granted use of was in rough shape and was further vandalized in my apartment complex's parking garage. I couldn't afford the repairs so I left it at the house for Bob and bought a truck, a new white GMC ¾ ton pick-up that could pull a big trailer. Dad lent me the down payment and the bank surprisingly approved me for a loan. Then I found a suitable trailer; a barely-used 28' long, three-horse trailer with a 12' short-wall living quarters, or LQ as horse people call it. It had all the abbreviated contours of a real home, but was three times as complicated. Dad lent me the money to buy it too, saying, "You deserve to be happy, honey; you've suffered long enough. This trip will be the adventure of a lifetime and you should do it before you're too old." I still hadn't come to think of SHLEP as an adventure, but was too grateful to correct him.

"Thanks Dad," I said, "I'll pay you back in December when I'm 59-1/2 and can take it out of my IRA without a penalty."

"I know you will. Don't worry about money right now, just get better. I'm sending you a VISA card to use too."

Dad had lent me a ton of money, I already owed him over $100,000 and I hated being in debt.

I'd planned a test trip to attend an EAGALA clinic up near Sacramento in July. EAGALA stands for Equine Assisted Growth and Learning Association. The psychotherapy sessions are held in an arena with a small herd of horses, a mental health expert and a horse expert that work as a team. I had become a believer in the horses' ability to read and help people with all kinds of problems, and hoped that this could be a rewarding career for me, even though I didn't expect to get rich from it. The clinic was my final requirement to becoming a certified EAGALA horse expert.

Caroline couldn't come on the test trip—she was worried about the summer heat making her sick—so I invited Teddy. He had a very busy social life; I'd doubted he'd give up a weekend to be with me, but to my surprise, he said okay.

Teddy was born horse crazy. He'd begged for a horse from the time he was three years old. When he was six, Santa gave him a horse named Ty. He was astonished and whispered, "I got a horse? Santa got me a horse?" His grin was ear to ear and I almost started crying I was so happy for him. When Teddy was 12, Ty died after colic surgery and Teddy quit riding. Three months later, Teddy was diagnosed with OCD and three months after that, Diabetes type 1. His pain and fear and heartache were excruciating for me to witness. Teddy rebounded from each trial better than I did; my pain lingered and I worried about him all the time.

The trailer dealer took a week longer than expected to finish installing the improvements I wanted, so I had no time to practice hauling it. I went to pick it up the day we were set to leave. It looked bigger than I'd remembered it being and I told my salesman, Jason, that I was nervous because I'd never hauled anything near that big before.

He said, "Oh, you'll get the hang of it. Just swing wide when yer turnin'; it is pretty long. One gal took out the fire hydrant at our entrance and had to pay the city to replace it." He laughed.

That laugh made me dislike him. Driving back to the house, I guess I didn't swing wide enough making a right turn and heard a small explosion as I blew a trailer tire on the curb. *I couldn't even get it home safely?*

I called AAA, who came and put my spare on for me. The mechanic said, "You're lucky the horses aren't in there, or I couldn't touch it. You should find a service that works on livestock trailers." I felt overwhelmed already. *What else hadn't I thought of?*

I parked by the backyard corral and waited for a mobile tire service to make its way through LA's Friday rush hour traffic. Once he arrived and inspected my tires, he said, "Your trailer tires are crap, you should replace all of them."

I heaved a sigh and called Dad, who said to put it on his card. By 6:00 I was finally ready to go, about 9 hours later than I'd planned. The clinic was starting in two days, and because driving the entire 450 miles in one day would cause my sciatica to flare up, I'd planned on taking two days to get there.

I texted Teddy, then loaded Dreamy and Wildflower. Teddy bounded down the million stairs from the house with his backpack slung over a shoulder. His hair was cut very short, showing off his handsome face with day-old stubble. "Hey mom, ready now?"

He gave me a hug and rested his chin on the top of my head. I sighed into his chest, "Yep, finally." I didn't want to let go; it felt so wonderful to be in his arms again.

I handed him my trip folder. "Here's our plans, the camp website printouts and Mapquest routes. We'll stay overnight at a place called Eastman Lake. About 300 miles from here; it should take us about four hours to get there."

I hadn't considered that I'd be driving much slower than the speed limit. I was so tense driving that my fingers cramped up from gripping the steering wheel so hard. The trailer was "extra wide," which gave the horses more room, but it made it more difficult for me to keep it between the lines on the highway. I stayed in the right lane the entire time, afraid I'd sideswipe a car if I tried passing anyone. I got so scared coming down the Grapevine Pass that I used the emergency trailer brake to keep it from pushing the truck down the hill too fast.

The brake made a loud metal scraping noise, which woke Teddy up, "What's that?"

"The trailer brake."

"You supposed to do that?"

"I don't know, but I think it's working."

We pulled into the camp after midnight, not ideal timing, but I rationalized that it had been a cooler haul for the horses. There wasn't a soul in camp. I backed the trailer for the first time into our site, with Teddy guiding me with a flashlight, put the mares into corrals, and went to bed in the LQ. I gave Teddy the queen bed in the gooseneck and I took the convertible dinette/bed. I fell asleep as soon as I hit the pillow.

In the morning, I let the horses loose with hobbles on to graze and waited for Teddy to wake up.

As the sun climbed higher, it got incredibly hot and I realized why we were the only ones there. Teddy got up around noon and we took a sweaty ride around the lake.

The once large reservoir was more like a puddle, the dry bed revealing the striated colors of the ground like a rainbow. California was in a serious drought and it was shocking to see how bad it was. The absence of water was disappointing but I found a subtle beauty in the dusty colors it revealed in the dry bed. The trail wound around the old shoreline with California Oaks occasionally providing shade from the blazing sun. Tall wild grasses blew in the breeze. I had decided I would also make a painting in each state where I rode, and I took some photos of Teddy on Wildflower with the dry lake bed in the background to use for my California painting. We had hauled, set up camp, slept in the trailer and ridden the mares. I was really doing it; I felt so accomplished.

We left that evening and headed to Placerville for the clinic. Much of the drive was on rural roads and I crept along in the dark as Teddy slept. At 3 am, I turned onto the single lane dirt road leading to the ranch. The road took a hard left and I barely cleared it, there were ditches and tall berms on either side. Then the road took a hard right. This time I didn't make it, and the trailer's back end got hung up in the ditch. Teddy woke up when I mumbled, "Shit!" He groaned when I told him what I'd done, but got out of the truck and helped me assess the situation. If I'd had 4-wheel drive, I might have been able to pull it out, but I hadn't thought of that when I bought the truck. I thought if the weight of the horses was out of the trailer, then maybe the truck would be able to pull it out. The doors at the back of the trailer for the horses were firmly embedded in the berm and wouldn't budge. I heard dogs barking from the house at the end of the dirt road.

"Well, there's an emergency door," I said, too brightly.

Teddy pulled all the horse gear out of the third stall as I stacked them on the dirt road. He asked, "What about the dividers, mom, they don't swing this way. We have to remove them somehow."

"Shit. I don't know how to do that. I guess you have to remove the hinge pins?"

Teddy figured out how the pins worked and was strong enough to manage the walls without whacking the horses with them. There's absolutely no way I could have done it. *What would I do if I had to do this alone with Caroline?* Thankfully Teddy didn't complain or criticize me, though I wouldn't have blamed him if he had. I handed him tools and watched him get it done.

As I exited the emergency door with Dreamy, a neighbor woman appeared with a barking dog in tow. "What's going on here? This is a private road!"

I explained my predicament and where I was going.

"I'll call John. He owns the ranch you're going to."

I felt guilty about waking John in the middle of the night but didn't stop her from making the call. He appeared shortly in the darkness from whence I'd come. *Was his place back there?!*

"Kathy?"

"Yeah, that's me."

"We expected you a bit earlier than this!"

"Sorry, I've had some problems."

"Well, ya missed our drive! We're back there." He pointed to a house lit up back before the first treacherous turn. *I groaned.*

"I used to drive a fire truck, I'll take over now. It's gonna be tough to turn around here."

I thought, *Turn around? Tough? More like impossible!* I handed him my keys and thanked him.

To my amazement, he did free up the trailer, then turned it around in a very tight space in his neighbor's gravel driveway. It took over an hour for him to execute it all. I put the horses in John's stalls as the sun was coming up.

John pointed to the covered arena and said, "It's about time for the clinic to start; you better get over there. I'm gonna go get some coffee." He looked exhausted and I apologized again.

I was beyond tired myself, but headed over to where he'd pointed. Teddy climbed in the trailer. I felt like an idiot.

Day 1 of the clinic was a blur. I had a hard time just keeping my eyes open. It had been a big expense for me to register for this clinic and I hoped that they'd still certify me.

There were more problems with my trailer. The a/c was not working well in the extreme heat there, which would be a problem for Caroline and her MS. The outlet in the barn I plugged into couldn't handle the load with the a/c on, so I ran the generator instead. I didn't think that the generator was working right either; it didn't appear to be charging the house batteries. It was going through propane very quickly, and I didn't have a spare tank for it. I couldn't get the trailer uncoupled from the truck so I could drive to town to get the propane refilled. The refrigerator "check" light was on, but I didn't know what I was supposed to check or do about it. The septic tank monitors indicated that they were full, and I had no idea how they got full so fast nor whether I needed to do something about it quickly or not. I had no idea how any of it worked, and it was dawning on me that I could never do this trip. Was it just the night before when I'd felt so accomplished? I now felt foolish and inept.

Day 2 of the clinic was more interesting, mostly because I'd gotten some sleep. I met participants that were already running their own therapy ranch businesses. They talked about the many challenges they faced, mostly to do with staying solvent. We played out mock sessions to practice our respective roles in therapy. In one session, I played the mother of a dysfunctional family who had come for a group session. One of my pretend daughters started fighting, for real, not a part of their role playing, with the pretend Dad. The girl came to me hysterically crying and I didn't know how to handle it. "He won't let me do it and he's not doing it right. He's scaring the horse."

I said, "Just breathe; stay here with me." I watched as the pretend Dad pranced around like a rooster, trying to push the horse down to the corner with little success. No way I was going to go over and confront him. It was extremely uncomfortable and I was relieved when the instructor told us to stop and come back to the circle for the review. He asked each of us, "So what happened out there?"

When it was my turn, I started by explaining the daughter/Dad conflict and how I felt helpless in resolving their problem because I hated confrontation with aggressive men. Then I burst into tears, "Oh my God, it's just like my real life!"

Everyone just stared at me, I hated letting people see

me cry.

The facilitator said to the class, "This always happens, that's why the therapeutic benefit of EAGALA is life changing. It's impossible for your brain not to find your life metaphor with the horses."

Feeling totally incompetent with my lack of any hauling skills and John's news about snow in Tahoe where I'd planned our next stop, I decided to head home after the clinic ended Sunday morning and do the haul in one day. I pulled off the I-5 for fuel when my tank approached ¼ full. I cautiously pulled up to the pump, remembering Jason's story of "a gal that took out the fuel pump and had to pay for it!" I filled up, and started pulling out. I was pretty sure that I had enough room to swinging wide back onto the road, but I didn't notice the steep angle of the driveway apron. Heck, I didn't even know that a steep angle would be a problem. I heard a loud scratching noise just as Teddy said, "What's that?"

I put it in Park and said, "Shit, I don't know, can you go check it out for me?"

He jumped out and came back saying, "The back end's hung up on the driveway apron, just gun it." So I did.

The newly installed horse ramp ripped off the trailer and crashed to the pavement. It pulled the C frame corner with it, leaving a gaping hole in the floor right where Dreamy's left hind foot could set down and break her leg. The horse door was bent so badly that it wouldn't open at all. I didn't know who to call for help. I tried AAA, the local police, and a couple of auto repair places my phone said were "near me." They all asked, "What exactly do you need? A tow?" Honestly, I didn't know exactly what I needed.

Teddy and I pulled all the horse stuff out of the 3rd stall, *again*, and then he removed the heavy-awkward dividers, *again*, as I handed him tools. We unloaded the horses through the emergency door, and tied them to a handicapped ramp railing at the gas station. *What the heck was I thinking? How could I possibly make this trip?* I felt like a failure and was near tears. Neither AAA nor the police ever showed up.

Then along came an angel, a man on a 4-wheeler. "Need some help?" he asked.

"Yes, I need help." I hadn't said that out loud in ages and it was humbling.

"I'm a pretty good welder and my shop's just a mile down that road," he said, nodding his cowboy hat toward whence he'd come. "I'll drive it for ya; you look a little shook up." *Yeah, well, I always look like this lately.* "Can your son drive a four wheeler?"

Teddy happily drove his 4-wheeler and I hand-walked the horses down the pretty country road. I passed a small farm and a beautiful treed pasture with horses peeking through the foliage at us as my horses nickered to them. We crossed a railroad track as the angel had said I would. I'd like to live someplace like this, I thought; it felt peaceful. By the time I got to the angel's property, I had calmed down a bit. The 4-wheeler angel was already at work on my trailer, bending the aluminum frame roughly back into place with his tractor bucket. His son and nephew were helping him. His wife, his elderly father and a few younger kids were milling about, offering us lemonade and snacks. They spent several hours working on it and put the detached loading ramp up on top of the trailer in the hay rack.

As I held the horses and watched the family, I was amazed at how naturally they worked together. This family worked. *So, it's not just a bullshit fairytale, how did they do that?* They simply enjoyed being with each other and helping me, a total stranger. When they were finished, this angel refused the money I tried to hand him, saying, "I'm just happy to help you."

I was blown away. I had not experienced such kindness in a very long time and I felt my heart relax, realizing that there were some truly good people in this world. My family had been a war zone for too long, and the angel's words melted some of my defensive wall. As we were driving away, I started crying. I wanted to do something big for him, like send his kids to college. I said, "That is the kind of family I had dreamt of for all of you. I failed you Teddy; I'm so sorry."

Teddy said, "Don't dwell on the past, Mom, just appreciate the present and try to think about the future."

How did my baby become so wise? He was right, my past was crippling me, I wanted to be rid of those chains. But how did I do that? I was reminded of Bob constantly; my mind kept weaving the story of our failure to the front of my consciousness and I couldn't turn off the negative chatter. *Bob did this to me! I'm damaged goods now, I hate him! He's going to fuck me over in the divorce! The kids are damaged from what they've witnessed; I should have left a long time ago! Bob's going to turn the kids against me with his lies and accusations! I'm going to die poor and alone!*

We got back to La Canada around suppertime and Teddy started texting on his phone as we approached our exit. He asked to be dropped near the Starbucks to meet his friends. He hopped out at the light and said good-bye. As I watched him jog across the intersection, I wondered what he thought about me after this weekend. Was his mom a raving lunatic, completely incompetent, bound to get herself killed on this journey? Or was he proud of me? I wondered if I'd see him again before I left for good.

I drove the trailer back to the riding club, relieved to be home without anyone getting hurt. I texted Caroline, "I made it!" hoping she would come visit. She asked how the weekend went and I told her the truth, "Horrible, I got stuck in a ditch going up and damaged the trailer in a gas station on the way home." I told her how the AC wasn't the greatest and how it sucked up propane. She stopped replying with questions eventually and I fell asleep. I wondered if she was going to bail on me.

In the morning I texted Caroline again, "I'm taking the

trailer to the dealer to get repaired. Want to come with me?"

She replied, "No, can't right now."

I hesitated then texted, "Are you still coming on SHLEP with me?" I sat in the trailer staring at my phone worrying why it was taking so long for her to answer.

"No. I don't think it would be wise for me to."

I didn't realize that I'd been holding my breath, and I let it out with a big sigh. Every ounce of excitement that I'd had about SHLEP flew out the window with my breath, leaving me empty and in shock. I was crushed and tasted a sour bitterness in my mouth. *How could I do this alone? I'd always hated being alone. It indicated to me that I wasn't wanted by anyone and that something must be wrong with me! Only losers are alone!*

I lay in the goose-neck bed and cried for a while, then mustered up the energy to drive the trailer to the dealer, rehearsing what I'd tell Jason. "I don't want it, it's way too big for me, I can't drive it, I have to trade it for a smaller one." *Be firm!*

Jason laughed. Then, poohpoohed me, insisting I could learn and I would change my mind once I got used to it. If I was going to live in it for a year, I'd need this much space. I caved in and left it there for them to repair. Luckily my insurance was covering it; the repair would be $15,000. I told Jason I needed it back by September 1st when I was moving out of my apartment and leaving for good.

I went back to my apartment and made lists of what I needed to do in my final month before departure. I realized it was foolish to start an adventure of this magnitude with virtually no hauling training. I found Dobson's Professional Truck Driving School and signed up for private lessons with a patient burly black guy named Ron. He could maneuver a rig like a professional and I was in awe of his skills. I used my bashed up trailer for my lessons while Jason waited on parts for its repair. I set up cones in the parking lot outside the Rose Bowl stadium and practiced for hours on end after my lessons.

Besides getting more comfortable with my driving abilities, this gave me an intense mind exercise, during which I never thought about all my problems. It took my full concentration, much like riding, and sometimes painting, did for me. Greg, a professional horse hauling friend, took me out for a few hours on small town streets in Altadena where street parking is allowed and then down Lake Avenue, which has an 8% downhill grade. He told me, "Switch to manual and put it in first gear. *Just trust your truck.*" Not touching the brakes when you're going down a steep grade with 7 tons pushing you is hard to do. But as Greg said, "You have to or you'll burn through your brakes."

Heather was really the only friend I had left in La Canada, the only one that continued to seek out my company anyway. She had gotten divorced a year before and was living in a loft in the same apartment complex as me while she remodeled her home. We'd hike with our dogs together, go to the movies and swim in the complex pool, the stuff I could afford to do now. She invited me to dinner and after we had eaten, we sat watching a movie on TV. Tucker and her dog, Kailie, lay by our feet. I was smoking my e-cigarette; we had gotten stoned and were sipping wine in the large open space. It reminded me of living in my loft in NYC; I liked the feeling.

Heather asked, "So, when are you leaving?"

"September 15th." I took a deep breath. "You sure you don't want to come with me?"

"No, I can't, the renovation will be starting soon and my son isn't going back to school this semester. He got an internship here."

"Oh, too bad." I was so scared of doing this alone. "I can't wait to get the hell out of here."

"How long do you think you'll be gone?"

"I'm not coming back," I'd said this so many times, but no one seemed to believe me. Not my kids either. "There's too many bad memories here, it's too hot, too expensive. There's no reason to come back."

Heather put her wine glass on the coffee table and sat up. Here we go again, I thought. "Kathy, don't say that, especially to your children. My parents moved away when I was in college and I felt abandoned. Don't abandon your children." I'd heard this shpiel before and was getting sick of it.

"Heather, I'm not abandoning them; they've got their father here if they want to come home from school."

"But he's a bad guy, that's why you left him. They don't want to be with him. You're *abandoning* them."

I stuffed my anger; I couldn't lose Heather too. Around 10, we hugged and I said good night. I took Tucker for a walk before heading back to my apartment and as Tucker searched for a good tree to pee on, I fumed, thinking about what Heather accused me of doing. Heather couldn't relate to my situation, her parents had recently died and she had inherited a lot of money. She didn't have to worry about being homeless or not being able to keep her horses.

Two weeks before I was to leave, I rode my mares down to the riding club and started staging my belongings in an empty stall they set aside for me. I decided I wasn't going to drive that damn thing back up to the house again. I would leave from the riding club where it was flat and there was lots of room to turn around.

A week before I was to leave, Heather threw me a send-off party at the riding club. As I spoke to the 50 or so equestrians in our historic stone clubhouse, a slide show of my trip preparations played on the TV, accompanied by the eclectic mix of music that I listened to. It ranged from 60's rock and roll to Eminem. I was now the black sheep member of the club full of lawyers, doctors and movie business people: I was single, unemployed and poor and I now felt intimidated by their stability and success. After I spoke about the superficial goals of my trip, the riding and painting parts, the guests asked me a bunch of practical horse related questions. Then a woman in the back stumped me with, "Why are you doing this trip?"

I took a deep breath. I'd wondered if anyone would be prying enough to ask me this and whether I'd answer it honestly or not. *What the hell, I'd probably never see these people again.* "Well, some of you know that I was in a really bad marriage and now I'm in a really bad divorce. My kids have all left for college and don't really need me here anymore and I can't afford to live here anyway and keep my horses and I hope my journey will help me figure out who I am again." *How crazy did that sound?*

There was a moment of silence and I felt very self-conscious. How did I get to this place? I was confused about what exactly had happened to me; all I knew for sure was that I had to get better and that this trip was hopefully going to do it.

I was going solo. The thought flipped my stomach upside down whenever I thought about it. But this fear felt better than panic or being depressed. At least I felt alive again. And I had a mission, a purpose, something to *DO*: I was going to spend the next year hauling to forest campgrounds, riding in all the lower 48 states and painting a landscape with my horses in it for each state. Brian would handle my divorce and said that I didn't have to be physically there.

Most importantly, I hoped that *something* along the way was going to heal me. I didn't know what or how or who would fix me, but I imagined that the peace of the forest might put me at ease, or the magical powers of my horses might give me back my strength, or the monumental accomplishment of just getting it done might make me feel more confident, or crossing the state line and putting thousands of miles between Bob and me might make me feel safe again.

Chapter 2

I woke up as the sun came through the small window by my bed up in the gooseneck of my horse trailer. For a second, I wondered where I was, and why was I fully dressed with my dusty hiking boots loosened, but still on my feet. I heard Tucker whine and his tail thump three times on something soft like a pillow. I jolted awake. Today was the day I was pulling out of California for good! As I got up to let Tucker out the door, it dawned on me that I hadn't mumbled my usual morning, "Shit I'm still alive."

My repaired rig was parked behind F barn at the Flintridge Riding Club. I'd been up most of the night packing all my stuff in it. I still had some other stuff in storage, heavy, bulky stuff like furniture and china. I wouldn't need any of that for at least a year.

I fed Tucker his pureed sweet potatoes, chicken, rice and prednisone pill, then tucked him in the back of the truck cab on my old feather bed. I started the truck and turned the AC on. Poor dog had no idea what he was in for.

When Emily left for college I got to keep Tucker. She'd fallen in love with him when they auctioned him off at the school gala; she begged for him non-stop. Bob hated losing anything, especially when it came to Emily, so he outbid all the other parents and won Tucker for $10,000. "Well, the money goes to a good cause, so it's okay, right?" he'd said.

"Right," I agreed, trying to do the "talking in one voice" thing that Bob was so keen on. Tucker was a soft round ball of fluff and fell asleep on my lap as the loud party carried on. He peed on my green taffeta gown, but I didn't care.

Tucker was now 11 and had become my therapy. My apartment complex hadn't allowed large dogs, so Lydia wrote a letter saying that due to my mental illness, I needed him as a therapy dog. He had helped keep me grounded the past year.

He even had a bright orange therapy dog vest that he proudly waddled around in. I could spoon up next to him and cry when I was having a panic attack and he wouldn't move a muscle as I'd stroke his soft white fur. He had a grapefruit-sized cancerous mass in his abdomen and had outlived the vet's prognosis by six months already. I hoped he'd survive for at least another year with me.

It was quiet outside, but for my truck's diesel engine and the soft sounds of horses munching on their breakfasts. It was already warm and the air smelled of hay, shavings and manure, a primal earthy smell that made me feel good. Seven years ago, a therapist had told me that I needed to be at the barn every day to experience this. I was very depressed back then and it had helped, but the peaceful feeling went away as soon as I encountered Bob. Even the familiar beep as he locked the doors of his BMW was a trigger; he was home, watch out! Why did I still feel intense fear just from thinking about it? Lydia said that was the PTSD.

I walked around the rig to check the hitch, turn off the propane, check the tail lights and be sure the many doors and windows were all secured. The entire rig was about 50' long and driving it still scared the crap out of me. It had been easier in the Rose Bowl parking lot without horses in it. I checked that the cabinet doors and windows in the LQ were shut tight. On my bed was a rust and teal colored Pendleton blanket given to me by my friend Jan, depicting Indians riding bareback. My white Persian, Nalla, was burrowed underneath it and I patted the lump she made. "Good kitty. Please don't puke under there," I whispered. She hunkered down and scooted away from my touch. I hadn't planned on bringing her but she'd stowed away in my rolled up bedding and I'd taken it as a sign that she should be with me.

While sitting on the toilet, I turned to shut the closet door behind me. A conservative navy dress and jacket hung in there beside my oil skin raingear and mud boots. Just in case there's a court date for my divorce that I need to attend. Or if Dad dies.

Dad had been diagnosed with stage 4 prostate cancer a year before at age 85. I was by his hospital bed when the surgeon told him, "you need to get your things in order." The first thing I told Dad when the Doctor left the room was to find a different surgeon, that guy had no bedside manner at all. Dad started estrogen therapy, which seemed to be keeping the testosterone-loving cancer from progressing so far and Dad sounded okay on the phone.

Dad was the first person I'd call when I'd secured a big print contract back when I was working. His "Atta boy! Ha ha, you're something else!" meant the world to me. When I'd needed to go to rehab in my early 30's, he arrived at my NYC loft in an hour's time, made all the arrangements, drove me there and had me checked in by midnight. When I needed legal advice, like the time when I lent Bob the money to buy his stupid company, Dad had me talk with his CPA and his lawyer, both of whom said it was too risky, but of course I did it anyway. Dad was a good listener and a great judge of character. He always made things better by either explaining it to me in understandable words or steering me the way of a trusted expert. My siblings felt the same way. "He's our hero!" we'd joke when we got together, even Mom, who'd divorced him over 25 years ago. When she'd needed a new car, Dad simply bought her one, not telling his second wife, Bobbi, of course. He supported my schizophrenic brother, Johnny, and my divorced bi-polar sister, Liza.

Since Bobbi died a few years earlier, he said he'd been lonely. Now he had a caregiver, Yvonne. I'd promised Dad that I'd spend Christmas with him. I whispered a quick plea to God, please don't let Dad die, I can't take any more in my storm right now.

I stared at the only dress I'd brought along and slammed the door. Nothing in the trailer just shut, you had to slam it.

My eyes scanned the 8' x 13' LQ space; this would be my home for the next year. It was roughly the same size as the master bathroom I used to share with Bob, until he moved to the guest bedroom. The bathroom was on the third floor and had a spectacular view of the peaceful but severe foothills surrounding La Canada. You could see Mount Wilson from there on a smog-free day. I had frequently locked myself in there to cry into a thick towel so that no one would hear me and I'd memorized those hills through my tears. I'd wanted to saddle up and ride straight out and never turn around. Well, I thought, now I was doing it.

I walked up the trailer ramp into the horse area. Two hay nets filled with timothy hay were hung, waiting for my mares, Dreamy and Wildflower. I opened the roof vents and slid open the windows so they'd stay as cool as possible on our haul to Las Vegas, where we would be overnighting on my way to Utah.

Dreamy nickered as I approached and politely slid her nose into her rope halter. I walked her out to the rig, where I tied her to a tie-ring welded onto the side of the trailer, and picked her beautiful unshod hooves. She had been barefoot for two years now and so was Wildflower. This way I could care for their feet myself, which saved me the money that a farrier would cost, plus I thought it was healthier for them. I rubbed my face on Dreamy's warm neck and breathed her earthy scent into my lungs. A tiny tear slipped out of my eye and I wiped it on my shirt sleeve. Wildflower was calling wildly for her buddy to come back to the barn, and I marched back to go get her. They were buddy sour and literally thought they'd get eaten by a mountain lion if they weren't together. You'd think that they would act loving towards each other because of this dependence, but they didn't. Wildflower pushed Dreamy away from the hay nets and would trap her in corners, telling her to stay there and watch for bears and mountain lions, which did occasionally stroll down the street. Dreamy tolerated it, so I'd ended up putting up a pipe corral wall between them.

Dreamy was my very first horse and held a special place in my heart. I'd bought her as a present to myself for my 50th birthday when she was just turning five. She taught me how to ride and made me fall in love with trail riding. She was a 15-year-old Quarterhorse Gruella mare, 15.3 hands tall and big boned. She was solid and bombproof, a perfect first horse.

Wildflower was prancing around her stall making it difficult to halter her. "Quit!" I said in my wimpy authoritative voice. She was now 6 years old but I still thought of her as a baby, my problem child. I had rescued her as a gangly legged 6-month-old from a Canadian Pregnant Mare Urine ranch. She had been pulled off her mom early and sent to a feedlot to be fattened up, cuz all the PMU babies are sold by the pound to slaughter. She eventually became a good trail horse for me, but she sure did keep me on my toes. She spooked at stupid stuff, but a lot of horses do that. She was pretty pushy too, invading my space on the ground; she'd kicked me more than once and turned to nip at me when I fastened her girth. I stroked the silky white fur on her neck as I haltered her. I remembered when she was a baby and terrified of people, her skin quivered at my touch. On our way down the barn aisle, Dreamy trotted in through the door dragging her lead rope with the broken tie ring clanging on the ground. She snorted as she passed us and made a sharp left turn into her stall. She looked pretty sound on that crooked left leg, I noted.

I groaned and walked Wildflower to the trailer, cleaned her feet, and loaded her. She made a couple more calls for Dreamy then set to work on her hay net. Food was a great distraction for her.

I walked back to the barn for Dreamy and wondered why she'd done that. She never misbehaved. When I got to her stall she looked at me sheepishly as I picked up her rope and untied the ½" thick metal tie ring she'd snapped like a toothpick. She heaved a sigh and let the air out with her lips loose, making a p-r-r-r-r-r-r sound that meant that she'd relaxed and was ready to comply. She loaded into the last stall of the trailer beside Wildflower, like the princess she really was, and I shut the back doors and pulled up the ramp.

The SHLEP party playlist was now on my tiny apple shuffle, which I plugged into the dashboard. Willie Nelson's twangy voice came through the speakers, singing "On the road again." I thought how Caroline had loved that this would be our departure song.

I buckled up and puffed on the e-cigarette Brad had bought for me so I'd quit smoking again. "Well Tucker, this trip is going to go better than the last one, right?" I said, as I swung wide at the FRC gates and headed onto the street at a diagonal to avoid bottoming out the back end of the trailer again, something that Ron, my truck driving instructor, had taught me. At least I'm getting better at this hauling thing, I patted myself on the back.

The truck muscled the 14,000-pound fully loaded trailer up the steep ramp to the 210 East and the traffic was thick. God, how I hated L.A. rush hour. The slow lane was rutted from all the trucks and I worried about my horse's legs. The traffic cleared up the further we got from the city. The semis were crawling up the long steep pass on the 15 North and we slipped past them easily. I just loved how powerful my truck felt and I patted the dashboard.

Adele belted out, "We could have had it all!"

Then I started to cry. Hauling and crying was not a good combination, but my lost dreams and lost love crashed over me like a wave. Maybe there was something I missed, something I didn't try, some way I could have changed or medicated myself into someone that could tolerate Bob without sacrificing my sanity. I felt like a failure. And I was a wreck, or wrecked for good. Maybe I was just crazy, like Bob always said. A memory started to replay itself as I sped north through the desert.

It was summer 2011; Brad was 20. I was in bed the lights were off, but I was still awake. Brad came into my bedroom; he said his car registration was expired and asked about getting it renewed.

All CA-DMV mail went to Bob's company in Glendale because everything that we owned was technically owned by Bob's company. Getting renewed auto registration cards had been just one of the recurring problems I had with Bob. I'd seen Bob sleeping on the sofa in his office before I'd gone to bed; he often slept there. In fact, most of <u>his</u> things were in there; suits hung from file cabinet handles and boxes of pressed and folded white men's shirts were stacked on top of the cabinets.

I didn't want to wake Bob; his reaction was always frightening. His whole body would jerk and I'd see a look of terror on his face when he first open his eyes. He'd gasp a couple times, then fly into a rage. The first time it happened, I thought I'd caught him in the middle of a nightmare. The next few times, I thought he had some kind of sleep disorder. By 2011, I'd thought it was just because he hated me.

I hadn't heard any of the kids talk about this happening when they woke him, so I told Brad if it couldn't wait until the morning, he'd have to go wake up his father. There was nothing I could do about it.

I heard Brad's footsteps go down two flights on the wooden stairs and across the tiled entry. I got out of bed and put on my bathrobe. I heard Bob screaming, and hoped he would calm down when he realized that it was just Brad and not me. But it continued and I heard Brad yelling back.

I walked to the hall. Brad ran into the entryway below me. Bob was hot on his tail and screaming at him. Brad turned and tried to reason with his dad; I could see that he was crying.

I yelled, "Bob stop! Look what you're doing to Brad!"

They were face to face and Brad tried to run up the stairs. Bob cornered him on the first landing. He was inches from Brad's face screaming insults at him, "You disrespectful little brat, why are you crying? What's the matter with you; you're spoiled rotten!"

Brad was cowering, crying and trying to speak, "Dad—" but Bob yelled over him. Bob was blocking the next flight of stairs, Brad's path to his room.

I ran down the flight of stairs to the next landing where Brad's door was, I was still a flight above them. I screamed, "Bob, stop. This is the only child that's your friend anymore; you're going to lose him too! Look what you're doing to your son!"

Bob looked up at me and shouted, "You stay out of this!" and went right back to yelling at Brad.

I thought he was going to hit my son!

Brad was six feet tall, but had never been a fighter; he avoided conflict as much as I did. I thought of calling 911, but knew that they'd never get there in time.

I flew down the next flight of stairs and squeezed between the two of them and told Brad, "Run to your room!"

Bob was caught off guard for a second and then his rage went to an all new level. His face turned beet red, his expression was menacing and frightening, the veins popped out of his neck, his fist were clenched at his sides and he was pumping his arms up and down as he screamed inches from my face, spit flying into my face with his words. I didn't care if he killed me.

I stared Bob in the eye and blocked out his words. I saw his fists clenched like he was squeezing a ball for hand exercise and I began saying to myself over and over again, "Hit me, just hit me, so I have a solid reason to leave you."

"Welcome to Nevada," read the sign. My first state line. I'd been hoping that crossing it would somehow magically heal me and I held my breath, but nothing happened. That was pretty stupid. I followed the handwritten notes I'd made in my SHLEP journal and pulled into the small dusty ranch outside Las Vegas as the sun was setting. The owner ambled towards me in a cowboy hat, kicking up pink dust in the glow of the sunset. He said, "You're late; I was just about to have supper."

"Sorry, I got a late start and I drive kind of slow. That and my water tank hose came off on the highway and spilled all my horse water, so I stopped to fix it."

He paused to let it all sink in. "Slow is better when hauling, no problem. Why don't you park next to the arena and turn your horses out in there," he said, pointing to the 100' x 100' arena.

"My horses fight over food if they're together," I said

"We'll just throw hay in each corner then." He helped me unload the horses, throw hay around the arena and fill up a muck bucket with water. After he went back for his supper, I sat on the pullout step of the LQ doorway and watched the mares roll in the sand, then get back up for a few bucks and laps of the arena. Wildflower started pushing Dreamy from one hay pile to the next as she always did when they ate together. Why didn't Dreamy put up a fight? Why was Wildflower such a bitch? And why did their relationship bug me so much?

Tucker followed me into the LQ and I rearranged the dinette to make a bed for him. The jump up to the goose neck bed where I was going to sleep was too high for him and I didn't want to hurt his abdomen by trying to pick him up. Besides, he was 85 pounds. The featherbed puffed up around him like a nest. My fingers played with his butter soft ear as I whispered my good night prayer that I used to say to my babies when I tucked them in: "God bless Tucker. Keep him happy and safe. Protect him from all evil." Then I said the prayer for Brad, Teddy, Emily, Dreamy, Wildflower, Tucker, Nalla and myself. I felt a slight sense of peace and promise.

I was really doing it! It was possible that if I just kept on, I could get to all 48 states, if I just took one step at a time, like they said in the Narcotics Anonymous "rooms" I'd been in in the 80's. I'd faced seemingly impossible challenges in my life before, like quitting cocaine and beating cancer. I'd endured 23 years with what Lydia had called "an emotionally abusive man," and I was still standing. I'd always come through the other side by remembering that simple slogan. I could do this trip one step at a time, one state at a time.

I whispered, "God, please make SHLEP work."

In the morning, my coffee creamer was warm when I took it from the fridge. I called the trailer dealer and asked for Jason, who'd sold me the trailer. Jason was a slick cowboy wannabe and intimidated me. He had not delivered the trailer to me on time, causing me to have to rush up to Placerville on my test trip, and was three weeks late finishing the repairs, which delayed my SHLEP departure by two weeks. He hadn't responded to my messages when I started panicking about having to be out of my apartment on September first. I'd paid him over $50,000 for the trailer and thought he should be nicer to me; I was a customer after all. I sat on hold for five minutes waiting for him to pick up.

"Hello." He sounded annoyed.

"Hi Jason, it's Kathy Roettig. I'm in Utah now," I said confidently. "The refrigerator's not cold and the check light is on; what does that mean?"

"It means it's not working." Duh.

"Well, what do I do about it?"

Jason heaved a sigh and said, "Turn it off and on again, listen for a clicking noise and a puff sound, which is the gas igniting. If it doesn't light, do it again till it does. Keep it set on "Gas" unless you're plugged into an electric source. And don't turn off the propane tanks when you're haulin'."

"I thought I was supposed to shut them off."

"No." He sounded exasperated.

"Ok, thanks. Bye, then." I did as Jason had said and the refrigerator went back on. My food seemed to be okay. I wrote down his instructions in my trailering journal for future reference.

The working systems on the trailer were so confusing to me. When I'd picked up the trailer, he'd given me an hour tour of it all and I'd scribbled notes and drawings in my journal as he'd rattled on. There were several possible power sources to use—two house batteries, an outside outlet, two house propane tanks and a generator, which started with its own battery and ran on its own propane tanks. Some appliances could run off all of these, some only ran on one or two. There was the microwave, stove, hot water heater, heat and AC, refrigerator/freezer and electric outlets inside the LQ. You couldn't power both the AC and the microwave at the same time or something would blow. Then there's the septic system, which drains into a gray tank from the shower and sinks and a black tank from the toilet. These of course, had to be emptied regularly. There was a house water tank or you could hook up to a water spigot. I also had a horse water tank up on the roof in the hayrack, where the generator was also mounted. A monitor by the microwave told me the status of some of these things. I was utterly confused by it all and my notes weren't very helpful. I was heading toward Idaho where a friend was going to teach me how to manage and understand it all better, so I just had to muscle through this next week in Utah.

I loaded the horses and left for my Utah camp by 10 a.m. I was still very nervous driving. Eight Rubbermaid tubs filled with horse supplies were in the truck bed and a few of their tops flew off on the highway. When I tried to pull into a gas station before starting the 7,000′ climb to the forest campground, I misjudged my turning radius and got jammed between the entrance curbs, tying up traffic until I was able to wiggle my way out. Other than that, it went perfectly.

The ranger at the forest's campground entrance pointed the way to the horse area. She said, "There's no other horse campers here right now, by the way." That was disappointing, but at least no one would be watching me do dumb newbie stuff. She handed me a map of the camp and adjoining trails. My assigned site was beautifully shaded by tall pine trees but had no electricity or water hook-ups for the trailer. This was called "primitive" camping and was probably a poor choice due to my lack of knowledge about how my trailer's systems worked.

There was a fire ring, a tie rail and only one small corral, something I hadn't anticipated. I walked around to see if any other sites had two, but they didn't. Shit! I put them both in the one I had and Wildflower kicked Dreamy right off the bat. I pulled Wildflower out, scolded her and walked her to the next site's corral and went back to set up camp. I thought it was stupid that they'd only built one corral at each site; didn't most people come with at least two horses? It reminded me of when there weren't enough beds on our Hawaii vacations and we had to get fold up cots because all the kids brought friends along. Bob had bought a time-share at a fancy resort in Maui in 2005; he'd said he could use it for entertaining customers, but we went there every year so I wasn't sure how he actually justified the purchase to his banks. There were two adjoining units facing the ocean that slept eight, but there were never enough beds. My last stay there, I slept on the floor. Dad was with us on that trip; he had a roll away cot to sleep on. How Bob thought that I should be grateful for this "luxurious vacation" was perplexing.

I remember sitting by the pool with Dad towards

the end of that trip.

Dad and I were by ourselves, lying on lounge chairs. He sat up, turned to me and very seriously said, "Kathy, no one deserves to be as unhappy as you are."

I thought maybe I did deserve it and said, "it's not that bad, Dad."

Bob upgraded all our tickets to First Class except my father's. Dad was 85 and nervous about a doctor's appointment he had coming up, something about his PSA. He was also claustrophobic and the assigned coach seat was by the window, so I traded seats with him.

As we crossed the Pacific, I walked into the first class cabin to ask one of the children to trade seats with me because my back hurt so bad. Everyone was sleeping and the cabin was dimmed.

As I was gently shaking Emily's shoulder, Bob jumped up out of his seat from the row behind her and started yelling at me, "What do you think you're doing? What's the matter with you? Get out of here! Go back to your seat!"

The kids and passengers all began to open their eyes with confused concerned looks on their faces. I saw Dad's face. His expression confused me, reflecting disgust and resignation, I think, but he didn't say anything to defend me. A steward appeared in the aisle between Bob and me somehow and pushed Bob away and back towards his seat, "Sir, sit down now and be quiet!"

I slipped behind them and walked back to my window seat in coach. Everyone was looking at me as if I were a criminal.

When we were collecting all our luggage at baggage claim, I told Bob, "I'm not going on these fucking trips with you anymore."

The next summer they all went without me. I spent the

gloriously peaceful week at home with my four dogs and horses organizing the house. I found a bottle of Viagra in Bob's office. Bob and I hadn't had sex in years; he slept in the guest room two floors down from me with a private entrance. That's when I called Brian, my divorce attorney.

The horses both were going crazy calling and running circles in their respective enclosures. The ranger pulled up in a golf cart with her husband and asked how I was doing.

I didn't think she was asking about my mental state, so I said, "I kind of have a problem with putting them together in this small pen."

I brought Wildflower back and tied her to the hitching rail and fed them their feed. I then put her back in with Dreamy and put hay in each corner, hoping to avoid any more kicking. Wildflower, the greedy little pig, couldn't guard all four corners at once.

When the sun set, they stood side by side at attention, ears perked forward. This was their first night in the forest. They had lived in controlled stable-like homes since they were young. It was cold and a full moon rose. The mooing sound of free ranging cattle nearby and coyotes howling punctuated the silence. Tucker and I sat by the fire ring watching my pitiful campfire where I'd stir-fried a frozen pasta meal. The log I'd cut wouldn't ignite so it was just sage brush that was burning, just kind of smoldering, and it smelled good. It reminded me of when I used to burn sage in the house after Bob and I had fought, or if he'd left on one of his business trips, trying to rid the home of the negative energy, like I'd heard the Indians used to do.

I looked up at the sky and was shocked by how many stars were in the sky. Bob used to tell the kids, "I love you more than all the stars in the sky." A sweet memory that made me sad for all I'd gambled and lost.

Thinking about Bob stirred up my insecurities, which was a problem since these memories popped into my head constantly. Everything I saw or heard seemed to trigger a Bob memory. I began doubting my ability to go through with this journey and worked myself into a panic. What the hell had I been thinking? I'm not that invincible woman anymore. I'm gonna die out here.

I used my DeLorme InReach satellite communicator to text Dad.

"I made it to Utah, but I'm not doing too good. I don't think I can do this."

He replied, "Sure you can! Come to Florida. Yvonne's a great cook and you can stay here as long as you want. I love you."

It was comforting to know that Dad still believed in me, but I didn't think he knew the extent of my damage. It was reassuring that he would take me in, but the fact that I needed to be taken in depressed me. I had always been so self-sufficient; what happened to that part of me?

I texted back, "Thanks, Dad. I'll be there by Christmas. Xxoo"

Next I texted Emily, "I'm in Utah now."

I thought that she probably wouldn't answer. I'd visited her at Point Loma just before I'd left California, to apologize. I remembered her tearing up and saying, "I forgive you, but that doesn't mean what you did is okay." I didn't understand, but I didn't ask for clarification, not wanting to provoke her any more.

To my delight, Emily texted back, "Good, how are you?"

I typed, "Afraid," and regretted it as soon as I hit send.

Emily texted, "Afraid of what?"

I texted, "Everything." My life, my future, what am I going to do, where am I going to live, will I end up homeless? Do you still love me? The uncertainty of my life.

I stared at the phone. She didn't reply.

I remembered saying, "Some Christian you are!"

It wasn't easy to live together in that little apartment in

Pasadena, both of us used to having a lot more space. Why had I said that? Had I expected her to "honor thy mother," the depressed mess that stood in front of her? Or exhibit some sort of gratitude for the pain I'd endured trying to keep her and her brothers' family intact? I hadn't done that with my own mother when I was Emily's age and found Mom curled up in a ball and sobbing, "I don't want to live."

Emily had exploded in tears, "How dare you question my faith! You have no idea what pain is! I've been going through hell since you moved out! It was my senior year, it was supposed to be special! It was the worst year of my life!"

I shot back, "I do too know what pain is!! You have no idea what kind of pain I've been going through for the last 15 years!"

She stopped cold, and looked confused. "What?"

"Your father abused me." I hadn't intended on saying it; I hadn't said it out loud to anyone. It had been on the tip of my tongue most of my waking hours for the past year, but I still thought it was my own fault, or I was exaggerating. I knew I shouldn't have said it to Emily; Bob was her father.

She shouted, "Liar!"

She was there, didn't she see it? Me, a liar? Bob was the liar, not me! This was the ultimate betrayal to me, the final slap in my face, my own flesh and blood calling me a liar!

I screamed, "Get out, get out now!"

My world fell apart as I watched her stuff clothes into trash bags and call Teddy.

I silently screamed at myself, "I'm a bad mom!" Just as Bob had regularly scolded me all these years.

I went out to our little third floor patio and curled up on the concrete, sobbing harder than I ever had before, whispering, "I want to die. God, just let me die."

Emily slid open the glass door and said, "I swear if this is true, I will never forgive him. Promise me you won't do anything rash, that you won't hurt yourself."

I'd thought I should say, "He never hit me." I thought that I should clarify, but I didn't have the strength to explain what emotional abuse was, I didn't know if I even understood it or believed it myself anymore. All I could say was, "Go, just go; I don't want you to see me like this."

A lone creature howled in the woods, bringing me out of my trance. I rapidly shook my head, trying to stop the scene in my mind. I took a deep breath and smelled the burning sage. I looked up at the stars, trying to bring myself back to the now.

I looked down at Tucker by my feet and stroked his head, "Let's go to bed, Tucker."

That night I had a dream:

A younger woman who worked for Bob was with me and we were cleaning the bedroom on Bob's boat. I didn't know that Bob had a boat. I could see Bob through the cabin porthole window with two other tall men. Bob was angrily typing on his cell phone then lifted his gaze and our eyes locked. He scowled and shouted, "What do you think you're doing!?"

Then we were in a truck that was towing the boat; the woman was driving and she pulled out fast saying, "Where can we park it? Oh, I know a lot where he won't find it."

I wondered why I was doing this; I didn't want his boat. I get seasick.

I woke up shaking. Here I was in another state in the wilderness and I still had to see Bob's face in my dreams? Who were his body guard friends? My boys? Who was the young woman helping me? The anonymous emailer? Or Emily? I got up and crawled down to Tucker's bed on the converted dinette seat, burying my face in his softness, trying to stop the panic I felt. I worried about Teddy still living with Bob and what Bob could do to him.

I remembered Dr. Anvekar's response during my visit just before I'd left California. I'd said that I was worried about leaving Brad with Bob. She'd said, "I think Brad will be okay; I'm more concerned about Teddy." He hadn't moved into his dorm for some reason. I felt ashamed that I'd left him in Bob's care. I sent him a text, asking if he was okay, but he didn't respond. I wondered if he was giving me the silent treatment, like Bob used to do. I'd spent the last seven years trying to be Teddy's nurse and therapist and school advocate and homework enforcer and protector from Bob, and then I just left; I abandoned him.

I said to myself, "Let go, let God. God, protect Teddy." It was all I could do.

When the sun rose, I rode Wildflower out for my first SHLEP ride. She jigged for most of the two hours we were out. We encountered free ranging cows and a large herd of deer bounding over boulders, both of which added to her apprehension. The trail entered the deep tall pine forest. It smelled wonderful, everything smelled more intense at altitude. The trail was skinny, rocky and hard to follow and I got lost, but soon found the Cracker-something trail again. I blamed the lame map.

Wildflower started calling back and forth with Dreamy as we approached camp just as my cell phone rang. Huh, I thought, cell service right at this spot, good to know.

"Woah!" I commanded as I answered the phone. She stopped for a moment.

"Hi honey, how ya doing today?" Dad said when I answered. I appreciated him checking in on me.

Wildflower was dancing around in circles, anxious to get back to Dreamy whom she could hear frantically calling her.

"Oh, a little better. I'm riding Wildflower and she's kind of a handful right now. Can I call you later?"

I put Wildflower in the corral and saddled Dreamy. Tucker joined us on a trail towards Forsyth Canyon as Wildflower went crazy in the corral, furious about being left behind. Tucker kept up for the two-hour ride, which made me happy; he must be doing okay. Dreamy scoffed at a water crossing where the sun was blindingly reflecting off the water. I figured she couldn't see the bottom. Tucker loved water and charged in. Seeing that the dog was okay, Dreamy followed him. Tucker's wagging tail floated on the surface a couple of feet behind his face. He looked so adorable and carefree, and I smiled. When we got back to the cell service spot, I told Dreamy to Woah and I called Dad back. I could hear Wildflower calling from camp and got annoyed. Dreamy stood stock still and ignored her. God, I loved this horse.

I told Dad about my problem with the horses being in the same corral, how I couldn't make a fire, that the trailer was cold, how I was alone there and worried about Teddy and my divorce mess and ending up homeless. Dad listened intently, interjecting occasionally with "Hmmm." I finally ran out of complaints and paused.

Dad said, "You can do this, Kathy, you're an amazing woman, don't forget that. And I'm always here for you."

I used to be amazing. I didn't forget that fact, but it was just a memory now, and I got mad at Bob all over again. "Thanks Dad, you're my rock."

He chuckled. What a good sound that was.

That night, as I ate my supper of a grilled cheese sandwich with lima beans, I realized that I did feel better than the previous night. Riding was magical for me and I wrote in my journal, "Remember, when depressed, RIDE LONG!" When writing down the date I realized Brad's birthday was the next day. He was turning 23 and had decided to finish college in

Madrid, Spain. I wondered if he would ever come back home. He'd said that he hated L.A. and wasn't coming home till the divorce was over. Smart kid. I sent him a birthday text and we texted back and forth a few times. I loved technology and how it had changed the world in the past twenty years, but not the texting part. It seemed impersonal to me and it was hard for me to type on my phone. But this is what my kids seemed to prefer. Probably because they didn't really want to talk to me.

Brad signed off with, "I love you, mom." It made my heart swell. I didn't have to worry about him; he was thousands of miles away from Bob. But that left Teddy alone to fend for himself, and it flipped my stomach upside down.

The next morning, I mounted Wildflower and grabbed Dreamy's lead rope to pony her with us. It was cold and wet. Tucker was tired so I left him in the trailer. We followed a trail up the mountainside. Once we'd gotten up pretty high, the clouds parted and the sun lit up droplets as they fell from the trees. I stopped and let the horses eat grass at a spot where I had a great view of the valley below. There was just one road into the valley that turned left when it hit the "town" of Pine Valley, which consisted of maybe 20 small buildings, houses and barns. The valley floor was carpeted with lush green grass and was surrounded by the mountains on three sides.

"Wow," I thought, "this was exactly what I'd pictured when I dreamed up this journey. I want to live here."

Tucker, being a typical lab, loved to play fetch, especially in the water. The lake was over by the RV campers and a short walk from our site, so I took him over there frequently. The mountain reflected on the brilliant blue surface as clearly as a mirror. As I tossed the stick over and over for Tucker, an Australian Shepherd wandered our way. His owner caught up to him and introduced himself and asked where I was from.

"I'm originally from California," he said. "I played

football for Utah State and loved it so much here that I just stayed after I graduated. Your dog reminds me of my old dog, Rex. I had to put him down recently."

"Oh, I'm sorry, what did he have?" I asked.

"My wife ran over him with the Suburban in our driveway."

I noticed he hadn't said ex-wife.

His teenaged daughter ran up and exclaimed, "Oh, Daddy, he looks just like Rex!"

I wondered if she'd called her mom a murderer.

I remembered when our dog, Toasty, had to be put down, Emily was maybe 6 or 7, and had protested the decision. For over a month afterwards, she stopped calling me mommy and referred to me as "the murderer."

Every time she said it, I thought of my two aborted babies and tried to picture what they'd look like if they'd not been killed. They would have both been in their early thirties by then.

After a week in Utah, I broke camp at night and went to bed early. I had a two-day haul ahead of me to get to a friend's ranch in Idaho and I wanted to get an early start. It got below freezing overnight and the ground was crusty with frost when I carried some hay to the corral, always the first thing I did in the morning. Both horses were covered in mud and looked like hell. I crawled in between the rough timber rails and inspected them more closely. Wildflower was okay, just a few scrapes on her and one slightly swollen hind leg. But Dreamy was covered in blood and there was missing skin on her withers and rump and by the sides of her tail. There was a hoofmark on her side and one deep puncture wound at the top of her right front leg, probably from the bolts that stuck out of the rails on the horse side. How could this have happened without me hearing anything?

"Did you do this, Wildflower?" I demanded.

I told myself, Wildflower is a troubled horse. She'd had a horrible babyhood. She'd been weaned early and sent to a feed lot for slaughter. It's not her fault, she's just fucked up.

I stuffed my anger and pulled out my "First Aid" Rubbermaid tub. I gently cleaned up all the open wounds and applied an antibiotic cream. None of the wounds looked like they needed stitches, thank God, something I would have needed a vet to do.

When I stopped for gas and offered the horses water, Dreamy wouldn't drink and her hay net was still full. "Oh, Dreamy, you have to drink," I said, as I offered her a carrot, which she refused. That scared me. I opened the back door and saw that she only had one tiny manure pile at her back feet. I was always on the lookout for signs of colic. That's how Ty died! Stress and lack of water can cause colic. I wondered why people didn't die from colic. Ty and Dreamy's colic surgeries had cost $15,000 each, something I could no longer afford.

At our overnight, I called Jack, my friend in Idaho, and told him what happened to Dreamy. He asked a bunch of questions and I described her wounds and told him that she started eating, drinking and pooping after I unloaded her. He reassured me that she was probably okay. "But there's a snow storm coming and you shouldn't waste any time getting here. It's going to get colder; do you have any alfalfa to feed?"

"No, just Timothy." I never fed alfalfa anymore.

I remembered Ty's surgeon calling me at 3am. He said, "We opened her up. There was alfalfa stem blockage; her intestines have already burst. What do you want me to do?"

I didn't know what any of that meant. I said, "Just fix her; she's my son's horse!"

Jack owned Challis Creek Ranch, the horse retirement ranch where Emily's horse, Tiara, had lived for the last few years. Last October, I'd flown up with a friend to visit Tiara and meet Jack.

On that visit, I hung out in the pasture with the retired horse herd, sketching. I hadn't felt such comforting peace in a long time and it had been a relief to know that I still had the capacity to feel wonderful. I remembered sketching Tiara grazing and swishing her tail at flies while the other horses tried to play with my folding chair and colored pencils. As I sketched that sweet little horse, I thought how Bob had told me to put her down a few years earlier just because she was too lame to be ridden. I'd mustered up a strength in that battle I hadn't been able to find in a long time, because there was no way I was going to have Emily calling me a murderer again.

Jack had been kind; he'd given us a tour of the nicely kept ranch and even cooked dinner for us in his log home. I told him I'd just filed for divorce and he shared that his divorce had been going on for five years already and he'd put the ranch up for sale, but doubted that it was worth half of what his wife thought it was, so it likely wouldn't sell. This scared me and I hoped my divorce wouldn't take that long. I admired Jack, sort of how I admired Dad, and wondered if we could ever develop a relationship. Already I'd started looking for a man to replace Bob, even though I knew it was way too soon and that I had a lot of work to do on myself before a good man would find me attractive.

Chapter 3

I felt again the promise of that peaceful feeling when I saw the sign for Challis, and hoped that this was God's way of telling me to settle down there. It had just stopped raining as I turned right out of the small town of Challis and headed into the green valley rimmed by the bare brown Rocky Mountains where Jack lived. One of Jack's ancestors had settled the area and the creek, town and road were all named after him. The sun came out and sparkled on the wide expanses of grass pastures. What was it about the color green, that I loved so much? Did it symbolize life?

In July, I'd shot Jack a panicking email, "Caroline bailed, do you want to come with me?"

He'd emailed me back:

Kathy:

Actually, I wish I could. However, this place cannot run itself and I could not put the total operational responsibility solely on my Ranch Manager for that length of time. Besides, my divorce predicament with the Ranch continues necessitating my being around here. Am I to Assume you have settled with your ex?

What I had been considering suggesting if your son was not able to go with you and you, in turn, were not going to go by yourself (something I think you should think long and hard about, considering the "dangers" you potentially could encounter if on your own), was you perhaps considering a trip back to Idaho. This way you could practice with your trailer while still being able to ride in new territory. Frankly I have refrained from suggesting this figuring the possible risk that I might well be accused of (using today's more common youthful vernacular) "hitting on you" (not that I wouldn't necessarily do that lol). I have a guest room, as you well know, plenty of space for your horses, a limited (due to the fire) but significant (if not unlimited) area for riding (trails or cut your own trails) and, again, plenty of space and places to practice driving your horse trailer, something frankly I could help you with. It's still occasionally smoky up here but tolerable. And while I could not necessarily ride with you all that much I would at least know where you were so if a situation did arise I would know where to look to find you.

Something you might possibly want to consider discussing further?

Jack

As I read it, I thought, man he writes long emails. "Settled with my ex?" made me laugh. I'd shot back, "Sounds great! Thanks!—K"

I didn't ask how long I could stay. I saw his invitation as a welcome sign of a possible romantic interest in me. I hadn't been "hit on"—the words he'd used—in many years. It made me hopeful that I was still hit on material and hoped that maybe I could now make a mature mate choice, one not instigated by physical attraction and that blinding chemistry thing, but by something more important, like kindness. Then I thought maybe I was reading too much into his words and I'd be stupid not to take him up on his offer to better prepare me for SHLEP.

Jack met me at the gate with his ranch hand, over whom Jack towered in height. He was a reassuring sight to me. He wore a plaid wool shirt, jeans and a baseball cap. He smiled and ambled over to my window. "You finally made it! Do you want me to take over from here? It's kind of steep and narrow down to the barn."

Steep and narrow scared me, so I said, "Yes. I'm beat driving this thing."

We unloaded the horses at the barn and Jack put Dreamy in the cross ties to clean up her wounds. He said, "Oh she's not too bad; she's lost a lot of hide but nothing serious."

I'd never thought of Dreamy's beautiful flesh as being hide and took a little offense.

Tucker couldn't come inside Jack's house. Jack had told me this beforehand and I had been anxious about it. Jack had two dogs that lived outside and he put them in a chain link enclosure at night to protect them from mountain lions. There was a huge doghouse in the enclosure that was stuffed with straw to keep them warm. I tried to talk Tucker into the doghouse, but he wouldn't go in it and scampered back out through the gate. Jack ran a cord to a space heater in my trailer, which he had parked by his home's front door. He took a look around at the mud and fur and hay in the LQ and asked, "Do you want to borrow my vacuum?"

I thought it odd that a rancher would notice dirt. "No, it'll just get dirty again anyway."

"Suit yourself. Do you like antelope?"

"I don't know."

As we ate Jack's stew, Tucker sat by the glass door and cried. I went out to console him for a while. After the sunset, Tucker started shivering. I went out and put him in the trailer and cuddled for a while. "I'm so sorry, Tucker. I love you." I tried real hard not to be mad at Jack.

Jack was seated in one of two matching Lazy Boys watching some violent cop show on his enormous screen TV. Overhead were several stuffed wild animals perched on the beams staring down at me. The carpet was white and spotless. I wondered if I could be happy here.

"Can I take a bath?" I asked.

He grinned and said, "Sure, let me show you how the faucet works," and he put the show on pause. Did I look that inept?

"It's one of those claw foot tubs that you can also use as a shower and it's not as simple as just turning the handle," he said. After his detailed instructions, I shut the door and used the toilet. It was an old-fashioned kind with a wooden seat and the tank suspended up high on the wall with a chain that you pull to flush. The water force was so strong that it sounds like a jet engine starting up and startled the heck out of me. I stripped off my filthy clothes and melted into the steamy hot bath. I reached up and ran my hand along one of the logs of the exterior wall.

This was a very comfortable home, I thought, neat and tidy with all the comforts you could want. I wondered what it would be like to live with a man who cared about domestic comforts and cleanliness. I wondered if Jack was a little OCD. There was a small window that looked out onto the 50-acre horse pasture but it was dark and I couldn't make out the horses down there. There was an antique wooden side table where I had laid my e-cigarette, pen and Sudoku book. I reached for the book and did one of the puzzles.

As the bath cooled down, I crawled out and faced myself in the full-length mirror on the door. I used to enjoy catching my reflection in a store window on the streets of NYC, my long dark hair up in a French twist, wearing designer dresses and heels, swinging a leather briefcase. That was when men still whistled at me, something I said I hated, yet secretly craved.

Looking at my reflection made me sad. Everyone used to tell me how beautiful I was. I'd always had a hard time seeing it in my own mirror and it was now impossible. If I had once been thin as a fashion model, I now looked more like a bony old witch. I had started cutting my hair myself to save money and it was a bit uneven. It came down to my shoulders and was salt and pepper except for a few inches at the ends, orangey brown from when I used to have it dyed. I admired the irises of my eyes, which were a yellowish shade of green with brown speckles—the windows to my soul.

My lips were less full than they used to be and I

remembered my high school art teacher calling them baby lips. The edges were now red and chapped. I smiled, just to see what that looked like, and it stung and made them bleed a little. I caught sight of the half missing tooth that I couldn't afford to get repaired so I closed my lips.

Emily had said that the deep furrows between my eyebrows made me look angry all the time; I'd said it was because the sun was too bright in L.A. and I was just squinting. I now lifted my eyebrows to try and minimize them and crooked crevices expanded on my forehead.

My laugh lines looked like crazed spider webs around the sides of my eyes. Why were they called laugh lines anyway? Mine didn't tell the story of all the time I'd spent laughing. Before I got married, I'd found it easy to laugh. I had a great career and a string of hot romances. I'd traveled around the world on vacations and never worried about children or money or a husband. I had the world by the tail, Dad used to say. I wanted to be that woman again. I wanted a do-over.

I remembered Bob saying, "You made your bed, now lay in it," and how I'd thought, that's better than sharing a bed with you. I was so sick of thinking about Bob every other thought; why couldn't I stop doing that? Because he did this to me!

I'd had my breast implants removed five years ago after they started leaking. I wondered what Bob had thought of that and if I'd done it out of spite. I tried to remember if we were still having sex then or not. What was left appeared dimpled and creased, no matter how far I stuck my chest out. Just to the south of that surgical mess appeared a nasty hip to hip scar from a tummy tuck I thought I needed after my third baby to remove the drapery of my stretched out skin. Why had I done this to myself?

I remembered mom saying, "I had a plan. I got a face lift, a boob job, bought a fur coat and graduated college. Then I filed for divorce.'" I'd sworn I'd never be anything like her.

I wrapped a soft thick towel that smelled like fabric softener around me and said to myself, "There's no way I'm ever letting anyone see me naked again."

I passed through the living room to tell Jack that I was going to bed.

"Sweet dreams," he said. Mom used to say that.

I lay there looking at the many stars through the window and after I heard the spiral stairs squeak as Jack climbed them to retire, I slipped outside into the frigid night air to my trailer. I wrapped my arm over Tucker and curled up on the dinette bench next to him to get warm. I buried my nose in the soft nape of his neck. No man had ever been this wonderful to snuggle with. I whispered, "I love you Tucker." Tucker's tail thumped a few times on the feather bed and we both dozed off.

Before the sun came up, I snuck back into the house and went to bed. I didn't want Jack to know I'd slept in the trailer; he would say I was too soft, Tucker was just a dog. Why did I care what he thought?

All was quiet in the house when I got up to pee. I smelled coffee coming from the kitchen but there was no sign of Jack around. I got dressed and went outside to feed Tucker and let him out of the trailer. Jack's dogs wandered up and joined us for a game of fetch. I was pleased that Tucker was still the champ at getting the ball first.

Jack pulled up on his 4-wheeler, a cloud of dust streaming behind him.

"Morning, sleepy head! Got some bad news, your truck's got a flat, a rock cut."

"A what? I've never heard of that. Rocks can cut through a tire?"

"Sure can, Idaho rocks are pretty sharp, and your truck tires are crap. You've got to replace them. I always replace the cheap factory tires on a new truck. I already called the tire store in town; they'll set you up."

"Oh, God. I can't afford that. I'm going to have to call my

Dad for the money."

"Well, let's go in and call him then. I want to talk to him anyway."

As I followed him into the house I wondered why he wanted to talk to my dad.

"Hi honey!" Dad answered, in his super upbeat voice.

I hated having to ask him for more money. "Hi dad. I got a flat on the truck. Jack says I need new tires."

"I thought you just got a set of new tires."

"That was for the trailer. Can you talk to Jack?"

"Sure, I'd love to talk to Jack!" His enthusiasm about talking to Jack surprised me, and I handed the phone to Jack.

I watched as Jack puffed up his chest and stood up straighter. He talked to Dad with authority about truck tires. Then about my rig. And the weather. Then about the horse's conditions. Then about me needing a gun.

I heard Jack reassuring Dad that he would not send me off until I was more prepared. This was interspersed with belly laughs and yes, yes, yes and occasional glances my way. It made me feel safe, these two capable men looking after me. I wondered what role Jack was taking in this conversation. Were they both playing the dad role? Or was it like a boyfriend talking to my dad? Finally, Jack handed the phone back to me.

"OK, honey, use my Visa card for the tires. Just do whatever Jack tells you to, okay?" He sounded so chipper to me.

"Thanks so much, Dad. I love you."

Jack said, "Let's go to town to get you some tires. We can stop by the store for a gun tomorrow. There's a new restaurant in town that I'll bet you'll like—very city like frou-frou kind of place; we can have lunch there while they mount your tires."

You can just go buy a gun at a store?

I knew how strongly Jack felt about this point and had taken two gun clinics to get over my fear of guns, as he'd insisted, before leaving California. I'd gone with Teddy who was a great shot. I actually had a lot of fun. I know this sounds sick, but I loved the "shoot to kill" exercise which was three rapid shots at the targets that depicted a person's silhouette. Two shots to the heart and one to the head. It was euphorically empowering and released the rage I'd been stuffing in my effort to not appear like the stereotypical angry divorcee that no one wanted to be around.

We went to the tire place and to lunch. He knew the people at every stop and introduced me to them as his friend from California, which he said was bad enough; he wasn't gonna mention that I was technically from New York City.

Jack said, "People are gonna be talkin' 'bout me an' you here; it's a small town."

"Oh," was all I could muster up. Was there something to talk about or was he just joking? I couldn't tell. I hadn't seen any interest on his part, or did I just miss it? As we drove home, I watched Jack's face. He was older than me and skin hung from his chin. He was wearing a ball cap as most men with receding hairlines seemed to do. I wondered what Jack had looked like when he was younger. There was no stirring of any sexual desire in my belly. I tried to imagine kissing him, but couldn't. I wasn't sure if my sexual desires were just dead for good or if I was a shallow person, not able to see any possible beauty beneath his skin.

I went out for a ride alone the next day, ponying Dreamy. I went straight up the nearest rise to enjoy the view of the vast Rocky mountain range, layer upon layer of mountains. The ground was full of those stupid sharp Idaho rocks and I worried about my horse's feet.

The hunting store didn't have the gun that Jack thought I should have so he decided to sell me his Colt revolver for $500. He said that he didn't use it much, preferring to carry his Glock, which was always by his side or on the kitchen table. He cleaned and loaded the Colt and handed it to me in a zippered case with a box of ammo. I carefully put it in a cabinet in the gooseneck by my bed, as if it might accidently go off. I wondered if it could go off by accident in the trailer if I crashed, if I'd be able to get it out of its case fast enough in an emergency. Its presence frightened me and I doubted I'd ever need it.

A few days later, Jack rode Dreamy and I rode Wildflower on a flatter route. We wandered around the gently rolling hills and viewed the bright yellow fall leaves on the trees along a stream and past a remote cabin with cows in the pasture. There were sharp rocks scattered all around and Dreamy looked a little sore to me, even though I'd booted her.

One morning as I was drinking coffee and setting up my art supplies on the counter to paint, Jack came in and slipped his boots off at the door as he always did.

He said, "I heard that Montana just got 6' of snow."

"What?! It's the beginning of October; I was going to go to Montana next."

"I'd rethink that if I were you. The Rockies have erratic weather this time of year. Oh, by the way, I might be going salmon fishing this weekend."

Would he still go if I was here? Or was he dropping a hint for me to hit the road? Dad used to say that houseguests are like fish; they start to stink after three days.

I thought about leaving. I was feeling more confident about driving and Jack had taught me a lot about the systems on the trailer and camping in general. And winter was definitely coming; there was snow on the tops of the peaks I could see out the living room window. If I didn't leave soon, I could get stuck there or have to haul in the snow, which I didn't want to even think about doing. I now had 500 pounds of alfalfa cubes loaded in the trailer's third stall, which would keep the mares warmer in the cold weather I was bound to hit, even though I'd change my route to head south.

Jack went back outside and I started my first SHLEP

painting. I chose a photo I'd taken in Utah of the mares grazing with the mountains in the background. I hadn't painted in such a small format in a long time; the panels I'd brought were just 10" square. My new acrylic paints were more liquid than the oils I used, and it was a learning experience mixing colors, but I liked the scene and stuck to it. I could lose myself while painting; I didn't worry about any of my problems and time would slip by quickly.

As the painting came together, I felt myself transported to the day I took the photo. I'd hobbled my mares and turned them loose with small cowbells on their halters so I could find them if they moved faster than me. I took pictures of them being free, something that I found very satisfying deep in my soul. The sky was that shocking vivid blue that you only see at altitude. The sage brush was thick and smelled heavenly. The bells clipped on their halters tinkled softly. There were tiny white and yellow wildflowers dotting the meadow as the breeze picked up the horses' manes and tails. Nothing about the scene reminded me of the fear I'd experienced in Utah; it was peaceful, wild and free and I yearned to experience it again. It was my only hope of healing and finding myself and I had to finish my trip. My final chapter in life was going to be my best one. My urge to SHLEP had returned and I called to make my next camp reservation in Colorado.

On the eleventh day there, Jack helped me load the horses and drove the rig through the retired horses' pasture and back up to the paved road. His ranch hand was there on the four-wheeler to give him a lift back to the barn. He gave me a bear hug and told me to stay safe. His embrace was strong and warm and I melted a little.

"Thanks for everything, Jack. I really appreciate it." I wish I could have been more open, but I was confused about how I felt towards him. It wasn't love or passion, but I didn't think I was capable of those feelings anymore. It felt warm and good. I just didn't know what to say and he didn't say anything.

As I made my way down the road, I felt my back and shoulders relax. I hadn't realized how tense I had been. I felt an excitement forming in my tummy. Tucker's head was by my right elbow, resting on the console. His tail wagged so hard his whole body swayed back and forth as if he was dancing to Willie Nelson's singing on the radio, "On the road again."

I smiled and said, "Just you and me again, Tucker."

Chapter 4

Three days after I hugged Jack good-bye, I crossed the Rocky Mountains in the afternoon, hoping the reported ice would be melted by the sun. I'd been on I-70 several times before, driving from Denver to Vail to go skiing. It was often closed in the winter because it was steep and dangerous in icy winter conditions.

After climbing the 7% grade up to Vail pass, I saw the ski resorts to my right, and thought how I couldn't afford to go there anymore. I remembered part one of our honeymoon at Beaver Creek.

> *My sister Liza and her husband Doug met us there and we stayed at a B&B. We all went out to dinner for Christmas. Bob took forever to place his order as the waitress stood there waiting. A few minutes later, he called her back, he now wanted manicotti without the cheese. He told a story about running over a ski instructor's skis and the guy threatened to pull his lift ticket because he was skiing out of control. He laughed about it. Somehow, we got on the subject of birth control being accessible to teenagers and I said, "Well if I have a girl, I'm just putting the pill in her orange juice once she gets her period."*
>
> *Bob said, "That's just giving her permission to be promiscuous."*
>
> *I said all teenagers had sex nowadays and I wasn't going to take any chances.*
>
> *He said, "Well, I didn't have sex as a teenager; I waited till I was in my late 20's."*
>
> *Liza later said to me, "I hope you guys never have a girl."*

Then the downgrade began, and my grip on the

steering wheel tightened. I shifted to Manual and put the truck in a lower gear. Tucker popped his head into the front seat as the engine began to roar. The highway was cantilevered into the mountain side, the opposing traffic was as well, but higher up on the wall to my left. The right side was a sheer drop off with the Colorado River raging below. The truck lanes were filled with semis trying to crawl down the grade. There were several tunnels, one of which is the highest and longest mountain tunnel in the US. This section is known for some outrageous truck signage such as "Trucks Don't be Fooled" and "Truckers You're Not Done Yet." My whole body was as tight as a fiddle string about to snap and I had to literally pry my cramped fingers off the steering wheel when it leveled out. But I did it, my rig did it; we all survived what would be the worst pass on my trip and I was proud of that.

I pulled into the Golden Fairgrounds, the closest horse camping to Boulder, where my young friend, Theresa, now lived. She had been our nanny in the '90s. I still remembered her bubbly personality when I'd interviewed her. Joy flowed out of her; you couldn't help but be happy around her. When she came for her interview, she sat cross legged on the floor, playing with Teddy and Brad. I knew Theresa would be a great influence for my children. More than anything, I wanted them to be happy, to see the glass half full instead of half empty. Theresa was in college then and could only work part time. I took all the hours she could give us. I hadn't seen her since I quit my job but we'd reconnected on Facebook and she'd insisted that I come see her when I was in Colorado. I wondered how she would react to the new, wet washrag me.

The Fairgrounds was called home by many recession-hit folks living in RV's. There wasn't another horse camper there at all. While eating supper, I looked out the window at a trailer nearby, from which yelling was coming. A woman emerged shouting, "You make me feel like everything I do is shit!" and she slammed the door, storming off in her little car. I caught my breath. I had said those exact words so many times to Bob and I felt that old rage take over my mind and body. That night, I had a nightmare that Bob was stalking around outside my trailer with a huge knife.

Theresa showed up the next day at noon, her long black curls blowing in the breeze. We hugged and both commented on what a gorgeous day it was. The sky was a vivid blue and it was in the low 70's. Tucker waddled up to us wagging his tail so hard he almost knocked himself over.

Theresa bent over to pat his head, "Well, hello there, who are you? You're not Toasty."

"No, Toasty died years ago. This is Tucker and he's pretty sweet too," I said. "You hungry?"

We went in the LQ and Theresa sat at the dinette drinking a beer as I cooked some quesadillas on the stovetop. We chatted about the weather and the flooding that had occurred there recently.

"You want sour cream?" I asked. Bob hated sour cream.

I retrieved it from the fridge and sat down across from her.

Theresa asked, "So, tell me, what happened? Why'd you leave Bob?"

I heaved a sigh, "It's still confusing to me. But basically, he was a shit head to me after I retired. He treated me like an indentured servant and criticized everything I did. Want another beer?"

"Sure, I'm off today."

I got up to get two Coors Lights from the fridge, stepping over Tucker since we'd taken his bed in the dinette. I wanted to be open with Theresa. I was no longer her boss, but a friend in need.

"I stuck it out as long as I could. My therapist says that he was emotionally abusive, but I have a hard time saying that." I took a big sip of beer, "All I know is that he was mean and lied all the time and now I'm half the person I used to be.

I'm hoping this journey will help me get better."

"I'm so sorry."

She didn't question the word abusive, which was a relief to me. I always worried that people would think I was lying by using that word; Emily had. I gave Tucker the rest of my quesadilla.

"I started having panic attacks and bouts of depression." I gave a quick smile as if to say, but I'm really okay. "I'm worried about money, too; all our assets were in Bob's name or the company's name, I'm not sure which, and he's stonewalling the divorce."

"Why? You're kidding me. After all you did for him? What an asshole."

"All I did for him?"

"You were running the whole show then; his company went under and he was broke!"

I'd almost forgotten, he'd said that he needed $100,000 and asked me to buy out his share of the house equity, the one asset that our prenup agreement said should be held jointly. Our "shared" budget now shifted the mortgage and repairs costs to my column as well as things like nannies, pre-school and maids, which he labeled as "discretionary" and "couldn't afford to" share the cost of. I'd give him the monthly list of our expenses and he'd just cross lines off and write a check for half of what was left.

"Bob says I'm making that all up."

Theresa cocked her head and scrunched her face, "Huhh?"

"Yeah, I know, it's weird; he lied all the time about stuff, made me think I was crazy after a while." I rolled my head and could hear tendons snapping over bones in my neck. "Then I lent him $100,000 to buy his new company in California so I could be a stay-at-home mom. I had enough foresight to put the loan agreement in writing and I put in the conditions that I'd retire, he'd share in the anticipated loss in selling the house too soon after just renovating it, we'd move to California and mingle our assets, he'd give me periodic financial reporting about the company and a few other things, like getting a vasectomy and his first marriage annulled."

Theresa laughed.

"Yeah, that was silly to put in a legal document but I wanted to cover all my bases. I was walking away from a lot of money so I figured it was my last chance to ask for something."

She nodded her head.

"The big old house finally sold and closing was a month away and Bob still hadn't gotten a place for us to live in California. We'd looked at a lot of houses but he found something wrong with every one of them. So, I bought this little old house across the street from St. Anne's for temporary housing. I thought it could be an income property once he found something and we moved. Bob flew home on weekends."

I fired up my e-cigarette and settled in to tell her the story. "During the week it was lovely; I was so excited about being a stay-at-home mom. I had fun fixing up and decorating the house. I was really happy."

> *I remembered how I loved being home with the children, walking them to school across the street. Brad's best friend's mom became my best friend and we ran together, or we took turns watching the kids and running. Her daughter was good friends with Emily. They all played well together, we had a fenced yard and a swing set with a fort and slide. Toasty played with them. They jumped on the trampoline, we'd take them to open gym night at the kid's gymnastic facility, swimming at the indoor pool at the YMCA in the winter. It was a drastically reduced lifestyle, but none of us minded one bit; it was wonderful in that little house.*

Theresa looked at me, and I continued. "I started getting angry and frustrated about our arrangement. He wasn't paying for any house repairs because I'd bought it and he said it wasn't his responsibility to fix my house. He paid the bills late; he still hadn't done anything about mingling our assets and he got angry when I brought it up. He got very 'mine/yours-conscious.' He hadn't gotten his marriage annulled; he did get a vasectomy, but complained about complications and pain, like it was this huge sacrifice, I thought it was just an excuse for being impotent."

Theresa made a sympathetic face.

"When he came home for the weekends, he started criticizing my parenting, calling me a bad mother. He acted like the Lord of the Castle, and he seemed to just dislike me. He was awful with Brad too."

"Man, I'm sorry," Theresa said.

"We tried marriage counseling again, but he dominated our sessions, interrupting me and talking down his nose at me. The counselor had us do this "Pleasing" exercise in which we were to ask the other to do something little that would please us. I asked Bob if he would pick up his dirty dinner dishes and take them to the kitchen sink. He said that he couldn't do that. Afterwards he said that we were quitting therapy."

I pictured the next week when I went to our session alone and told her that we were quitting. She'd said, "You seem so different than when I've seen you with Bob."

I wasn't sure what she was talking about. She explained, "I've never had a patient refuse to do the Pleasing exercise."

I said that I thought Bob might be OCD or a germaphobe.

She said, "If you follow that man to California, it will be the biggest mistake of your life."

I thought she was overreacting, just because he wouldn't take his dish to the sink? I said, "No, we love each other, I have three children to think of and a divorce would hurt them."

I drew a long breath as I told Theresa, "That counselor said, 'That man will kill you.'"

Theresa exclaimed, "Oh my God!" Her eyes were wide open and her jaw had gone slack.

"Yeah, it shocked me too. I still wonder what made her say that. But I figured she didn't know how strong I was. Then I got this obscene pocket dial call from Bob. He was in his car, I could hear the radio and he was saying horrible things about me, screaming really. I freaked out and called him back and told him not to come home. He denied everything."

"Of course," Theresa said.

"I saw a divorce attorney downtown after that. I was so stupid. Saying it all out loud now makes me feel like such an idiot."

"Kathy, you were strong! You were such an inspiration to me!"

I straightened my spine and a spark of energy brought my chest up in pride. "I didn't know that."

"Are you kidding? You were so-o-o successful! And a great mom!! I really looked up to you."

I really had been like that. It wasn't just an inflated memory; she'd seen it too. It meant a lot to me.

Theresa went on to tell me about leaving her husband and moving to Colorado. She had been terrified but was now incredibly happy that she did. She talked about the new love in her life, Chad; he was a musician and they lived together. She said she wanted to be a nanny again, that she couldn't have children and she wanted to be around them again. She asked about my kids and told me that she'd kept in touch with Teddy.

She said, "I told him he has the most amazing mom in the world."

"Oh, I bet he doesn't think so now. I feel so guilty that I left him living with Bob."

After lunch, we went out for a ride. We roamed the grassy hills around the fairgrounds together and could see the Denver skyline to the east and the Rocky Mountains to the west. I got a dramatic shot of Theresa coming down a hill on

Dreamy, the sun glinting off the mare's golden dapples and lighting up Theresa's fair skin. I knew the sharp contrast of her red t-shirt and the blue sky would make a great painting. Dreamy slowly picked her way through the rocks, knowing that she had a beginner on her back, and stopped frequently to munch on the tall grasses blowing in the wind. I had a lovely day.

The rest of the week I rode alone in the same grass hills and once I rode in the rodeo arena. I was booting the horses every time now because it was rocky in the Rocky Mountains.

I hiked with Tucker in the hills too, but he seemed exhausted if we went too far, walking slowly and panting more than usual. I thought the altitude was affecting him. He was still wagging his tail, which always made me smile and reassured me that he wasn't in any pain.

I saw Theresa two more times while I was in Colorado. She took me out for a steak dinner at the kind of restaurant I couldn't afford to go to any more. We had a bottle of wine and lingered at our table until I started getting sleepy.

Another night I joined her, Chad and another young couple for a night out in Boulder. Chad seemed like a real nice guy. He had very long hair and his beard was the same length. We all got stoned on the way there; recreational pot was now legal in Colorado and I told them how cool I thought that was. We had dinner and then went to a coffee house-wine bar. There was local art hanging on the walls and a live band. Theresa laughed often. She put her arm around me for a selfie, kissed me on the cheek and said, "I love you so much!"

Chad got up and did a set with the band. Theresa stood and danced alone on the dance floor, something I would never do in public unless I was drunk. I admired the wonderful free spirit she still had. I used to be like that. And for the first time in years, I thought that maybe I could be like that again.

After I left Colorado, it took me three days to get to Tin

Acres, an overnight bed and barn in rural Colby on the western edge of Kansas. Kansas was flat as a pancake, with miles of fields filled with corn stalks ready to chop down and plow under for the winter. The ranch looked run down, but the owner's house appeared brand new. There was a spanking new living quarters horse trailer as big as mine parked in front with all the doors open. A goat stood by the house's front door nibbling on potted plants and a few dogs were running around as I rang the doorbell.

A woman appeared from around back, greeted me and told me to follow her to the barn.

"I'm not the owner, Jane is. She's a super nice lady; I just help her out here. My name is Kathy too. Jane's gone off to get some stuff for a trip she's going on."

She led me into the dilapidated barn. The sun peeked through the slats of the walls. There were several large round bales, usually used for cows, being stored in the common area and a few horses were nibbling on them. The dirt floor was hard packed and pocked with holes.

Kathy filled a water tub and said, "A tornado hit this last year." She shut off the hose and we headed outside.

"A tornado?! Oh my God, how scary!" I'm in Kansas now! The Wizard of Oz tornado scene flashed in my head, I heard that dum da dum da dum dum wicked witch song that scared the crap out of me as a kid.

"Jane and her late husband had kind of let this place go. He was real sick and Jane nursed him for years. He just died last year."

"Oh, that's so sad." I remembered worrying about becoming widowed when one of Emily's friend's father had a massive heart attack and died.

> *I'd asked the girl's mom if they were going to have to move and she'd said no, they'd had the house in both their names and it was turned over to her.*
>
> *My name wasn't on the deed to our house. Bob*

had just come back from a run, we were both in the back yard.

"Bob, I was talking to the mom in Brownie's that was just widowed and I was wondering, do you have a life insurance policy?"

"The banks holding the loans on the company have one."

"What about me and the children?"

"You don't care whether I die or not, do you? All you care about is my money."

He was so sensitive, how did he turn that around? I mustered up the courage to ask another question.

"Bob how am I supposed to handle the company if you died?"

"Oh God, you just don't give up do you? You'd just call Wayne Silverman."

"Who's that?"

"My accountant in Chicago. You met him at our wedding; don't you remember anything?"

I'd sent out the invitations, Wayne Silverman wasn't at our wedding.

I brought myself back to the present moment.

"Well, Jane's a real trooper," Kathy was saying. "A couple of months ago, her favorite horse was bitten by a rattlesnake in the pasture and died too. She's been through a lot; that's why I help her."

"You have rattlesnakes in Kansas?" I thought I'd left those nasty critters behind in California.

"Yeah, and no one checked on the pasture horses for a few days when she was out of town, so it just died."

She didn't have someone to check on her horses when she was away? I was overwhelmed with this tragic story. How could she carry on? Why would God do all this to her? I just stood there with my mouth open.

"Well, I'll leave you to get settled in. Jane should be back soon."

As I led the mares to the barn, I continued dwelling on what Kathy had just told me. What kind of resilience did one need to endure all of this and then head out on a horse camping trip solo? I couldn't wait to meet her. I threw a few flakes of hay into the stall and headed back to make supper.

As I was washing the dishes, Jane called and said, "Kathy? My friend Kathy just told me that you're there already. I'll be right back. I've been dying to meet you and hear all about your amazing journey."

She knocked on my trailer door an hour or so later as the sun was setting. She had short reddish hair that turned golden as the sun hit it. Her smile showed off her perfect white teeth. Her green eyes twinkled. This was a very high energy person before me. I stepped outside and answered her rapid-fire questions about horse camping and where I'd been already. The sky was ablaze with color behind her and it had cooled off considerably.

"So, you're a horse camper too?" I asked, nodding to her new rig and an even larger one by the road with a for sale sign on it.

"No, I've never gone horse camping before! This will be my first trip without my husband. We used to use that old big one for horse shows. My husband raised quarter horses."

We walked around my rig and she showed me where there was an outlet to plug into.

"Kathy told me about losing your husband, I'm so sorry."

Her smile broke for a second. "Thanks." She quickly recovered and said, "I've never hauled a horse trailer before; my husband always did the driving and heavy work when we were going to shows. Actually, he always did everything around here; I'm an insurance agent."

I followed her to a pipe coming out of the ground and

she told me I could dump my tanks there.

"Oh, I used to be in sales, but that was a long time ago."

"You could sell insurance. State Farm has a great mentoring program that I'm involved with."

"Oh, I think I'm too old to get a job offer now; I've tried already. Where are you going camping?"

"You're not old! It's a Fall Colors ride in Missouri! I'm so excited about it. You should come with me! We can ride and you can tell me all about your SHLEP; that's what it's called, right?"

I was surprised that there wasn't an ounce of fear in her voice. I had been so fearful before my first attempt at this. And she wanted me, a total stranger, to go with her.

"Really? But, I was going to ride here for Kansas."

"This will be way more fun than riding the cornfields here; it's pretty boring. My friend says that it's the best ride she's been to. It's at 4-J in Duke."

"What's 4-J?"

"It's a private campground on the edge of the National Forest. They put on organized weekends for trail riding; there'll be tons of people there. Oh, you gotta come!"

A private horse campground? Fun? I could use some fun in my life. Jane's enthusiasm was contagious; maybe I could learn something from this amazing woman. It was getting dark and I wrapped my arms around myself to warm up.

"When are you leaving?"

"Crack of dawn. Come up to the house at 6 for breakfast. You can meet my other guests, there is a couple due in late tonight. But they'll be staying in the house. I'm gonna go finish packing my trailer now. Don't forget 6:00 sharp for breakfast!"

I got up early and fed the mares and put fresh hay nets in the trailer. Jane answered the front door in her exuberant style and introduced me to the four guests that were gathering in the spacious kitchen area. There was a Christmas tree decorated with Halloween ornaments next to the table. Numerous photos of children and grandchildren hung on the walls. The vast counters and buffet area were filled with homemade omelets, bacon, sausages, muffins, quiche, fruit and anything else you could ever desire for breakfast.

"Your home is beautiful."

"Thanks. I built it to withstand a tornado! The only thing that was left was the chimney," she said as she pointed toward the two story high stone fireplace in the great room.

I wondered what you had to do to a building to make it withstand a tornado. "It smells delicious. When did you have time to cook all this?"

She laughed, "Last night!"

"Do you ever sleep?"

She laughed again and said, "Not much."

During breakfast, she told me that we'd be overnighting near Kansas City at her friend's house, who was going with us in her own rig. We'd also be meeting up with another friend between there and 4-J.

We pulled out a couple of hours later; I followed Jane to a nearby ranch where she picked up her 4-year-old horse that she had in training there. She called him JJ, which I noticed were also Jane's initials. She drove fast on the country roads and I nervously kept up. She didn't seem to have any trouble hauling that thing for the first time.

We drove to the other side of Kansas on a flat, straight interstate, passing more cornfields and turbine windmill farms. We got to her friend Nancy's house around dinnertime. Nancy was an endurance rider and was bringing her gray Arabian mare. She had shoulder length dark brown hair and a bunch of freckles scattered across her face. She was wiry and tightly wound. Her rig was just as big as mine. Jane slept in the house, preferring a real bed, she said. I opted to stay in my trailer, explaining, "I'd rather sleep with my dog; besides, it's my home now." I'd declined going out to dinner with them also. Nancy talked to her husband with disdain, similar to how I had talked to Bob, and I didn't want to be around the two of them together.

The next morning, we stopped for breakfast in the middle of nowhere and met up with Barb, who had a ginormous rig too. Barb looked very country to me, like she belonged on a ranch—short and strong looking, her dirty blonde hair cut blunt at her chin. This was getting cooler and cooler for me. We were a women's convoy of four big rigs now and I started singing that goofy convoy song from the 60's as we made our way to 4J.

At the end of a long narrow winding dirt road, we finally pulled in. I was exhausted from five days in a row of hauling. I got out to stretch my legs and looked down to the green field below where at least 100 big rigs were parked. Wow, lots of people are into this horse camping thing. It made me feel less like a loner.

I checked in and was told where to find the mess hall that served breakfast at 6:30 and dinner at 6, the laundromat and the showers. I was told about the dance and the ride times too. I felt foolish that I hadn't thought about looking for private horse camps before. I wondered if there were places like this in other states. The only thing it seemed to lack was a trail map if you wanted to ride on your own.

At 6 am I woke to music blaring "The Cowboy Song." I'd never heard it before and it was kind of catchy. I guessed that it was the breakfast call so I got dressed and fed Tucker and the horses and walked up to the mess hall. There was an all you can eat cafeteria style buffet and I was starving. Funny how I didn't usually eat breakfast but when it was put in front of me I dove in. I sat with my new girlfriends who joked about how much I ate and how did I stay so skinny.

Jane and I opted out of the group rides and rode together. On our first ride, Jane said, "I've never seen anyone ride as well as you do. You have a great seat."

"Thanks, I've worked hard on becoming a more balanced rider. I have a crooked spine and only have one functioning ear for balance so I have to concentrate hard on it."

On another ride, she asked me to come live with her. "I won't charge you, and your horses can stay there too." I was tempted, I really had nowhere to live now and I liked her so much.

"That's really generous of you, but I want to finish SHLEP. Maybe when I'm finished."

She drove a hard bargain. "I can teach you the insurance business; you'd be really good at it, I can tell. And you can teach me to ride."

Over the next days, she talked about her marriage, how wonderful a man he was, how they were so in love, about her many children who had all moved away, and how surprised she was to find herself longing for a man already. It was sad that he died, but I thought she was lucky to have had a loving husband. I told her how my marriage had slowly died and how it had made me never want to be with a man again.

Jane said, "That will change."

I doubt it, I thought, but said, "Maybe."

One afternoon, while hanging by the rodeo arena, watching other people ride, she said, "There's a man in California I've been seeing when I go there for meetings. I can't sleep with him, ya' know, 'cuz we're not married."

"Jane, that doesn't matter anymore."

"It does to me. I'm Catholic."

I was stunned. People our age still followed that rule? How could you even consider marrying someone that you hadn't shared a bed with? But then, that hadn't worked so well for me, had it?

In the evenings, Jane, Nancy, Barb and I sipped wine around the campfire, trading stories about our very different lives. Nancy had adopted two girls from China, one with an attachment disorder, and had started a support group for others in the same boat. "It was so frustrating; the child wouldn't show any affection towards anyone, and none of the adoption agency people could help us. We found out that the babies, all girls given up by their parents in the hope of having a boy, are raised without any love or affection in the orphanages. They are left alone in their cribs for most of the day."

She got up and added a piece of wood to the fire, sending sparks up towards the stars. Left alone in their cribs all day? I felt like crying.

> *I remembered an early therapy session when I was in college. I was lying down and sobbing with my arms outstretched. Dr. Baker let me cry for a few minutes like that, then said, "What's this about?"*
>
> *I said, "I don't know, but I feel like a baby longing to be picked up."*
>
> *He said it didn't matter if I remembered where the feeling came from; simply recognizing the emotion was enough.*
>
> *But that wasn't enough for me and I asked Mom if she had any idea what it could be about. We were in my apartment in New Providence. She had a startled expression on her face as I told her what happened.*
>
> *"I was afraid to pick you up when you were a baby." She paused. "You seemed so fragile."*

I'd made sure to hug my kids a lot, but I still felt an ache in my chest. The wind shifted and the smoke was blowing in my face, so I moved my camp chair and Tucker moved with me, settling back down by my feet.

Nancy then started talking about going to vet school, but not starting a practice after passing her exam. I asked how she could walk away from that and she said that she just couldn't put animals down. I hadn't thought of that.

Then they all started talking about the Bible. I hadn't talked about God to anyone but Emily and I'd never read the Bible, so, I just listened.

Every morning I walked Tucker down the trail to the river and played fetch with him in the water. He was walking slower and his hind end seemed unstable, but he could still swim well. I loved watching him swim for the stick and thought about how much he meant to me. He followed me everywhere around the busy campground and never bothered anyone. He was the best dog. He was wagging his tail most of the time, something my vet, Megan, had told me to watch for to indicate his level of pain. His poop was coming out squashed now, oval-like instead of round and I emailed her about that. She replied that the tumor was squeezing on his intestines and I should double his prednisone dose and give him more pureed sweet potatoes to keep it moving. I asked how I would know when it was near the end, when I should find a vet to put him down. I was holding onto him for dear life, I couldn't bear to part with him, but I didn't want him to suffer either. Megan replied, "You'll just know."

Jane and I went out on a ride one day and got lost. I was ponying Dreamy and hadn't booted either horse. We found a gravel road and began following it, hoping it would lead to civilization. My horses started stumbling and walking in the brush on the sides of the road, looking for relief from the gravel; they were now sore. Jane and I got off and started walking the horses; we'd been out for a few hours already and we were all tired.

"This is sure beautiful, isn't it? Look at that!" Jane said, pointing to yet another tree aflame in color. She bent to pick up a bright yellow leaf. Her chipper personality lightened up the fear I had about being lost.

I silently cursed my navigating skills, my muddled mind for getting us in this situation, and my rotten luck. Jane probably thought I was an idiot.

Eventually a guy came along on a four-wheeler. He had on a ball cap on and a bandana hid his face. He was covered with dirt. He stopped at a distance and just looked at us as the dust he'd stirred up settled in his wake.

Jane smiled and said "Yeah!" then a second later she whispered, "This is a little scary."

I thought so too; I wished that I had my pepper spray or gun with me.

The man still hadn't moved. I walked towards him with my horses in tow and said, "We're a little lost and trying to find 4J camp. Do you know where that is?" As if being two women alone and a "little" lost in the wilderness wasn't a huge big deal.

He just sat there looking at us, and I was getting scared. I stood my ground and stared at the dirt between us. I wondered if I could use the horses to protect us, I could turn their butts to him and back them up if it got ugly. My adrenaline was pumping. After what seemed like an eternity, he pulled down his bandana and said, "Yeah, I work there. Your horses are barefoot and sore. I'll call Jay to come get you when I get home."

I breathed a sigh of relief and wondered how far that was but didn't ask him. He said to stay on the road and something about "the old cabin."

I said, "Thanks." And he took off in a cloud of dust.

About an hour later as we were trudging up a hill, Jay appeared with his stock trailer rattling behind his truck. I realized that I'd met Jay when I checked in; he was the owner of 4-J, the big burly guy in the flannel shirt and cowboy hat that rode around camp on a palomino.

Jay stopped. "I been lookin fer ya'. Why'd ya' go so far? The cabin was back where ya' came from and ya' could'a crossed there."

I didn't know what to say to that; we never saw a cabin, and cross what? The river? We loaded the horses and got in his truck. It felt so good to sit down but I felt humiliated.

We rumbled down the rough road pretty fast and I wondered how the horses were handling it. As we passed a dirt driveway, Jay said, "Good thing ya' didn't wander down there; there's a meth lab cabin and ya could'a got shot."

Wander was a good way of putting it. I was just aimlessly wandering around in the woods, wandering around the states, wandering around in my search for healing. I could get killed with all this wandering. I needed to be more thoughtful and purposeful. But I didn't know how.

Jane and I went out for another ride the next day and asked a group of riders that we encountered if we could join them. They were all middle-aged and said that they were all vets. They said sure, but that they liked to go fast. Jane and I agreed that fast would be better than lost so we tagged along.

It was a ride neither of us will ever forget. It wasn't just fast, it was extreme and probably just plain reckless. We were out for four hours and were rarely on a real trail. Their horses were gaited and we had to trot to keep up with their walk. The vets called what we were doing bush-whacking. I spent most of the time on Wildflower's neck avoiding getting smacked in the face by branches. JJ stayed glued to Wildflower's butt; he was clearly terrified and found comfort in being close to her. Wildflower's leg got tangled in a vine and I had to dismount to try and get it off without getting kicked, as she continued thrashing in circles. The finale was a long slick hill that the vets excitedly called a mule-slide. The horses had to basically slide down it on their butts. Jane's saddle slid up onto JJ's withers and we stopped at the bottom to adjusted his saddle. I was exhausted when we finally got back to camp and Wildflower was just plain pissed. I told her I was sorry and would never do that to her again. I felt so stupid for getting us into another potentially dangerous situation, continuing to blindly follow the vets when I knew it was too tough a ride after the first half hour. I couldn't afford to put Wildflower at risk like that.

I had never been one to follow the crowd, but had done

so anyway because I'd been afraid of getting lost again, finding safety in the first people we happened to bump into. Thinking that I could outride anybody, that Wildflower could power through just about anything. I had to watch out for those proud stupid thoughts in the future. After all, hadn't I taken the same approach to my marriage after it became clear to everyone else that I should get out?

The last night there, I got an email from my divorce attorney about my support being reduced now that Emily had turned 18. She was still my dependent as far as I was concerned; I was paying for her tuition and housing even though I wasn't there. In fact, I was paying for all three of my kids' tuitions. Everything about this seemed unfair and I hated how it made me feel like a victim. Of the legal system and of Bob. Bob used to sarcastically say, "Oh you're such a victim!" I'd never been a victim before; I was the strong one, the leader, the fearless woman. The one that he'd been attracted to in the first place. The one that Jane admired. I needed to relocate those traits with in me; they must be somewhere inside of me still. Why couldn't I tap into them now?

I had awful dreams about buildings blowing up but I couldn't remember the details. I'd hoped I would wake up feeling better but I didn't. I put one foot in front of the other like a robot, fed, mucked, started laundry, walked Tucker to the river, drank coffee, smoked (my e-cigarette was broken) and avoided any social contact. I felt no joy, no hope.

As I made my way around camp I saw that everyone was packing up their trailers in preparation of leaving later in the day. I wasn't ready to go yet; I didn't even know which state I was headed to next. It made me feel left out; they were all going back to their normal lives, their jobs and families. All the things I wanted but didn't feel like I had any chance of having again. Dreamy was sore and I felt guilty for her pain since I had taken her on the road. What was I doing this stupid trip for? I missed having a "normal" life, even though my life back in CA had been far from normal.

I missed my kids a lot; I was sure they all blamed me for blowing up the family and now I felt distanced from them. I missed the predictability of my days even though they were not very happy there. I didn't know what I was going to do, where I was going to live, how I was going to make ends meet financially. I felt out of place everywhere and with everyone.

I wandered into the mess hall while waiting for the dryer cycle to finish. Jane, Barb and Nancy were there. I knew that my eyes were red from crying. Nancy stood as I approached and asked, "Can we pray for you?"

No one had ever asked me that before. I'd never felt that desperate to ask anyone to and doubted it would help, but I nodded my head yes. We sat around the table and held hands and I started crying as Nancy prayed like I'd never heard anyone pray before.

"Dear heavenly Father, we ask You today to have mercy on our friend, Kathy. She is in great turmoil and needs Your loving embrace. She is lost and searching for your healing powers. We pray that you heal her mind, quiet her fears about her future and guide her steps on this quest. Keep her safe from all dangers on the road and in the woods. Keep her horses, Wildflower and Dreamy, and her dog, Tucker, safe as they accompany her through Your kingdom here on earth. Protect Tucker from his cancer, free him from any pain that he may be experiencing. Through the power and beauty of all that You have created in nature, let her see You and be inspired. Bring God-loving people onto her path to help and encourage her when she needs help. Let her be reunited with her children, whom she misses and loves dearly."

Nancy said much more, then Barb and Jane did too. All I could do was cry and join them with "Amen."

Jane handed me some tissues and I blew my nose. Each of them offered me a place to stay with my horses. They asked me about my finances and said that I could afford to live in the

Midwest and suggested some places to look. Barb gave me a campground suggestion in Arkansas, which was the next eastern state on the path towards my Dad in Florida, and told me to avoid Pig's Trail in getting there.

I felt vulnerable and said, "I feel stripped of my defenses and it's scary. Thanks for being my friends and sticking with me even though I must be such a drag. I've never really talked about God before, except with my daughter. I know he gave me the strength to leave Bob. I just don't know why he lets go of my hand sometimes."

Nancy said, "Maybe you let go of his hand. God is always by your side."

Something told me she was right. In fact, I was pretty sure I'd dropped His hand a couple of times in my life.

Nancy hugged me and said, "Barb and I are ready to go, so this is our good-bye now. Safe travels and happy trails."

As I went back to get my clothes from the dryer I tried to remember when and why I'd dropped God's hand. When I was thirty-five, about to get married and told that I couldn't have children because I had cervical cancer and needed a hysterectomy, I begged for God's help. He heard me and blessed me with three Miracle babies. My gratitude and devotion was rock solid for the next sixteen years.

I prayed for God to make me the mother that they deserved. I prayed for God to fix my marriage and keep my children safe. I prayed for God to fix Bob. I took the children to church and sent them to Catholic school. I'd prayed over my children every night of their lives, whether they were away on a sleep over or I was away on business.

I remembered at bedtime, holding Teddy in my arms, lying in his bed, drawing a cross on his forehead with my finger and praying: "God bless Teddy in the name of the Father, the Son and the Holy Ghost. Make Teddy grow up happy and healthy. Protect him from all evil. Amen." But in 2006, Teddy was not growing up happy nor healthy.

Teddy was sitting at the kitchen butcher block island, his head on the wood, cradled in his small arms. He was sobbing.

I embraced his small frame and asked, "What's the matter Teddy, where does it hurt?"

Silence. I asked again.

"I'm a mass murderer," he whispered.

"Oh no, no way, honey, you're a good boy. The sweetest boy ever. I love you Tom-Tom."

"And a rapist!"

There was no consoling him or convincing him any differently. I called my psychiatrist. As his phone rang, I racked my brain to remember if this was how my brother had behaved when he had his schizophrenic breakdown. God no, please, not Teddy!

Dr Lasarow finally picked up, I tried to explain what was going on and he said, "Let me talk to Teddy."

I handed the phone to Teddy. He didn't pick up his head.

He said, "No."

He repeated, "No."

His head still on the island, he handed the phone back to me and continued sobbing.

Dr. Lasarow said, "Teddy can't 'contract for safety.' You have to take him to Los Encinas."

I asked, "Where's that?"

"It's a psychiatric hospital in Pasadena. I'll let them know that you're coming."

I took Teddy's hand and walked him to my car. My heart was breaking but the adrenaline in my veins gave me God-like super focus that night.

I called Bob, "Teddy is suicidal, Dr. Lasarow said to take him to Los Encinas."

"What? Lasarow, that quack?! What's the matter with you?"

I hung up, I didn't need his shit now.

Teddy and I sat in an office; there were a couple of others there. A doctor was asking me questions. Bob stormed in and glared at me, "You're something else, what's the matter with you?!"

He picked Teddy up and barged out of the office. I started screaming at him, he screamed back. Teddy was crying; orderlies appeared and tried to reason with Bob. Bob threatened them with a law suit. We all ended up on the front lawn. I felt like I was living in a nightmare.

Teddy was eventually admitted. Bob and I went home to battle about permitting medication for Teddy's symptoms. Bob said the only thing wrong with Teddy was that he had an unstable mother. I was overreacting; Lasarow was a quack; psychotropic drugs were a conspiracy by the drug companies. I called him evil, abusive and an ignorant bastard. I scoured the internet and picked other people's brains: Had anyone heard of a child thinking this awful stuff about themselves. My sister Liza had her Masters in Psychology and had started her internship, so I called her too.

She said, "I disagree with the hospital's diagnosis. It sounds more like Pure Obsessions to me, a form of OCD."

I Googled it; my God, she was right!

On the third day of Teddy's hospitalization, Bob signed the permission to medicate after I threatened to report him to Child Welfare Service for withholding treatment for a medical need. And in case he didn't take that seriously, I also told him I'd leave him.

Teddy was released after a week's stay and I took him to "interview" a few Cognitive Behavior therapists.

At the Cognitive Behavioral Therapy office in Glendale, Dr Boone met with us and then spoke privately with Teddy. He recommended Elsa, a new young female doctor in his group that he thought would be a good fit for Teddy.

Elsa exuded palpable empathy and asked Teddy if it was okay if his mom left the room so they could talk privately. Afterwards, Teddy told me that he liked her and he started sessions immediately.

While I focused 24/7 on Teddy, Bob drove me crazy, insisting that nothing was wrong with Teddy; he just needed to pull himself up by the bootstraps. He said I was unstable, that this was all my fault; I was an unfit mother. He ranted on in front of Teddy, undermining his doctors and psychotherapy in general.

In my mind, Bob had gone from being a mean husband, to being simply an evil man.

In a couple months, Teddy started feeling and functioning better, not cured, but better. Then he was diagnosed with type 1 Diabetes. The doctor at Huntington Hospital said that this rarely happened when there's no family history of the disease and that it was probably stress induced.

I grew terrified of Teddy dying in his sleep from low blood sugar or injecting too much insulin or going blind or becoming impotent or losing his feet from high blood sugar. Bob wasn't involved or helpful with any of Teddy's diabetic care either. Because of my fear, I hyper-focused on taking care of Teddy and simply forgot about God. I stopped dragging the kids to St. Bedes on Sundays, saying that it was too exhausting to do it without Bob's support and later, that the priest child sex scandal had turned me off to the church. Was I mad at God?

If it hadn't have been for Emily inviting me to church last summer, I'd still be running around in the dark. Then I thought, Emily saved me!

Before I pulled out the following morning, instead of plugging in my shuffle, I put the CD that Emily had given me for Christmas in the cd slot. I looked at the cracked plastic case, where she had drawn with pink paint markers, “God Songs.”

I folded my hands and bowed my head. “Thank you, God, for giving me Emily. Turn me into the mother that she deserves. That they all deserve. Keep them safe and happy till then. Amen.”

Chapter 5

I couldn't glance at a map when hauling my precious horses, so I blindly followed the annoying voice on my trucker's GPS. She was driving me nuts, repeating over and over "Warning! Winding road ahead!" I was getting more and more anxious.

I passed a campground called "Pigs Trail Campground." What an odd name I thought, and it sounded familiar. Then there was a "Pigs Trail Bait Shop." Wait, wasn't that the road Barb warned me about? Shit, was I on Pig's Trail? The warnings were coming non-stop now and interspersed with "Warning! Serious downgrade ahead!" There were three cops standing by their cars outside of "Pig's Trail Café," sipping their coffees. Their heads swiveled in disbelief following my rig as I passed, and I gripped the steering wheel even tighter.

The road descended sharply and coming up quick was a switchback. I swung as wide as I could, then checked my mirrors to see where the trailer was. Not good, it was in the oncoming traffic lane.

The trailer weight was bearing down on me; I was afraid to shift into Manual and downshift, thinking I might damage the gears. I'd recently investigated the meaning of a dashboard button that had an icon of what looks like a puff of air. My manual had told me that it was for the "exhaust brakes," which I didn't fully understand, but it said if you tap the brakes the transmission will slow the truck down with the engine. I pushed the button and tapped the brakes. It shifted down low, the engine began roaring and held the trailer back much better than the brakes had been doing. The switchbacks kept coming but thankfully there wasn't much traffic coming up the mountain so I didn't wipe anyone off the road.

Arkansas was my sixth state, I proudly mused as I pulled into Lonesome D.

"Six down, 42 to go," I said to Tucker.

He lifted his head and thumped his tail in response. "God, I love you Tucker," and I reached behind and ran my fingers over his silky fur.

I went to the office to check in and get a trail map. I told the owner how 4-J didn't have a map and I'd had to be rescued.

"Yes, we do have a good trail map here," Mary said, as she wrote her cellphone number on it, "just in case you need help. The trails are marked with colored ribbons tied to tree branches along the way."

My first couple of days of riding were frustrating, even with a map. Ribbons were missing or I was just blind. I kept getting lost, but always managed to find my way back to camp with the help of my buddy sour horses. They knew how to get back to each other if I just gave them a loose rein.

When I got back from one of these frustrating rides, Mary walked up to me and told me there was a package for me in the office. I took off Dreamy's saddle and went to collect it. It was from Nancy. I excitedly cut open the small box to find an assortment of tiny loaves of homemade breads. I was so touched at her thoughtfulness; she must have known how much it would mean to me. I opened one up and ate it while I painted my Missouri painting, feeling her friendship inside me. I worked from a shot that Jane took of me walking through knee deep grass with my horses grazing at 4J. Dreamy's head is turned towards my feet, half buried in the grass, and I'm looking down at her. My right hand is on her neck and my left is on Wildflower's. The wind is blowing their manes and tails. In the distance are the fall-colored bluffs. I particularly liked this one, maybe because I was in it and it told my story.

On the third day, I went out on Wildflower in the afternoon. I was following the Red trail, and after being out for an hour, I couldn't find any more red ribbons. It began raining and I was getting cold. Wildflower was getting her knickers in a bunch wanting to just simply turning around. I got pig-headed and said, "No, we're not turning around, we're doing this damn red loop. Listen to me!"

It was getting dark when I started getting scared. I found a cluster of hunter's trailers but they were padlocked and no one was around. I didn't have a cell signal to call Mary at camp. It was pouring when a pick up came along and stopped to help me. His phone worked and he called Mary. When he hung up, he told me they were sending a trailer to come get me, and he gave me directions to a closed State Campground to meet them. Once I got there, I tied Wildflower to the hitching rail and stood in the pouring rain trying to console her; she was fit to be tied, literally. Eventually a red truck pulled in with a stock trailer rattling behind it. My second rescue; this was humiliating.

Frankie jumped out of the cab. He was a handsome older man. Fit and dressed in snug jeans, worn cowboy boots, an oil skin jacket and dirty white cowboy hat. *I had to get rescued by a hot cowboy? Shit, I'm such an idiot.*

Wildflower was wild by now and was starting to scare me. Frankie grabbed her rope and got real close to her face, tapping the brim of his hat on her nose; she froze and then followed him onto the trailer. What was that, I wondered.

We got in the truck and as he put it in gear he said, "That mare of yers is a bully. I can help you with that."

I'd never thought of Wildflower as anything but a troubled baby before, but bully was pretty applicable now that I thought about it. Bob was a bully; I hated bullies!

He started talking about horse therapy, and I told him a few things that I'd learned in my EAGALA clinics, like how they can read our story and help us find the answers we're looking for. He said he worked with troubled kids and horses, and to make money he worked at the stockyards.

"Ya' know, there's bubbles around people and animals. And sometimes those bubbles touch; ya' can bounce off or back up or sometimes the bubbles merge and you share the energy with each other. Like there's this bubble around me an' you in this truck and it's getting squashed 'cuz its kinda tight in here."

This seemed too intimate and I got scared. I wanted out of the truck, but I needed the ride back and it was pouring. So, I changed the subject, "I've often felt this energy with my horses, when riding in the mountains, when everything feels perfect, and my legs begin tingling and I'm filled with strength and power, the power of my mares. It's exhilarating; it's why I ride."

"You got the gift, girl!!" he shouted so loud, I jumped.

"I don't really talk about it much, I figure most people'd think I was odd."

"Don't talk about it at all! They'll think yer crazy!" and he laughed hard. "But yer not!"

Yes, I thought, I'm not! Maybe I'd over reacted. He seemed like a nice guy, and I relaxed into the seat as we rumbled over the beat up road back to camp.

I rode with Frankie for the next few days. He'd talk the entire time about trail safety, trailering safety, truck safety, horse safety, on and on like he was on a mission to save me from any SHLEP hazard I might face. I mostly just listened; his advice made logical sense to me and I adopted all his rules, but was resistant to one.

"Those horses are sore. They need to be shod for Arkansas rocks."

Most folks shoe their horses; I was used to people voicing their opinion on this issue. I was proud of their beautiful bare hooves, but they had been having trouble ever since Idaho. Not every horse can go barefoot and it takes a horse a year to grow a new hoof for a new harder rockier footing. So, I caved in and said I'd talk to his farrier, Wayne, when he came later in the week to shoe Frankie's horse.

I got a text from Teddy. He was invited by a college friend to go home with him to South Carolina over Thanksgiving break. He'd asked Bob to pay his airfare, but hadn't gotten an answer from him yet. I knew how that was; Bob rarely gave me a direct answer. But I got my hopes up, I could head that way and possibly see Teddy. This gave me something to look forward to and Thanksgiving was just a few weeks away. I sat down with my atlas and SHLEP journal, planning my route and picking campgrounds to stay at. My next stop would be Tennessee.

Wayne came to shoe Frankie's horse and set up shop in the dilapidated small barn. He was a kind old guy. Wayne seemed knowledgeable as he talked to me about the horse's hoof anatomy while working on Frankie's horse. I then had Wayne shoe my mares and he said he'd come check them before I left. He told me to soak their feet a few times a day in Epsom salts and I did. They were still sore the next day, but were markedly better the following day.

I started breaking camp; I'd be leaving the following day for Tennessee. Tucker was wandering the campground when I noticed he hadn't touched his breakfast. He hadn't finished his dinner the night before either. This was odd; Tucker loved eating. I whistled and walked around looking for him. He was on the dirt camp road, walking very slowly towards me. His head hung low and his tail was not wagging. He squatted to poop and fell over. He recovered and kept walking towards me. I felt something crack inside me.

I sat on the ground and tried feeding him by hand, something that had worked when he'd been sick before. He wasn't interested and lay his head in my lap. I knew.

I picked up Tucker, swaddled in the green velvet blanket he was lying on, and put him in the truck cab. I unhitched the trailer and drove to town. I found a vet office and Tucker ever so slowly followed me in. A woman behind the counter said, "Oh poor baby." I filled out forms for payment and was told that they could not dispose of the body if he was put to sleep.

The old vet gently helped me lift Tucker onto the exam

table, "Oh, there, there, you poor boy," he said. "All his internal systems are shutting down. I'm sorry."

"I don't want him suffer." I lay my face into the warm fur of his side. I could feel his heart beating, his labored breath, I started sobbing and stayed like that as the vet worked.

A few minutes later, I lifted my eyes to the vet and said, "Is it over?"

"Yes, it was over a long time ago, as soon as I got a vein."

I lay my head down again and continued crying.

"When you're ready, I'll help you get him back into your truck."

As I pulled into camp, Mary's husband was standing there and said, "What's wrong?" He opened his arms and I fell into his embrace, sobbing on his shoulder, telling him what I'd done, that I had Tucker's body with me and I didn't know what to do with it. All the while he patted me on the back and said, "There, there."

I followed their daughter, Delicia's SUV to a field; she followed her husband, Dub, who was driving an excavator. Her kids stayed quietly in the car as we hugged and cried together, watching Dub dig a six-foot hole and bury my sweet Tucker, wrapped in my old green velvet quilt cover from when I had a real bed. Dub placed a boulder on top of the mound and they all left. I painted Tucker's name on the boulder with a small heart, then cried onto it until I had no tears left. I felt broken inside in a way that I'd never broken before.

Wayne came by later to check on the horse's feet and told me they were good to go now. He brought me a jar of his wife's homemade Muskadine jam and wished me safe travels with a big bear hug.

"Ya' know," he said, "Frankie cleans up real good."

"I bet he does," I said. I'd thought he looked pretty good dirty.

"He could be a real asset on your trip, ya' know."

I raised my brows slightly in surprise. Wayne was trying to set me up? How sweet. I smiled at him.

"That would be nice, but he's already left," I said. I'd gone looking for him after I buried Tucker, hoping for another shoulder to cry on, but his campsite was empty. I stood where his trailer had been and hurt even more. "He didn't even say good-bye."

My last night in Arkansas, I had a dream:

I was flying! Just because I felt like it and I could, riding the wind currents and gazing down at the peaceful landscape below me. If I wanted to go higher, I simply willed it so. It was effortless, I was weightless. It was exhilarating.

I woke up feeling euphoric and sat up looking for Tucker. The dinette bench bed was empty and I remembered. The thought struck me that Tucker was in heaven; God was taking care of him better than I ever could. Tucker must be wagging his tail, running around on clouds, his body strong and youthful again. I was happy for him, but I missed him horribly and had an empty feeling inside. If I felt this bad about losing a dog, what was going to happen to me when my Dad died, or if Mom died, or God forbid a child? I knew that Dad was going to die in the near future; there was really no hope with stage 4 cancer. I knew I needed to somehow prepare for that blow. But I couldn't think about it much without getting overcome with panic, so I shooed it out of my mind when it popped up.

I left early that morning heading for Tennessee and my God Songs started playing when I started the truck.

One song told about forgiveness and how it sets you free. I wondered if I could ever forgive Bob. Another one was about being thankful for everything in your life, including every breath you take.

I thought I had nothing to be thankful for, but I was thankful that I could still breathe, so I said a thank you prayer. "Dear God, Thank you for this breath."

Ugh, it sounded like the thank you letters that mom made me write to Grandma. I breathed in and exhaled slowly, trying to get in touch with the miracle of how a breath keeps me alive and noticed that my heart was beating.

"Thank you for my beating heart, my physical health, for surviving cancer, for my three children and their health and well-being, my amazing horses and the bond I share with them, for my truck and trailer."

I couldn't think of anything else and paused. There were a million things I wanted to ask for; like saving my Dad, taking away my anxiety and fear, securing my finances and getting this divorce over with, but this was a thank you prayer, so I dug some more.

"Thank you for giving me the strength to leave Bob. Thank you for saving me from destruction and thank you for this journey I'm on." Then I couldn't help but ask for something, "Please make it work. Amen."

I felt my shoulders relax and thought I was on to something. I repeated it whenever my anxiety crept up on me. To my surprise, it calmed me down quite a bit.

The first few days at True West Campground, near Jamestown, Tennessee, I rode with other campers I met there. Then the owner, Donna, had asked if I'd like to ride with her to her favorite spot, Charrit Creek, on her day off. We used her stock trailer to haul to the trailhead and headed down the hill, me on Wildflower. We came to a stream crossing and stopped to take some pictures of each other and I asked her about how she came to own a horse campground.

She laughed, "We came down here from New Hampshire for vacation and I just fell in love with the area; then I saw this place for sale."

"So, you just up and moved your entire family here?"

"Yep! We quit our jobs and moved; actually, I still work remotely for my job, but that's just because it's been so hard to make a profit. We overpaid for the place and the previous owner had run its reputation into the ground, so it's been a tough road trying to bring it back."

"But I saw you on the Horse Trails and Camping Across America site; you're rated 5 stars."

"Well it's taken a few years to get that. Actually, we are rated #1 right now; I'm pretty proud of that."

I couldn't help but think how lucky she was that her husband, Shaun, had supported her dream, or maybe it became his dream too. They succeeded together, which I thought was amazing. I couldn't imagine how wonderful it would be to be married to a real partner like that. I remembered how I'd thought that's what I was doing when I'd moved to California, but once I got there with the children, Bob kept his business dealings and finances secret from me, and there was nothing I could do about it. I'd walked right into his trap.

"You should be! It really is a nice campground and the trail system is amazing."

"Yes, it is. But, wait till you see Charrit Creek Lodge!"

The lodge was a cluster of weathered wood buildings originally built in the 1800's as a hog farm. It had been restored and was now a lodge for hikers and trail riders, providing bunk beds, stalls and meals cooked over a cast iron stove that also heated the dining hall. The caretaker was an attractive, talkative young man who lived there alone most of the time and told us that he'd placed an ad for a mail order bride to come help out.

"You can still do that?" I laughed. I was still looking for a way out of my life and thought about answering his ad; it would be so cool to live there.

Donna and I left the horses in the wooden pens there and hiked about an hour up to the top of the naturally formed sandstone bridges called Twin Arches, from where there was a 360-degree view of the surrounding mountains in a spectacle of fall colors. There were a lot of other hikers up there admiring the view and snapping pictures. I knelt down and carved "KB" in the rock with my pocketknife, where others had done the same.

Donna said, "I thought your name was Roettig."

"It is, but I'm going back to my maiden name," I declared. "Burns. It's a lot easier to spell," I laughed.

I'd been thinking about it for over a year. Emily had objected, because it was her last name too, she said. But I wanted my father's name back, to always have him as a part of me. And I didn't want to be reminded of Bob every time I signed my name or opened my mail.

A few mornings later, I got a text from Brad. "Bob says you're trying to put our birthright company, out of business."

I noticed that he hadn't said "Dad says..."

I hadn't asked or demanded anything; I was just hoping for a settlement offer. Besides, hadn't we agreed not to talk about the divorce or each other to the children during the process? It was even handwritten into our separation document; I'd assumed that Bob had insisted on it being there. I couldn't stop thinking about this strange accusation.

Birthright? What a strange word for Bob to use. What about his first son, Alex's birthright?

I texted back, "That's crazy, why would I do that?"

Brad didn't reply.

On the dirt drive into the cabin at Bear Creek Resort in Strunk, Kentucky, I couldn't make the turn and crunched my awning on the barn roof. I was more concerned about damaging their barn, but it was okay. I wasn't upset about my awning getting dented and ripped, because I never used it anyway.

A perky black lab greeted me and dropped a stick at my feet when I hopped out of the truck. I laughed. He reminded me of Brandi, one of the three dogs I had to leave with Bob when I moved out. I wondered how Brandi was. I hoped she was spending her days down the street with that German family that she'd decided was her home away from home. I picked up the stick and tossed it; the lab tore after it and dropped it again at my feet a few seconds later. This dog liked fetch as much as Tucker had; I wondered if he had a home.

I continued tossing the stick as I set the horses up in their pens and unloaded some of my clothes and food into the cabin. He never lost interest and it made me laugh again. As I sat on the sofa to watch *The Man from Snowy River*, the lab sat at the front door watching me, like Tucker had at Jack's house. He had tags on his collar; he probably had a home. I fell asleep right after my favorite scene, the one where Jim is riding a horse that looks like Dreamy and he follows the herd of wild horses down a long steep mountainside. I slept like a baby.

The next morning, I spread out my art supplies on the big kitchen table. I had two paintings to work on, Arkansas and Tennessee, and spent the better part of the day finishing them. The Arkansas painting was of Wildflower tied to the hitching rail in the closed campground where Frankie rescued us. In the Tennessee painting, I was looking up from the ground at Dreamy who was tied to a tree, with brilliant fall colored leaves all around her. I played God Songs on my laptop as I painted, stopping often to dance and sing along to some of my new favorites.

I called Dad, who sounded good, so that made me happy. He talked about activities we'd do when I got there, like go to a polo match in Wellington, go to the spa and get a massage, get a Christmas tree, maybe play a little golf. He said he was looking forward to seeing me.

Then I called Teddy and was surprised when he answered his phone. It was wonderful to hear his voice and it made me want more of him; I wanted to see him.

He said, "I'm not sure if Dad is going to pay for my ticket to South Carolina or not."

"Oh. Did he say no?"

"Not exactly."

I knew how this went, Teddy wouldn't know until a day before he was set to go. This happened whenever we traveled together.

"I'm sorry, Teddy, just keep asking him till you get a real answer. There's nothing I can do about it. I wish I could, but I just don't have the money."

I asked him how school was going, if he was okay. Fine and yes, but no details were offered and I didn't want to pry. I asked if he'd moved into the dorm yet and he said, "Sort of." He asked how I was doing and said that the pictures I'd posted on Facebook were beautiful and that I was lucky to be seeing so many cool places.

I said, "You could join up with me for summer break if you wanted to." He didn't really answer me, and I was sure he'd never do that, especially after our test trip.

Teddy said he loved me; I said I loved him too and we hung up. Speaking to him was so much more satisfying than texting. But now I ached inside, and figured he must be aching too.

I emailed Brian, my lawyer, to ask how the court date scheduled for yesterday had gone. He had been terrible about responding to my emails and calls and I remembered how he'd told me at our first meeting, "I'm a great lawyer, but not a terrific hand holder."

At the end of the day, I turned up the hot tub and slipped in, melting my knotted up back muscles in the scalding water. I emerged after 30 minutes and stumbled to bed, falling asleep as soon as I hit the pillow. I woke up earlier than usual the next morning and it was pitch black outside. I took my cup of coffee outside to look at the stars. With a quilt wrapped around me I curled up in a rocking chair on the porch. I could hear the horses walking around but couldn't see them. It felt so peaceful. I lit a cigarette and felt the rush of nicotine relax my body.

I thought about SHLEP. The word schlep was one that I'd used in New York among my Jewish friends. It means to drag your shit from one dull place to another, which technically I was doing. I'd initially chosen Party for the "P" to entice Caroline into coming along. But Party didn't fit me, I didn't feel like partying and this trip wasn't turning out to be anything remotely like a party.

The one thing that stood out to me so far was that God was now with me and was helping me heal somehow. The God Songs CD was a big part of why I thought that. I used to listen to mostly female rock vocalists singing songs about survival, angry at their man, showing them how they will move on, get over them, show the man that he will be sorry he left or hurt them. The angry lyrics used to energize me. My shuffle held a collection of these retaliation songs and had been my primary hauling soundtrack. God Songs were about redemption—hope when the world is caving in on you, love when the whole world is hating, life when you think the world is going to end. God's love could make the bad, good. And no matter how broken you were, he could make you whole again. Then it hit me. P was for Praise.

I enjoyed my rides alone while I was at the cabin. I'd pony sometimes, or just ride them separately. The horses were in fine shape now and frisky with the nippy weather, so I went for longer rides than usual. I enjoyed the little lab hooking up with us every day. He obviously had a home because he went somewhere at night.

I got another text from Brad: "Bob has been saying things like, 'Your mother is gallivanting around the country on some glamorous trip, while I'm working 100 hour weeks and taking care of all of you.'" I briefly wondered when it was that Brad had stopped calling Bob, dad. But then I flew into a rage that scared me.

It was about time Bob took care of his children! Not so easy, is it? Gallivanting? Glamorous? I'm broke, in the middle of a stalled divorce because of that asshole and living in a fucking horse trailer that's smaller than his bathroom! I posted a long rambling rant on my blog, which wasn't as satisfying as I thought it would be. All my rage came back full force, a toxic emotion that I was so sick of and I knew served no good purpose, but I couldn't suppress it. I was a mess all over again. More than anything, I resented that Bob still had the power to do this to me.

Later in the week I got lost coming back from the Piggly Wiggly and stopped to read my map. A woman knocked on my window, scaring the crap out of me and said, "You shouldn't just stop any old place around here, you're gonna get shot." That kind of shook me up.

During my last two days at the cabin, I had to move back into my trailer because the owner and some friends were coming for the weekend. The first group arrived and helped navigate me out of the driveway so I didn't hit the barn again. They asked a lot of questions about my journey and seemed amazed by me. It made me feel special.

Before retiring, I checked my email. Brian replied that the court date had been continued because Bob had failed to produce any financial documents or separation date. I didn't know what "continued" meant and tried not to worry about his lack of a separation date; was he still trying to say that we were separated a few years earlier? Would anyone believe this crock of shit?

I tried to not panic and said, "Let go, let God." I missed hanging on to Tucker in times like this.

Before I got into my sleeping bag, I took my gun out of the cabinet, removed it from its zippered case, checked to see that it was loaded and placed it next to my pillow. I wasn't afraid of it anymore; in fact, I found it comforting.

There's a show I used to watch on RFD-TV called *Best of America by Horseback.* Their main sponsor was

Leatherwood, an equestrian community near Ferguson, North Carolina that had miles of maintained trails and a horse campground. As I pulled into the driveway, I thought it looked just as beautiful as the commercial. Rustic-style homes were scattered on the forested mountainside above the equestrian facility and lodge. The campground was across the road along a stream.

I woke up the next morning shivering; it was mid-November and 27 degrees outside. The horses were standing by their water tub just staring into it. It had frozen on the surface and I knocked the ice apart with my boot heel then drove to town to buy a space heater.

I bundled up with long underwear and gloves for my rides, which were quite spectacular. The cold made the horses frisky. Most of the leaves had already fallen off the trees and carpeted the trails, but there were still some bright colors on the surrounding hills. The trails were steep, lots of ups and downs and rarely flat, but the footing was good.

My septic tanks were full and there wasn't a dump at Leatherwood. I hooked up the trailer and drove about a half hour on a narrow curvy road to go dump the tanks at a state park campground. On the way there I heard a strange grinding noise coming from behind me, but I didn't stop to investigate. I entered the empty park, dumped my tanks and was putting the hoses away when I noticed that the goose neck hitch looked odd and I'd forgotten to put the safety chains on. I couldn't believe I'd forgotten that and scolded myself as I started to climb into the bed to clip them, then I realized that the trailer's goose neck stem was not fully set! It was just resting on top of the ball. Horror and adrenaline shot through my body.

I dropped to my knees and thanked God that no disaster had happened. I'd never dropped to my knees before; it was a reflex, something I had no control over. I couldn't believe I'd driven off without double-checking everything. I couldn't believe that simply the weight of the trailer resting on the top of the ball had held it in place on that winding road. If it had come loose it could have killed someone behind me. I couldn't believe I was so stupid, yet lucky. No, I was blessed!

When I got back to Leatherwood, I made a cardboard checklist that I vowed to go through twice before I ever moved the rig again.

I rode alone and spent my days and nights alone. I danced with my headphones on outside, knowing there wasn't a soul around. I sang, loudly and off key, to the horses when I was riding. I was having fun again!

I spent a day painting my KY and NC paintings while listening to the local Christian Rock radio station. They had several preachers talking about marriage. I thought that maybe I could learn something so I kept it on. They talked about "holding each other up." I think they meant to support and respect each other. I don't think Bob or I ever did that. Listening, I started to think that our failed marriage was at least partly my fault. I hadn't had God then; He wasn't in my heart and maybe that would have helped me handle the situation better. I'd fought back with hurtful words. I swore at and insulted him; I wanted to hurt him back, though it never seemed to have any effect on him. I'd be miserable for days after a big fight, and he'd be like, "What's the matter with you?" as if nothing had ever happened. Maybe if I could have been move civil, less reactive, he would have softened or been nicer.

I'd tried to forgive Bob. I'd heard that forgiveness would free me of resentment, and since I still resented him I guess I had failed. I didn't think I would ever be able to forgive him. Was that so wrong? Did I really need another thing to feel guilty about? Did I really have to forgive him to get over my rage? That didn't seem fair. But I wanted so much to move on, I had to try.

Shame on you! I'd heard this my whole life, from Mom and the Catholic Church. I felt like I was going to explode. I got up and changed the channel.

I fumed a while longer. The radio preachers not only sounded unreasonable, but dangerous and sexist. My new God wasn't unreasonable; he loves us! I'd been grappling with the contradiction of being in the middle of a divorce as my Christian faith was growing. How could they condone staying in a marriage that's abusive? Or if a partner is lying or cheating? Or evil? Or controlling and cruel? How can you justify not only hurting the victim but the children witnessing it too? How and why should a victim forgive the monster that's punched her or worse, fried her brain? It sounded like victim-blaming to me—just accept that punch, you deserve it! Doesn't he have to even show some remorse? This is bullshit! And what the fuck does "lift him up" mean anyway? They're condoning a woman becoming a doormat? I'd left; it was the right thing to do. Getting angry felt better than feeling shame. I wasn't going back there again.

The second to last day there, while riding to a trailhead, I passed the arena where two women were with their horses. As I approached they asked if I was the one riding all around the country. I stopped and chatted a while and they asked if they could ride out with me because one of their horses was better heading out with a calm horse. I smiled and patted Wildflower's neck, and decided not to mention that my calm horse was back in her pen. One woman, Karen, was very interested in hearing about my journey and rode alongside me asking questions. My answers were the usual, and when she asked the why question, I felt confident using the word abusive.

"I left my abusive husband and couldn't afford to stay in L.A. so I headed out with my horses trying to find myself again."

"Is it working?"

I did a quick mind scan of how I felt at that moment and said, "Yes, I think it is. I'm reconnecting with God." I was a little shy about the God part because my friend, Jan, had recently called me a Jesus Freak and it sounded like we weren't friends anymore because of it.

"That's great!" she said.

I smiled and thought, I'll find better friends!

At the top of a rise my phone dinged. I pulled it out of my back pocket and saw two bars on the screen, "Oh great, I have cell service! I need to make a call, okay?" I sat back and said "Woah" and Wildflower stopped.

As I dialed, I said, "It's my mom's birthday. I was worried I wouldn't be able to wish her a happy birthday, I don't have any service here."

"Oh, neither do we."

Mom answered, "Kathy darling? Well, hello there, honey."

Her Jitterbug must have caller ID. "Happy Birthday, Mom! Are you having a fun day?"

"Oh, thank you, thank you, that's so sweet of you to call. It's okay, but I'm having a little car trouble."

"What's wrong with your car?"

"Oh, they took away my license."

How was that car trouble? "Why'd they do that? Can you get it back?"

"It's some technicality. How are my darling grandchildren?"

Technicality? Like what, a DUI? "They're okay; I actually haven't seen them for a couple of months now."

Why does everything she say piss me off?

"Why not? Of course, they're in school. How silly of me to forget. How's the weather there?"

Her questions were throwing me off track; I was trying to be nice. My heart started racing; why did talking to mom do this to me? "Kind of cold, I'm in North Carolina now."

"North Carolina? What are you doing in North Carolina? Charlotte lives there."

What the fuck is the matter with you? Didn't Charlotte

die? "I'm on a trip around the country riding my horses, remember?"

There was a slight pause and I noticed that I was breathing too fast. I felt like a rotten daughter when I got annoyed with mom. Everyone says she's such a sweet, kind woman. What's the matter with me?

"Of course, I remember! How could I forget about a thing like that? Your Wild adventure! I gave you the book, remember?"

"Yes, Mom. Well, I'm riding right now and just got cell service so I wanted to wish you a happy birthday. I'm going to have to go now, Mom; I'm with other people and if I move I'll lose you. I love you."

"I love you too darling! Give Dreamy a kiss for me; she's such a sweet thing."

I softened. I had gotten mom up on Dreamy last year when she was visiting us. She was thrilled. Mom sat pretty good on a horse and I told her so. She'd quipped, "You know I had a pony when I was a girl." She'd leaned forward and hugged Dreamy's neck. It was quite touching to me. Mom loved all animals, even more so as she'd gotten older.

I hung up not knowing what to make of our conversation; something seemed off. She was either confused or tipsy. For the last few months, my sister had been emailing me about mom "declining" and that she needed to move to assisted living, but I hadn't taken her seriously.

Karen asked, "Everything okay?"

"I don't know; it was a strange conversation. Okay if we head back?"

"Sure, it's getting dark anyway."

On the ride back, they invited me to dinner. They were part of a group of five women staying in a friend's house there and she said they wanted the others to meet me. They were having steak and had enough for us all.

I accepted, "That would be lovely." I knew being alone

in the trailer would make me start dissecting my relationship with Mom again. Dinner with a group of horsewomen that didn't think it was bizarre to tell a stranger that she was reconnecting with God would be a good distraction.

Two women were on the porch when I walked up; one was tending the charcoal grill and smoking a cigarette. The other gal handed me a bottle of beer and we all introduced ourselves. Karen had told them I was coming and they said they wanted to hear some more about my journey.

As we sat down for dinner one of them led us in grace. I hadn't said grace in a very long time, and when I had it was the short memorized Catholic prayer I'd learned as a child. This grace lasted several minutes long and was an awesome Thank You prayer. Once again, I was impressed at how some people had such a talent for hitting all the specific things that we should be thankful for and all the requests we had for God. Karen took her time and spoke about the needs of each person at the table, as if she was reading their minds and speaking their words; it showed how well she listened to others when they spoke. I wanted to learn to pray like that. She prayed for my horses' and my safety on my journey and that I would find healing and happiness along the way, and affirmed that He would guide my path.

She added, "And should she write a book about her journey, that it be published and an inspiration to others in need."

We all said, "Amen," together.

Me, inspiring? I had been writing a blog, but it was more like a poorly written diary; I'd had to take a remedial English course in college and I still couldn't put sentences together very well. I had said that I was going to turn it into a book someday, but I'd pictured more of a travel guide thing.

Most of the dinner conversation revolved around SHLEP. They asked about my biggest surprise and I told them it was finding faith in God again; they all smiled. Two of the women shared painful memories from their divorces, both much worse than mine. One ex-husband had dragged her into an evil cult and she'd risked her life escaping.

I remembered when Bob called a church that I wanted to go to a cult. I'd gone there on Good Friday with our baby-group and was very moved by the service. Willow Creek was a Christian megachurch; how could he have considered it a cult? That Scientology group he worked with, that was a cult! I remembered being at one of their functions and they were doing a reading of some goofy science fiction book. They were so dramatic and solemn, as if they were reading the Bible. I wore a gold cross necklace and my fingers played with it all night, like I was warding off vampires.

After dinner, we sat around the fireplace on some old comfy sofas. The walls were constructed of old barn wood and displayed pictures of horses. One asked me, "So what's your book going to be called?"

"I guess SHLEP, that's what I'm calling the trip."

They all frowned and shook their heads. I started to explain what it stood for.

"Noooo, that sounds soooo boring. It's gotta be like *Wild* or *Eat, Pray, Love.* Did you see that movie?"

"No, isn't it a romance?"

"Well, in the end it is. But you gotta see it. We have the DVD here somewhere; you can have it. We watched it last night!"

She rummaged around the coffee table and handed it to me. "Do you have a TV in your trailer?"

I told them I could watch on my laptop. They all said how much they'd loved and been inspired by it.

I looked at the case: Julia Roberts, a youthful beauty, in exotic locales, with a handsome man. I couldn't relate to this at all, but I thanked them anyway and promised to watch it.

I rode Dreamy on my last ride at Leatherwood. I set the reins down on her neck. I had my God Songs on my shuffle now and I asked Dreamy to move out. I felt tingling in my legs and it coursed through my body. It felt euphoric. Dreamy was frisky and we flew over all sorts of terrain, through water, over bridges, up and down the hills. God was with me in the saddle that day and it was exhilarating.

That night as I started to break camp, Susan pulled up in a blue pickup. One of the owners of Leatherwood, she was young, tall, lean, blonde and beautiful. Her cute little dog followed her every step.

"I heard about your journey and I had to meet you before you left. I'd love to see your paintings." Her eyes were a piercing blue color and looked right through me.

"Sure, come on in the trailer." I pulled the wrapped panels out of the cupboard and removed the newspaper around them.

As she was leaving she asked, "Do you believe in God?"

I looked up to the darkening sky, a deep shade of blue and said, "Yes, I love the Lord!"

I had never said those words before in my entire life. I hadn't told my mouth to say them; they just flowed out and I felt strange, as if I had just divulged a deep dark secret.

"That's great. God bless you."

Early the next morning she drove back up as I was about to pull out.

"I'm glad I caught you! I have something for you." She handed me a small spiral book. I read the cover, *Jesus Calling*.

"It's a devotional," she said.

I didn't know what a devotional was and I flipped it open. Each page had a short understandable message about God, one for every day of the year. "It's my personal copy, but I can get another one. You should have it."

"How special. What a perfect gift, and a perfect ending for my stay here too."

She pulled me in for a hug and whispered in my ear, "Stay safe. I'll be praying for you."

"Thank you, I need all the prayers I can get."

When I stopped for gas, I listened to a voice message from Dad. "Hi honey. I know how much you want to see Teddy and since it doesn't look like Bob is going to pay for his ticket, I will. Try to get a good fare and use my Visa card. I love you."

My nagging anxiety about whether or not I'd get to see Teddy evaporated. My hero saved the day again!

I called Dad back to thank him and then excitedly tapped out a text to Teddy, "Great news! Grandpa will pay for your ticket for Thanksgiving! XXOO mom."

Teddy would surely answer my text this time.

Chapter 6

I felt my tires losing traction on the soft white sand road that cut through the pine forest leading into the H Cooper Black Recreation Area in Patrick, South Carolina, so I rolled through the stop sign. I unloaded the mares by the barn and turned them loose in a large round pen beneath tall pine trees. They dropped and rolled over and over in the fluffy white sand as if to tell me, "Finally, some soft ground!" There was a lot of activity going on in camp, but I didn't see any other horses or horse trailers. Three rifle blasts sounded in the distance. Dreamy jumped up from the ground and stood stock still, staring off to where the noise came from as Wildflower frantically ran circles around her. Lots of people were milling about in the direction of the gun noise and I saw a few large white tents pitched over there. Pickup trucks with metal box like inserts—which I found out later were dog kennels—in the truck beds and fancy RV's were parked everywhere. The barn was on a slight rise and the surrounding area revealed expansive golden grass fields lined with the pine forest. The smell of pine was strong and refreshing. My boots crunched on the pine needles as I walked into the office to check in.

"You look pretty full here; what's going on?" I asked.

"A couple more horse campers are due in a few days, but everyone else is here for the National Field Trials finals this week. I hope your horses are okay with gunfire." *Not really.* She handed me a trail map with an X marking where I was to park my rig. "You'll need to stay off the fields when they are being used. The competitions will be rotating fields."

"Okay. What are field trials anyway?"

"It's a competition for retriever dogs."

Retrievers? Like Tucker? I hadn't seen any dogs so far; I wondered where they all were. Seeing them was probably going to make me sad. I still didn't know what trials meant, but she looked busy.

I parked beneath a canopy of tall pine trees and put the horses in two pens at the back side of my site. A large muscular black lab wandered over to me wagging his tail and I reached down to pat his head.

"That's Champ," a male voice said. I looked up to see a tall man walking towards me, extending his hand for a firm shake.

"He sure is beautiful. Is Champ in the field trials?"

"No, not any more. He's just my spoiled dog now so he gets to stay with me; all the competitors stay in kennels. Champ's made the finals a few times in his youth."

I asked him what the trials were. He explained that 3 or 4 pheasants are released and shot down in the field and dogs then run out and find them one at a time. Their handlers direct them with whistles and hand signals. The fastest time wins. They were mostly black labs like Champ.

"This is the Super Bowl of field trials, ya' know," he said.

"How much do they win?"

"The real reward is that the champion's stud fees will fetch around $200,000."

"Wow, that's a lot! What about the females?" I asked.

"Bitches rarely make it to this level," he said. I bristled at the word bitches and the inference they were inferior.

"So, they shoot live pheasants?" I said, trying to calculate how many poor birds would die this week.

"Sometimes they just fire the rifle and throw one out that's already been shot." As if that was somehow more palatable.

"Come on, Champ. We gotta get to bed. I exercise the dogs at 5 a.m. Hope I don't wake you."

Champ trotted alongside him to the RV parked next to mine.

A couple of days later on a crisp sunny afternoon, I headed out on Dreamy. Galloping toward us was a cowboy with two dogs following him. I stepped off the trail for him to pass.

He thanked me as he passed and said, "Just running these two annoying strays back to the ranger; my group is back there, why don't you join us?"

A bit further along I met up with two women and a man. They were all around my age and I introduced myself. As we waited for Ron to return, they told me that they had just arrived and were from Virginia. Ron's wife, Penny, was super friendly. "We saw your California plates. You're a long way from home. You here alone?"

"Yeah, I'm solo. I'm trying to ride all 48 states."

"Wow, what number is this?"

"Eleven."

"You should stick with us here. We know the trails pretty good; we come here all the time," she said.

"Do you ride fast?" I asked, thinking about Ron galloping down the trail and reminding myself of the crazy vets Jane and I had hooked up with in Missouri.

"No! We ride s-l-o-w!" They all laughed. "We're all on quarterhorses."

When Ron got back, we headed down the trail; we were out for a few hours, all at a walk. Penny told me that they had a ranch and horse campground in Virginia. Their lives revolved around horses.

"I didn't start riding till I was 50. But now it's my lifeline. If I am ever unable to ride, you might as well shoot me," I said and then laughed. She didn't find it funny.

"That's a stupid thing to say," she said and she glanced over at Ron who was on her other side.

Stupid? I was dead serious. Riding was my lifeline. I couldn't live without riding. Why did she say that? Didn't all horse people feel that way? Trying to unruffled her feathers, I said, "Well, it's my only joy now."

On the way back, we passed an active field just as shots fired out. Key and his wife's horses spooked and reared up. Dreamy trotted off about 10 feet before I got her back. Ron, who had been leading, said, "Oops. Didn't know they were here, they must'a moved fields."

I checked my phone whenever I had a signal, to see if Teddy had responded. I thought about calling him, but didn't want to bother him. I thought about why I felt like this; I'd always been the mom in charge with him before I moved out of the house. But now I wasn't so confident in that role. Teddy had a choice; he wasn't a minor any more. He didn't live with me; he lived with Bob. God knows what Bob had told him about me.

Maybe I'd lost all three of my children for good. I couldn't fix any of this; I was too unsure of myself, unsure of their love, of my own abilities to mother, to be a productive member of society, someone they could come to in times of need. I couldn't even dial Teddy's number! How had this happened to me? Every aspect of my self-esteem was in wreckage because of how Bob had treated me, and I hated myself for letting it happen.

I hung out with Penny's group for all my meals and rides for the next few days. Penny gave me a tour of their trailer that Ron had converted himself. It had two slide outs, a full-sized fridge, two ovens and a mudroom. Penny said she needed two ovens because she loved to cook.

"Must be nice to have such a handy husband." I said.

"Yes, he's a keeper."

On our last ride together, Penny told me, "Ron's staying in the trailer today; he doesn't feel well. He doesn't want folks to know, but he has MS."

I thought about my stupid comment the other day and felt terrible.

"Oh, I'm so sorry. The woman who was supposed to

come with me has MS."

I thought about Caroline, and how it was good that she hadn't come along. I thought about all the crying and raging I'd been through; my emotional rollercoaster would have been awful with someone else along.

I never got the nerve to called Teddy and he never responded to my text. He wasn't going to come, and he wasn't even going to let me know. My chest ached from the disappointment.

I wanted my children to forgive me. I didn't think they ever would. I'd had no compassion for my mother when she left dad. I felt myself falling into a black hole of depression.

The weather forecast said it was going to snow so I decided to skip Georgia for now and head straight to Dad's for the holiday. Dad had started chemo; the hormone therapy wasn't working any more. He said the first session was easy, but now he was having three days of extreme fatigue after the sessions. He was so excited when I told him I was accelerating my arrival. He found a place for me to keep the horses nearby and gave me Marion's number. I called her to make the arrangements.

The last night I was there, the Virginia group had buried a chicken and slow cooked it all day. What an effort just to eat, I thought, but Penny loved to cook. I remember Mom telling me that cooking and housecleaning was "shit work"; I'd found out for myself that cooking for kids who turn up their noses at dinner and a husband who rarely made an appearance made it shit work for me too. I'd quit preparing meals altogether the year before I left.

"I'm headed down to see my Dad in Florida; he's battling stage 4 cancer."

"Oh honey, that's rough," Penny said. Ron was by her side with his large brimmed cowboy hat on. He tilted his head to watch the ground as we talked.

"I don't know what I'm gonna do if he dies," I said.

She gave me a hug. "We're probably gonna leave early too; the ranger said they're getting cancellations because of the weather."

Ron raised his gaze to me and said, "You're the bravest woman I've met." He grabbed me for a bear hug and I thought, me brave? I was anxious most of the time; that was fear of the future, right? Could you be brave and fearful at the same time?

Penny said, "We want you to come to our camp in the spring. We don't advertise, it's by invitation only. We have great trails there; please come, it will be fun."

I felt honored and agreed to be in touch. "It's been really great meeting y'all."

Y'all? I hadn't said that since I'd lived in Georgia.

I left the next day and hauled through Georgia. As I crossed into Georgia, I read the sign welcoming drivers, "We're glad you've got Georgia on your mind."

I wasn't glad about it. We had lived there for less than a year, when I was sixteen. We had moved twice in the previous two years and I was a miserable teenager by then.

> *Moving to Georgia was like moving to another country to me. I had a hard time understanding the thick southern accents and expressions.*
>
> *Ann was the first girl at school to say hey, so I latched on to her. She lived in an apartment with her mom who was rarely home. Ann had just come off a year of being grounded for getting pregnant and had an abortion. She had long straight dark hair and a voluptuous figure, which lured young men wherever we roamed. I still looked like a boy. Ann introduced me to LSD, which I ended up taking almost daily.*

The Christian Rock station turned to static on my radio and I searched for something else to listen to. I found a Christian Talk show and settled on that. They were going to interview some Catholic priests about how the church was trying to get "fallen" Catholics back to church. Dad stopped taking us to church when we'd moved to Connecticut, or was it before that?

The priest on the radio was talking about the new Catholic Church policies being more relevant to today's society. I knew I'd never return there. My Catholic upbringing had been all about being afraid of God's wrath, the many ways you could offend Him and end up in Hell. When I was very young, I kept a list of my sins in my nightstand drawer and would bring it to confession with me so I didn't forget to confess something.

But later, I believed there were some sins I could never confess.

The stirrups were cold. The doctor said, "You're five months pregnant."

I confidently said, "That's impossible."

Mom blurted out, "Did you at least have an orgasm?"

The doctor left the room.

"What's that?" I asked.

Mom started to cry and didn't answer me. She said, "You were a love child you know. When I was 19, I got pregnant with you and had to get married. I had to give up my dreams, and I resented it."

I knew it! She really didn't want me. I wondered what dreams she'd had that I'd ruined.

The Catholic priest on the radio was talking about bringing men in particular back to the church and what God's idea of a good man was. How important the father's role is in the family and how the church needs to support the men. What about the women, I wondered. They were the ones stuck getting pregnant and raising the children primarily on their own. What about allowing birth control to help them out?

Mom said, "You're going to get an abortion."

That was murder. That was a mortal sin. So, who

would the murderer be? Me? The doctor? My mom? Or all of us? Would the baby go to Purgatory?

I felt I had no choice but to agree. I didn't know who the father was, so I obviously couldn't marry him, as she and dad had done.

I was taken to two psychiatrists and a physician for interviews to declare me an unfit mother and rule out the possibility of adoption because LSD caused chromosomal damage.

The abortion was done in the hospital. I woke in a room with a woman and her newborn. My parents had left a small bouquet of baby's breath and tiny pink rosebuds on my nightstand with a little card saying they loved me.

It still pissed me off that no one asked me how I felt about it afterwards. No one discussed birth control with me either. Dad barely spoke to me for a year afterward. I don't remember even seeing him till we moved back to New Jersey.

The Florida border was coming up and I shook my head to erase the memory, like shaking an Etch a Sketch. I stopped at the Agriculture Inspection to show them my horses' papers.

The officer examined them and said, "These are expired."

I'd forgotten all about needing to do this every 30 days. I was ordered to have the horses put in quarantine for two weeks at my destination and have a state vet inspect them at that time. The guard filled out the papers and explained that the horses needed to be kept away from touching other horses for the two-week Quarantine. That should be easy to comply with in Jupiter, since they'd be in their own pasture. I tucked the Quarantine order into my horse papers folder and got back on I-95 South.

I was exhausted. I was weary of traveling and living like a vagabond. How old would my dead baby be now? Forty-three.

I now accepted ownership of my abortion; I used to blame mom. But I'm the one that got pregnant in the first place and I hadn't objected to having an abortion; I could have run away from home. I wasn't able to confess those sins until I was in my mid-thirties, but even then, my feeling of guilt didn't go away. I wanted to *feel* God's forgiveness, if that was possible. Maybe then I could forgive myself. I needed spiritual guidance and decided to find a church in Jupiter.

Dad's black Genesis was parked in front of Marion's house when I maneuvered the rig into the circular sand driveway, trying to avoid the low branches and hitting any of the tall trees that lined the way. Dad walked toward me with his usual big grin on his face and his arms open wide as I slid out of the truck. He enveloped me in his arms and said, "Oh honey, it's so good to see you. I love you and I'm so proud of you."

He was as big around the middle as before so he hadn't lost any weight and I was relieved. He held me tight and rocked back and forth like he was rocking a baby, I felt so safe in his arms. There were tears on my cheeks. I noticed gray hair on his shoulders. My rock.

He grabbed my shoulders and gave me an Eskimo kiss, "Now let's see this fancy trailer!"

"Okay, but let me unload the horses first." Marion had come out of the house and offered to help. I handed her Dreamy's rope saying, "She has very good manners, I'll take the other one."

We all walked around back and put them in their new temporary home, a large sand paddock; they both dropped and rolled. I threw in some hay and Dad patted Dreamy's neck as they dug in. "Such good horseys." he said.

I gave him the grand tour of the rig that he had

financed and he was thrilled by it all, but obviously tired. "You finish up and I'll see you when you get home."

"Okay, love you Dad." I kissed him on the cheek.

Marion was about 10 years older than me with short curly hair, glasses, and a trim athletic physique. She raked her hair with her fingers, scrunched up her nose and pushed her glasses back up with her finger. "I want to know all about your trip, but we can do that on the trails together; you must be tired now."

"I sure am. I'd love to ride with you, I've ridden alone so much lately, it'll be great."

I unhitched the trailer and drove about twenty minutes to Dad's gated community in Jupiter. A uniformed guard walked out of the stone guardhouse. I rolled down my window and the humidity hit me like a wet towel. I heard the rush of water from the entrance wall's waterfalls.

The guard said, "You must be Mr. Burns' daughter, welcome!"

He handed me a barcoded window sticker and I wound my way through the precisely manicured streets, past the golf course and luxurious homes. Dad's house was just as pretty, but not as large as most of them, it had just been the two of them when he and Bobbi had moved there in the early 90's. I parked the truck on the cobblestone driveway and rang the bell.

A short round black woman opened the door and exclaimed, "She's here! She's here!" She had a thick Jamacian accent.

I disliked her immediately. "Hi, you must be Yvonne, I'm Kathy." I extended my hand for a shake and she grabbed me for a hug and peck on the cheek. I cringed.

"I'm going now; see you mañana! Your supper's wrapped up on the counter."

Dad sat with me while I ate, his elbows on the table, leaning towards me. "So, how are you, really?"

"Good, now that I'm here, it's been rough going."

"What? I can't hear you."

"Do you have your hearing aids on, Dad?" I said louder.

"No, I got them wet, I need to get them fixed."

"It's been kind of tough." Talking louder was hard to do, I didn't have enough air in my lungs.

"Well, you're home now, you can stay as long as you want."

I thought I should stay forever. It's the only thing that made sense now.

Between bites I told him about the last two months, which had seemed much longer to me. The problems with my generator, my self-doubt and physical exhaustion. The kids' not staying in touch and being angry at me about abandoning them. That I wasn't sure if this was such a good idea after all.

"What's going on with the divorce?"

I smirked, "Nothing at all. I don't wanna talk about it."

"You can't let him get away with this; you need a different lawyer."

I sighed. He didn't know how hopeless I felt about this by now. There was no speeding things along with Bob; I'd lose anyway. He didn't know the whole story; only Lydia knew it. And I really didn't want to talk about it.

I hadn't realized how hungry I was and cleaned my plate. To change the subject I said, "Are you still playing golf Dad?"

His face dropped and he said, "No, I'm just too tired." Oh no, I made him sad. I hadn't realized he'd stopped; he had played golf for as long as I could remember.

"But I play cards a few times a week and have lunch with my friends on Tuesdays." He added with a smile. "And I go out on Marty's boat; he lets me use it whenever I want."

Marty's "boat" was a yacht with a crew of two. I hated Marty. "He and June will be back down next week for Thanksgiving; we'll be having dinner with them, okay?" June was his trophy wife. Ugh. “They come down from NYC every two weeks now!”

This was horrible news, I thought they were in NYC for the winters. How was I going to be polite with that creep?

I’d met Marty at his sister’s, my step-mother’s, Bobbi’s funeral service. So, he was my step-uncle? He was on my left, and Emily, who was ten, was on my right. A woman was speaking about her dear friend Bobbi from the podium.

Marty leaned over to tell me something and cupped his hand over my ear and said, “She likes to take it up the ass.”

I scooted closer to Emily and put my arm around her.

Dad said, “Kathy, he’s my best friend, I love him like a brother.” I hated how Dad could read me so well.

“That’s nice Dad, I’m glad for you.” And changing the subject again, “How are you handling the chemo?”

“Well, I have a few bad days afterwards but other than that I’m fine.” He sat up straighter and smiled as if to prove his point. He added, “But, I’m losing my hair,” as he stroked his fingers through his curly white locks.

I remember Teddy as a little boy doing the same thing; Dad’s hair was irresistible. I smiled.

“It will grow back.” I said.

He leaned in again, “Have you spoken to your mother? Liza is very concerned about her memory. And she’s cracked up her car several times now.”

“I talked to her a few weeks ago on her birthday; she sounded tipsy.”

“She’s lost her driver’s license too.”

“I know. Poor Mom, she probably shouldn’t be driving if she’s drinking anyway.”

He continued, “Liza goes down several times a week to

help her. I think she is handling all her finances now."

Liza's helping with finances? With her history of manic spending, wasn't that a little risky? She had the nerve to insinuate that I'm only interested in money? She'd asked me like she was my therapist, "What was with your drive for success back then?" I wonder if she's reconsidered that, now that I'm living in a trailer.

"I go to bed early now honey. I'm tired, so sweet dreams Kath, I love you."

He kissed me on the cheek and realized I'd been staring at my plate a bit too long. "Love you too Dad. Sweet Dreams." He gave me a quick squeeze and headed towards his huge double doors.

I walked outside to get Nalla and the black trash bag of clothes out of the truck. It was dark now and the humidity was still overwhelming to me.

Our family already had so much brokenness; now me, too. Thank God Dad didn't ask, "Have you talked to Johnny lately?" How was Dad facing death with so many loose tangled ends with his children? It must be breaking his heart. I wished I could show him that at least I was okay.

I walked into the guest room where a dozen long stem roses in a vase were waiting for me on the dresser. Nalla scampered under the bed and I stuck my nose in one of the flowers, it smelled sweet, like heaven must smell. The card read, "Welcome home, honey." I started crying.

A few days later, Dad went for chemo and I came along. Yvonne announced to the receptionist, "I'm Mr. Burns' nurse." What a bold faced lie, I thought, she wasn't a nurse!

We were led to a semi-private treatment room. Dad was hooked up to an IV chemo drip and I opened my laptop and as Dad says, *punched up* Pandora's "Smooth Jazz" station and handed Dad the earplugs.

Dad was sharing the treatment room with a woman who said that she had cervical cancer.

I said, "Oh, I had that, but I had a hysterectomy."

She told me she'd had a hysterectomy too, but the cancer came back anyway.

I got scared and went outside to email my doctor to ask if that could happen to me. I started missing my kids; it had been three months since I'd seen them and I checked on airfares for Emily and Teddy to come visit over Christmas break. Even after New Year's, tickets were still over $800 each. I checked on airfare for me to go to L.A. over New Year's for just a few days to see them and found a $400 fare. I couldn't afford any of this, so what was I even doing it for? I went back inside and held Dad's hand till his treatment was over.

I wanted to pay Dad back, now that I was now 59½ and able to withdraw money from my IRA without incurring a penalty. We went to Fidelity to do the paperwork together and the rep said, "You know your IRA is not going to last you for the rest of your life. What are your plans?" I wanted to punch him.

Later in the car Dad said, "You know you're going to inherit some money when I die."

I said, "I can't talk about that, please." I didn't want Dad to die so I wouldn't be poor!

> *Money. It had always been an issue for me and Bob. We used to have monthly lunch meetings that took me days to recover from, but I refused to do them anymore after Los Encinas.*
>
> *I remembered Bob wanted me to meet him at Panera's in late 2010. He insisted there was something very important that he had to talk to me about in private. He was seated at a booth looking at his cup of coffee when I arrived. I thought he looked different; there weren't any papers on the table, nor his phone. When he looked up and saw me, he didn't flash his usual nanosecond half smile, he just got up and walked with me to the counter to order. Was he depressed?*
>
> *"Hey, how are you?" I asked.*

He shook his head and bemoaned, "I'm running in front of a freight train."

I thought how that freight train had been bearing down on him for over ten years now and I wished it would just hit him already.

We ordered our food and took our number back to the booth where Bob had left his battered overstuffed briefcase and cup of coffee. We sat and just looked at each other. I felt uneasy and on guard as usual, but something seemed different. I tried to hide my apprehension.

Bob said, "The new lender wants me more invested in the company. They want me to put my IRA into it."

I gulped. "You're not going to do that, are you?"

"I had no choice."

I opened my eyes wider and he looked down and calmly took a bite of his salad with no dressing. I thought, you already did this? He took a sip of coffee.

I took a deep breath and asked, "How much?"

He looked up at me and said, "All of it, $350,000. It's not enough; they want more."

I thought, are you crazy?

The waitress brought our food to the table and asked if we needed anything else, I shook my head and she left.

I said, "You could just leave the keys on your desk and get a job somewhere."

He looked annoyed. "I can't do that, I can't work for someone else."

I asked, "Why not? It would be better than going bankrupt!"

He smirked and said, "I'd never be able to support our lifestyle on what I'd earn working for someone else."

I said, "Screw our lifestyle. We should sell the house, it's too big anyway."

He said, "I'm not selling the house, that's separate anyway."

Of course not, it's your castle! I looked at my sandwich, I picked a piece of avocado off it and put it in my mouth.

He looked at me with a blank matter-of-fact face and said, "The new lender wants you to put your IRA's $700,000 into the company."

I choked on the avocado. You treat me like shit for years and you want me to give you my retirement fund?

"My IRA? How do they know about my IRA?"

He looked annoyed and said with disdain, "They know you're my wife!"

I said, "No."

He looked sort of satisfied, "That's what I thought you'd say."

He was chewing his food as he said, "You have to cut the budget in half then."

I felt nauseous. Did he make all this up to get me to cut the budget in half?

"And I don't want the children to know about any of this either."

"How am I supposed to do that?"

"Cut the nonessentials, the horses and the therapy."

I thought, of course, everything that I did was non-essential. What about Emily's horse, Teddy's and Brad's therapy? How do I explain those cuts to them? What about your BMW, Porsche, Dodger VIP seats, 5-star restaurants and vacations? He kept talking and I stopped listening; all I could hear was my mind saying, "You're a failure, you're a failure, you're a failure."

I started crying and got up to leave.

He followed me outside and hugged me on the

sidewalk. He said, "We'll get through this together."
Together? You're taking us all down with the ship! You care more about your stupid company than your own children and me?

I Googled churches in Jupiter and listened to a few on line sermons. I particularly liked the one I saw on Christian Family Church's website. That Sunday, I went to their service. The rock band was good and Pastor Steve was a passionate speaker with a South African/British accent. His message was entitled "Everything's gonna be alright!", which was projected in script on the screen behind him as he spoke.

During the service, Pastor Steve asked everyone to bow their heads and close their eyes. He asked if anyone was ready to give themselves to God, if they were tired of trying to live their lives without His help, and if they did to stand up. I felt my legs straighten and stand, tears streaming down my cheeks. I don't remember all Steve said, but I felt he was talking directly to me, to the mess of my life. I knew it was only going to get worse without some divine intervention.

When the service was over a woman came over to me and handed me a Bible and a tissue. She asked me where I was from and how I'd found their church and I blurted out, "My Dad is dying and I am in the middle of a long drawn out divorce. I am lost and so afraid."

She took my hands and bowed her head and then prayed for me; she asked God to help me find my way, for Him to heal my father, to enter my life and guide me. I was shaking and touched and started crying again. She handed me more tissues. I thanked her, wiped my face and exited the worship area. As I was leaving the building Steve stepped in front of me and introduce himself and I blurted out that my father was dying and started crying again. He held my hands, bowed his head and prayed for a miracle, "Heavenly Father, we pray to you today to wipe the cancer from John's body!" He said it with such passion and conviction that I thought it might possibly work.

I started attending services on Wednesday nights and Sundays. Besides teaching me about the Bible in plain English for the first time in my life, I thought of it like my therapy, my support group. It lifted my mood immensely and gave me enough hope and strength to just keep on breathing. I felt alive at church, but had trouble maintaining it once I'd left the building. I thought about how different everything could have turned out with our family if Bob hadn't refused to join Willow Creek Church back in the beginning of our marriage and it made me sad.

I got the horses' shoes pulled and they went back to being barefoot again. The trails in Florida were all soft sand which was perfect for their transition. The mares got sort of used to the tropical wildlife on the flat sandy canal trails. There were turtles plopping into the water, gators trying to snatch low-flying, big-winged, stork-like birds, pelicans, and wild pigs. Wildflower took me for a run or two, and Dreamy even did once as well, when a dirt bike came flying around the bend towards us. But they got better about it over time.

Dad had frequent doctor appointments, which Yvonne and I would attend with him. He played cards at the clubhouse a couple of days a week and had a weekly lunch with his buddies. He got up around 10:00, took a long afternoon nap and went to bed by 9:00. We had most of our meals together and watched TV at night. He never felt up to doing much else. I was not included in any of his personal care; Yvonne did not want help and said that Dad was very private.

"I'm going to clean him up now," she'd announce as she'd lead him past the huge double doors that led to his bedroom and bath. She'd emerge and say, "He's sleeping now, don't disturb him."

I felt useless. I'd thought he had needed me there but maybe he just wanted my companionship. "Well, I can do that,"

I thought.

After Christmas I went back to riding every day. Dad was asleep much of the day anyway, and I needed the kind of therapy I could only get in the saddle. I took to going for long walks on the beach, too. I was bored and lonely much of the time, with too much time to worry about my future. I had one internet date, but backed off when the guy tried to hold my hand; I just wasn't ready. Other than Marion, I made no friends. We rode together a few times a week and I'd hang around her house afterwards, drinking soda or beer and getting stoned.

After New Years, I flew back to California for four days to see my kids. Dad paid for my ticket and I stayed at my friend Rose's in her beautiful La Canada home.

The first afternoon there, I drove to the Flintridge Riding Club, to meet Brad and Teddy for lunch. They were late and I waited on the stone porch under the shade of the big old oak trees, where I'd sat hundreds of times in the last twelve years, yet I now felt out of place. I was no longer the same person as when I'd left. I felt sad that I wasn't a part of that place anymore, but I also didn't really want to be. It felt pretentious.

I remembered back to 2000 when Bob had sat on this same porch and called me at the little old house in Illinois.

> *"Kathy, I'm sitting under a huge oak tree on the patio of FRC in La Canada having lunch. It's so beautiful! You'd love it here; people are riding horses and there's this quaint old club house with a kitchen. We'll join and bring Ty here for Teddy."*
>
> *He went on to tell me about two houses that he'd just seen that he really liked, how good the schools were there and that it was an easy commute to Glendale for him.*
>
> *I'd already looked at houses in La Canada but Bob had said they were too expensive. I thought about if I really wanted to "follow that man to California" or not.*

"I've got a ticket booked for you this Friday, get a sitter for the kids."

His realtor picked me up at LAX. He had a sign with my name on it as I came down the escalator and introduced himself.

"Bob wants me to show you the two houses he saw the other day plus anything else that's on the market in the same price range. There's only one though." He handed me the listing sheets.

As we drove to the first house, I looked at the papers he'd given me. They were all over $1,500,000! Three times what our big old house sold for. I'd had no idea that Bob was making that much money. At the end of the day, Bob met us at the "one more for comparison" house and as we walked through the 5,000 square feet and numerous tiled patios and balconies, he staked claim on the Family Room as his office and said that he wanted to make an offer on it.

I asked, "Bob, can we really afford this place?"

He said, "I'll get it for less than that, don't worry; it's for the sake of the family."

I thought, but the children don't want to move, and I don't think I want to either, but he was acting pretty nice right now; maybe he'd be more like this if we moved?

Brad and Teddy finally pulled up in Bob's red convertible Porsche and walked towards me laughing. My heart started racing; they both hugged me and I didn't cry and, after ordering lunch in the kitchen, we went back to sit at a table on the patio.

Teddy asked, "Are you going to be back for the summer?"

I said, "I don't think so. I can't afford to live here." I wasn't ashamed to say it any more.

Brad pulled up some apartment listings on his phone

and showed them to me. I said, "I can't afford any of those, honey. I feel guilty about not being here for you all. I miss having you around, but I rarely saw you when I was here. If you aren't living with me, I don't see you much."

Brad said, "That's because you were never home. You were always riding."

I got confused; the horses were in the back yard for the last few years. Was he talking about high school?

"That's so unfair, Brad. I was always there for you guys when you needed me; I rode when you were in school."

Indignant, he said, "Well, my image of you is always with your animals."

I swallowed hard, and held his accusatory gaze. Did he really feel this way or had Bob convinced him of it?

I said, "I wish I had a home here with rooms for all of you. I wish I didn't have to worry about money so much. I wish I had a good job. I wish I hadn't had to break up the family to save myself."

Nobody said anything. I felt like dying. I'd thought my SHLEP would heal me faster than it was, make me see what I was supposed to do. Help me handle confrontations better, but what was I supposed to do now? Should I finish my SHLEP? Was the prospect of writing a book and selling my paintings a possibility or was it a pipe dream? Should I just buckle down and somehow get a job and come back to California? Was that a possibility or another pipe dream? I felt an urgency to do something. Something important, meaningful, responsible. Would that make a positive difference in my children's lives? Would they love me again if I did that?

Brad said, "Bob's an asshole." It was still strange to hear him call him Bob. "And he's so cheap. You should see the house, it's disgusting now."

So, Brad hated both of us now.

Teddy said nothing and neither did I. Teddy's silence made me think he was level headed and mature now. Or maybe he was just beaten down? He was living with Bob instead of at the dorm where he should have been. This was so fucked up. Did I do all this? Was it really all my fault?

Teddy checked his blood sugar, and I felt better about him not dying from diabetes in my absence. We ate and the boys talked between themselves. I felt like a third wheel. We hugged and they drove off. I felt hopeless as I watched the red Porsche drive away from me.

Lying in Rose's luxurious guest room made me feel even more poor and homeless. Not on-the-streets homeless but never the less home-less. I felt so unsettled.

I kneeled by the bed and prayed, "God, I am begging you to show me the way. I need direction now. How can I guide my children when I can't guide myself?" I asked God to open my eyes and ears and heart and mind to see the path that He was making. I knew that He was making a way for me. "Help me just see it and be open and trusting enough not to be afraid."

The next few days I found myself going from here to there without any advance planning. Like I was in a trance or on auto-pilot, like I was making sales calls again. I wasn't sure if God was guiding me everywhere or if I'd tapped into my Dale Carnegie skills. I found myself having a glass of wine and bowl of pot with Caroline in her backyard. I visited Heather. I even stopped at Jan's house to ask about rentals she might have in the area. She said they were out of my price range. I saw Charni, my riding trainer, at the club. The last time I'd seen her was at my send-off party when she'd said that she was proud of me, which had made me feel better after I'd spilled my guts answering the "Why are you doing this trip?" question. I sat in Brian's office until he came back from lunch; he said that nothing's happened but he had a plan. I'd been nervous before I came about seeing some of these people. But I was surprised how well I got through it and I was pretty sure that no one saw the pain inside me.

I went on Monster, Ladders, and a few other job websites. I submitted a bunch of resumes. I started to feel confident. I looked online at real estate rentals, and when I thought about dropping my horses off in Idaho at Jack's—because there was no way I could afford LA board prices—I didn't fall apart at the prospect of living without them. I thought how that would give me so much more time to concentrate on building a career from the ground up again; this thought that used to paralyze me seemed doable for the first time.

I went to our La Cañada home to pick up Emily for lunch the next day. Our once gorgeous Spanish styled home had become a real dump the past year, but I vowed not to dwell on the negative. The bell was broken so I knocked on the front door. As I waited, I remembered when we had moved in, back in 2001.

> *Bob picked us up at LAX and took us to the empty house. It took a week for the truck to arrive and we all slept in the only carpeted room, which became the boy's room. The kids were at school. Bob gave me a new Visa card with his name on it and said that it had a $5,000/month limit, and a checkbook with his name on the checks, which he said he'd fund with $5,000 a month.*
>
> *"What about the mortgage payment, isn't it more than that?"*
>
> *He laughed, "Yes, but I'll take care of that separately,"*
>
> *I thought, Separately? And I realized that he hadn't asked me to attend the closing. My name wasn't on the card or checks either.*
>
> *"Bob, the house is supposed to be in both our names."*
>
> *"Our other houses weren't in both our names."*
>
> *I said, "We bought our first house together and then you asked me to buy out your equity because Redson*

went under and you needed the money, remember?"

"That's not what happened; all you care about is money, I'm taking care of everything, I'm doing this all for the family! Don't be so selfish."

I had not stood at the front door in one and a half years because of the restraining order Bob had filed based on my so-called "violent" art and "hacking" his computer. He was a master at turning the tables on an adversary. I felt like an intruder until Brandi ran out the doggie door wagging her tail. Sweet little Brandi had gotten very fat, but she was the survivor, I crouched down to hug her, "Oh Brandi, I missed you so much."

Bob finally opened the door, and when I went to shake his hand, I somehow hugged him instead. It felt good, and I realized how much I missed being hugged by a man.

I said I was sorry and that it had been a horrible year.

I heard Bob say, "...love you."

My heart skipped a beat and I pulled back. In the past Bob would say to me, "Do you love me?" and if I said I did, he would say it back. He never offered it first.

I said, "What?"

He said, "The kids love you."

Oh. I said, "I'm here till Friday if you want to talk."

Did I really say that?

I didn't know how he interpreted any of this and I didn't care. I didn't feel angry or afraid. I felt at peace in his presence and I was thrilled! I talked to my boys and Emily after he left the entryway. Man, the place was really a mess; there were piles of boxes and papers everywhere. Bob's hoarding had crept out of his office now that I was gone.

I found myself telling the kids that I was going to cut my SHLEP short and finish it later. The words blurted out of my mouth without being filtered by my brain. I hadn't planned any of this. I heard myself say that I would stay with Grandpa through April for his chemo, then head back to California, find a job and home in the area and they were welcome to live me then.

"I don't want you to think I've abandoned you."

Where did these words come from? Were these God's words? I had a million questions for God, most of all how would I keep these promises? But I was not afraid.

On the kitchen counter sat an opened FedEx envelope from Fidelity addressed to me. I grabbed it on my way out with Emily. It contained the first of two $50,000 checks made out to Dad that I had ordered when we'd gone to Fidelity together. Son of a bitch, Bob, you haven't changed at all.

I felt peaceful as I sat down next to Bob at Starbucks a few nights later, but I couldn't believe I'd initiated this meeting. He had his usual stack of files on the table, along with his Blackberry which dinged and he referred to regularly.

He gave me his crooked nanosecond smile and asked, "So what did you want to talk about? What do you want?"

It dawned on me that he thought I wanted to talk about a settlement? He'd never asked me what I wanted in twenty-three years; I couldn't come up with an answer. I hadn't ever thought about any details; I just wanted out. I wanted a judge to figure out a fair split. I looked at his face. It wasn't handsome any more, it was mean. He still took me for a fool.

I calmly said, "No, that is not what I wanted to talk about."

We then "talked" about the kids, mostly Teddy. Bob began blabbing on in his familiar gibberish with clichéd sayings, elongating every sentence with extra words – his usual key words, business-type, catch-phrase words – as we talked about our children. I couldn't understand most of what he was saying; Dr. Lasarow said it wasn't me; no one could. Bob complained about his business; he was running in front of a freight train. He scrunched up his nose and did that fast wiggle thing with his mouth. He gave me his take on what was wrong with the kids, and told me what I should do to get Teddy back on track; he said Teddy thought I'd abandoned him and that's why he dropped out last semester and I should write him a letter.

I had to blink a few times to keep from screaming at him. *How dare you say I abandoned him! You left us in Illinois for four years; you screamed at him like he was the scum of the earth! You and your fucking letters, you write it! It's your fault he's got OCD in the first place!*

Bob jumped subjects mid-sentence, and I struggled to follow along. I sat there listening to this one-sided communication, his ranting speech, as if I still did it every day. It made me feel like there was something wrong with me all over again.

Bob said that Teddy was going back to college so I'd need to pay his tuition bill, and he'd move into the dorm.

Funny how he could be clear when it came to getting money. What a load off my mind that Teddy would be out of that crazy house. I didn't think to tell him to pay the tuition. I had to be sure it got paid and Teddy got out from under his roof. There was no way one could not be negatively affected by living with Bob. But there was nothing I could do about the past, and I would have a home they could come to soon, I hoped. I prayed, God make this happen.

My short trip changed my focus dramatically. When I got back to Florida I was obsessed with finding a job and devoted eight hours a day to it. I was on the internet or phone, job searching in the way that people did it these days; apparently no one wanted to meet you face to face anymore. I concentrated on print sales in southern California but eventually applied to other fields and expanded to a nationwide search. I gave it a valiant effort for the next three months, till April 1st when Dad's chemo was over.

In January, I hauled up to R O Ranch in Mayo , for a three-day *Best of America by Horseback* ride; that was the TV show where I first saw the ad for Leatherwood, North Carolina. I froze my butt off because my generator didn't work. And I started second guessing my promise of getting a job, quitting SHLEP and returning to California. I thought maybe I'd not seen God's plan accurately.

Upon return to Dad's I took the trailer to a dealer and they rewired the generator. They told me it had been installed improperly and I was lucky I hadn't gotten electrocuted. I sent the bill to Jason, that cowboy in California who sold me the damn thing. I never heard back and so I just paid it myself.

In February, Emily skyped me. She was crying and Dad flew her in for Valentine's Day. At lunch she asked, "Can we get a puppy when you get back to LA next month?"

I was particularly fragmented during her visit and said, "I'm not going back now because I haven't found a job yet, I can't afford the area without an income. And Grandpa needs me here now. I'm staying through April to finish up his chemo treatments." Wasn't this what I had told her in January? I did not want to let my children nor my Dad down. Yet I didn't feel capable of really helping anyone, I was so down myself.

Emily looked like she was going to cry and wouldn't look at me for the rest of the meal and for several hours after. When we got back to Dad's I asked, "Do you want to talk about it?"

She replied, "What for?"

I said, "OK, I'm going to bed then," and lay down for a good cry.

A while later she came in my room and lay down with me and said, "It feels like you've chosen Grandpa over me. You haven't been there for me for such a long time. I was so looking forward to you coming back to California and living with you on breaks. But I want you to know that I understand your decision."

"Oh, Emily, I am so sorry. I am such a mess. I can't find a job and it's so depressing. I never should have left my career when you were two."

"But Mom, I'm so glad you did stay home with us. It would have been awful if you were working."

"And I never should have moved to California."

She looked puzzled, "Why?"

"Because I lost all my self-esteem after that," I cried.

"But then I wouldn't have gone to LCHS and met all my friends. It was a great place to live and I got such a good education so I could go to a good college," she said.

She didn't mention my self-esteem and I was offended but didn't point it out.

"You know Teddy dropped out of school mid-semester don't you?"

Not again!! Another $20 grand down the tube? I took a calming breath, "No I didn't."

We hugged and cried for a while then she went back to her bed. I was in shock from our conversation. Everything was so fucked up. I had no control over any of it either. I started thinking about putting the muzzle of my gun in my mouth and pulling the trigger, but it was in the trailer at Marion's. I was not the strong woman I used to be. I would probably never be her again. I was ruined. I quit.

I had enough therapy to recognize the state that I was in. How could I pull myself out of it? Did I even want to anymore? What's the point? Everything I did turned to shit.

I took Emily to the airport on Tuesday and still felt like shit.

I hated Yvonne by then. Besides misrepresenting herself as a nurse, she professed to be religious, but her proclamations of, "Prayers work, hallelujah" sounded phony to my ears. Cooking to her meant that she heated up a prepared meal she'd picked up at Whole Foods. She talked with her mouth full. She said that she was "deathly allergic" to my cat, who never came out from under my bed, and my e-cigarette vapor, which no one else could even smell. She had talked Dad into paying for her dental work. She went grocery shopping daily and to Costco once a week, and didn't bring in all the bags and packages either. Dad was paying her $1,600 a week under the table, which seemed high to me since most of the day she slept in the Lazy Boy watching Judge Judy or was out shopping. She bragged to me about taking care of wealthy people and that the family members were jealous of how the dying person loved her more. Dad's housekeeper, who he'd had for 30 years, hated Yvonne, and so did my sister. The only people that seemed to love her as much as Dad were Marty and June; they were the ones who recommended her in the first place. The whole think stank to me.

But Yvonne had Dad hooked. Dad told me one day, "You have to be nicer to Yvonne. I love her! She's promised to stay with me till the end." I took this statement as a rejection and it hurt real bad. But it did give me the freedom to leave without guilt.

Dad started offering suggestions on my job searching, "You should call that guy back again." or "You should send that company another letter." Or, "Did I tell you about the time that I got hired because I called the guy back twice?" He would sit down to chat and peek at my screen as if he didn't believe that I was job searching on my laptop. I started getting very annoyed by it all.

Liza visited and I took her for a ride on Dreamy, but she got sore and walked back to Marion's. Later, she referred to Marion as white trash, as if she thought she were better than Marion, who had become my friend. I got angry and looked at Liza differently after that remark.

Dad went over his will with us and showed us a camera bag in his closet with $30,000 in cash in it to get us all through the first month or so. I didn't think it was a good idea to have that much cash in the house but I didn't tell Dad that. Dad explained to me how Johnny's Special Needs Trust was set up and what my role as Trustee entailed, but I didn't really understand. I resented that Liza had resigned from this position a couple of years ago; the alternate was Marty's wife, so I was stuck with it forever.

In a moment of despair on a beach walk, I texted Bob and asked him if he wanted to reconcile. I regretted it as soon as I hit send, but he didn't reply anyway. Shortly after that our La Canada house sold for $1,800,000 and after paying off the mortgage and broker, it netted $1,000,000. Bob tried to get me to sign a Quit Claim without going through our attorneys and I was reminded why I'd left him. Usually the proceeds would go into a court account and stay there until the divorce was finalized but Bob wanted the money now so in exchange for agreeing to that, I was awarded $200,000 of it. I felt better about being able to get the kids through college now.

> *When the boys were in high school, I asked Bob if he'd followed up on the kid's college savings plans and could I see the statements. We were standing outside the kitchen, I'd just dumped a bag of garbage in the trash.*
>
> *I'd stopped making annual deposits to the college funds when I'd retired and it was probably only about half of what three degrees were going to cost.*
>
> *Bob said, "Don't worry about it; the house equity will be used for their tuition."*
>
> *"The house? Where are we supposed to live?" and thought to myself, Wasn't the house half mine? How was this his contribution?*
>
> *He looked at me like I was an idiot. "I can borrow against it."*

I had one in-person interview, which I thought went well, but they called a week later and said, "We've decided to go in a different direction."

Liza started texting me regularly about Mom's mental decline, which she now called dementia. I told her I'd support all her decisions and that I'd be there in June to help her. She seemed to be handling it better than I could have at this point anyway.

I took Dad to Christian Family Church a couple times but he wasn't into it, saying that he thought Pastor Steve looked like a hippie and that churches prey on dying people to get a bequest in their wills. I was disappointed that he didn't find some comfort in going to church, but it was very different than a Catholic Mass, so I understood. He continued battling his cancer but said he wasn't going to do any heroics like fly to South America for a new treatment. I was beginning to think that chemo was possibly heroic but didn't express that to him.

I prayed constantly while driving, walking on the beach and in bed. I listened to Christian Rock with earphones in my ears all day long. Then I took a baptism class. I didn't talk to anyone about what I'd learned and what I was planning to do; it was too personal and private to me. I wanted to be washed of my lifetime of sins. I wanted to feel freedom. I wanted my shackling chains shattered. I was totally devoted to following Jesus and this was a declaration to God that I was 100% devoted to Him. I'd be born again. I'd get a do-over. I knew without any doubt that God had brought me through those awful years I'd lived with Bob; I couldn't have survived if He hadn't. He had a big plan for me and I was going to do it, whatever it was. I promised Him.

After service one day, Steve walked a group of about 20 of us, along with their family members, across the street to a church member's pool. I didn't talk to anyone else; I just watched as they huddled with their loved ones on the patio. Steve walked down the steps into the pool and shivered. "Chilly," he pronounced. I'd never witnessed this type of baptism before. I watched as a long-haired young man covered in tattoos was baptized. Then a buxom woman in a skimpy bathing suit top was baptized, with her young child and boyfriend watching and cheering when she came back up to them.

When my turn came, I stepped into the cold water and stood alongside Steve. He asked me, "Do you believe that Jesus Christ is your Lord and Savior?"

I said, "Yes, I do."

He told me to hold onto his arm and said, "I baptize you in the name of the Father and of the Son and of the Holy Spirit." He leaned me backwards and I held my breath as I went under water.

> *I remembered getting dunked playing Crazy School with Dad. He played the role of a deranged swim instructor that dunked his students when they least expected it. Our entire neighborhood loved playing Crazy School, "Again, again!" we'd shout.*

As I surfaced I physically felt a darkness leave my body and dissipate. I felt freed from the crippling shame that had dragged me down and made me feel worthless for so long. I was a child of God and He loved me just the way I was.

It was much more profound and powerful than I'd anticipated. I felt like I was glowing and, as I walked back to my truck, I thought it must be visible to others. I was on the right path now, the path that I had been asking God to show me for so long. I didn't know where that path would take me or what was going to happen along the way, but He was by my side now and guiding my feet; he was going to take care of me forever and I'd see him face to face in Heaven one day.

I felt safe. I knew I wasn't perfect. I'd fail again, but I'd try harder not to and God would forgive me. I thought about the sixty years I'd wasted and how much nicer life could have been if I'd found out the truth about God's forgiveness and love when I was younger.

In mid-March I got a voice message from a recruiter in the printing industry:

"Hey Kathy, Steve Soltan. I did get your resume. You haven't worked since '96, (laughs), Wow, that's obviously 18 years ago. I am familiar with Alden Press, but the industry has changed and not for the better, so I don't know what to tell ya'. It's tough enough placing people who have a loyal client following, but placing people who haven't been in the industry for 18 years is—I guess the word I'm trying to use is impossible. I appreciate you sending me your resume anyway. I wish you well, take care, bye."

I cried, then I got mad because he'd laughed and used the word "impossible," then I felt thankful that at least he called me back and was honest. No one else had done that. It confirmed what I'd been starting to assume. I played the message for Dad and he hung his head at the word "impossible."

I decided that I'd call myself "Retired" instead of "Unemployed" because of the stigma. I'd never been lazy or unambitious. I also thought it just wasn't in God's plan right then but it could change. I firmly believed God had a plan for me. So, coupled with the fact that Dad wanted Yvonne to care for him at home till he died and Yvonne and I under the same roof were going to create unwanted stress in his life, I started planning my next leg of SHLEP. Since I'd promised Liza I'd be in NJ by June, I had two and a half months to make my way there. I'd visit sixteen states on the way. I was in no rush to get there; dementia isn't life threatening and Liza seemed capable of handling it on her own till then.

The day before I was heading out to resume SHLEP, I drove to Peggy Adams Rescue to adopt a stray I'd found on the internet. His photo looked so pathetic; his black lab eyes pleaded with me. He looked like the little black lab that befriended me in Kentucky.

The greeter at the shelter asked me, "Is there a particular dog that you're here to see?"

I said, "Yes, his name is Jessie."

Her eyes opened wide, "Oh no, you don't want Jessie!"

He was like a whirling dervish in the small meet and greet room; he acted much younger than the year-old they said he was. He was emaciated and I could see his ribs. His fur was a mess and full of dandruff. I scratched his butt and shook my fingers out releasing gobs of black fur.

"He won't let us brush him," the employee said.

The dog and I bonded instantly. I thought, "Nobody wants either of us anymore, but we want each other."

I lied a white lie and said that I lived at my Dad's address, knowing my gypsy life style wouldn't comply with their adoption rules. Jessie gleefully jumped into the truck when I opened the door. I laughed and thought, "You have no idea what you're signing up for!"

When I got back to Dad's it was dark. Dad was standing on the front porch as I got out of the truck. He slapped his thighs a few times and baby-talked, "Oh hello little puppy!"

Jessie's hackles went up, he curled his lips, showing his enormous scary teeth and growled deeply for a second, then charged, barking his head off. Luckily, I had a good grip on his leash or he surely would have attacked Dad. I thought, "Shit, this dog is scary!"

Dad just grinned and said, "What a good doggie! Honey, I'm so glad you got him. I feel so much better about you being safe now."

I didn't know he'd been worried about my physical safety. I wished I could say the same about how I felt leaving Dad in Yvonne's care.

I left early the next morning before the sun was up. Dad got up to say good-bye. We hugged for a long while as he slowly rocked me back and forth like a baby. Speaking into his shoulder I said, "Thanks for everything you've done for me, Dad. I couldn't have done any of this without you. You're the best Dad in the whole world."

He made that soothing "Hummmm," sound that you

make when you feel too good to spoil it with words. "It's my pleasure to help you, honey." And he squeezed me tighter.

"You know I'll fly back if you need me to. Don't hesitate to call me, please."

He pulled back and held me by my upper arms. "Don't worry about me! I've got Yvonne now." His whole face was smiling.

It took all my self-control to smile back at him.

Chapter 7

Jessie must have not driven in a truck much; he jumped into my lap, nearly giving me a heart attack, so I pulled over and tied him to the backdoor handle with his leash. He scared the crap out of me barking his head off and growling at motorcycles, trucks and black people. His bark was throaty and frightening. He really had it in for the toll booth collector. Eventually he conked out. He was nothing like Tucker. Instead of helping me calm down, he doubled my anxiety. Whenever I slowed down, he seemed to think it was about time to stop and get out, so he'd begin panting like crazy and whining, no matter how much I told him to cut it out. What did I get myself into with this mutt?

I arrived at Mingo's Trails Horse Park in Toomsboro, Georgia the next afternoon and set up camp. I began painting at the dinette table, with Jessie underneath chewing on my boots. I heard a rig pulling in and peeked through the window to see a woman around my age and a young girl get out of the truck and unload two horses. I stopped what I was doing and walked over to say hi.

She said her name was Katherine, "And this is my godchild, McKensey."

"Hi Miss Kathy," Mckensey said in her southern drawl. I found the southern respectfulness charming now that I was an adult.

Katherine had given her the rescue pony that she was tacking up. They'd come to Mingo's often for day rides, Katherine explained. "These day rides are real important to maintaining my sanity. I have a 23-year-old disabled daughter at home who requires 24/7 care."

And I'd thought my children required a lot of care. When McKensey was out of earshot Katherine said, "McKensey has a mom problem and I've taken her under my wing since she is just bonkers for horses and I've got a few. I just call her my godchild."

"What do you mean by mom problem?"

"She's a meth addict," she said with disgust.

I opened my eyes wider in disbelief and said, "And she still has custody? That's insane!"

"That's Georgia's messed up child welfare system. Meth, welfare and child abuse are a big problem here. And it's nearly impossible to take a kid away from their mother, no matter what's going on."

Katherine and Mckensey came again a few days later and I rode out with them.

"McKensey is really taken with what you're doing." Katherine said. I thought to myself that McKensey might need a journey of her own some day with what she'd endured. Thank God for Katherine coming into her life.

We got back to camp and I put Wildflower back in with Dreamy. I threw together a peanut butter and jelly sandwich and joined them at a picnic table by their rig to eat lunch together. I liked their company and loved listening to their southern accents.

McKensey asked, "Miss Kathy, do you know what Tourette's is?"

"Why yes, I do. It's a form of OCD, which my son has."

She said, "Oh, I've got that too." Like it was no big deal. She then went on to tell me about her best friend who had Tourette's and how kids made fun of her, but of course she added, she'd never do that.

I remembered kids teasing me at school; they'd called me "branches" or "stick." It didn't sound so bad now, but it hurt my feelings; I knew they were making fun of me.

Katherine had been taking care of the horses and then joined us to eat. She pulled out her phone and showed me a picture of her daughter. She looked just like Katherine and was seated in a wheelchair with a huge grin on her face.

"She's now 23. She was born premature with severe brain damage. My other daughter is in the army now."

"Really? How does she like that?"

Katherine laughed, "She joined because she said we were too strict. Her boot camp letters home were interesting. You could wring the tears out of them."

Katherine was a nurse and did hospice care. I told her about Dad and asked what it was exactly that hospice did. She said, "You wouldn't believe how many old people there are in nursing homes and have no visitors, ever! Most of 'em are so lonely, facing death all alone. I just wanna make them more comfortable and die with some dignity, knowing that somebody cares about them."

I took "comfortable" to mean without pain, so I assumed it meant you had to be a nurse to administer morphine. I thought about Yvonne introducing herself to all Dad's doctor's as "John's nurse" and my stomach turned over.

Another camper joined our table. She'd overheard Katherine talking about hospice and said that she was the sole caregiver for her ex-husband who was an invalid. I wondered if she was a nurse.

"That would be my worst nightmare," I said.

"He used to beat me; that's why I left him. But he needs me now; there's no one else, so I'm glad to do it."

I was speechless. How can you forgive someone who's punched you? How can you care for someone that's too weak to punch you but probably still wanted to?

One night I had supper with the Chatahoochie Trails group that had come in. Every one of these women had a tractor and knew how to use it. I was used to women asking about the amenities in my living quarters, but not one of these women brought that up. They were mostly interested in how much my trailer weighed, what kind of engine I had or how I cared for my horses.

They were shocked that I had never gone horse

camping before I decided to do the trip. And that I'd bought my truck before I knew how much weight I'd be pulling. When they eventually asked why I started SHLEP in the first place and I told them that my therapist thought I should do it, they burst out laughing and couldn't stop. I felt foolish for a few seconds but then joined in their laughter.

I could laugh at myself now. I had turned a corner.

It was Dad's birthday the next day. I had to remember to call him and sing Happy Birthday to him when I got up. He had never forgotten to do it for me.

At the Heart of Dixie Trail in Troy, Alabama, Dreamy and Wildflower were in a 40x40 rough timber paddock under a row of blooming tulip trees. It poured hard the first night and all the lovely soft pink petals made a fairytale scene in the morning. The paddock was carpeted with pink petals that also decorated the horses' rumps and manes. I took a bunch of pictures, deciding that it would be a pretty scene to paint.

I unhitched the trailer and went to the Piggly Wiggly to get chicken, eggs, bacon, ground beef, and spam, along with my regular stuff, to shore up on my protein intake. In the check-out line, a child sitting in the grocery cart in front of me, kept whispering in his mom's ear and pointing at me. The mom walked a few steps towards me and politely said, "Do you know that your shirt is inside out?"

I blushed. I'm sure I looked like a wreck, but I hadn't stood in front of a mirror since I'd left Florida, and I didn't really care about my appearance anymore. I smiled and said, "Yeah, thanks, I know. I'm camping." I thought about how I used to primp and dress, even for riding. Now I couldn't remember the last time I'd combed my hair.

I had cell service in town and called Dad to sing "Happy Birthday" but it went to voice mail so I sang to the machine instead.

In a few more days I headed to the Trace Trails in Utica, Mississippi. It rained several times while I was there; I was parked on low ground and it flooded. On my last night there, it poured again all through the night and I continued to worry about trying to get out in the morning.

As I went to sleep, I thought how worry was such a useless energy draining emotion. How could I stop doing that? Was it in direct correlation to my feeling incompetent, was it a self-esteem issue? If I trusted that God's will was for my own good, then maybe my tendency to worry would go away. What a relief it would be to trust Him that much. But I was new to this faith thing, I prayed for stronger faith and dozed off.

As I'd anticipated, the rig was seriously stuck in mud when I tried to pull out of camp. I cursed myself again for not getting 4-wheel drive. I dug away all the soupy mess around my rear drive tire but it didn't help. I laid branches down in front of both rear tires, but the tires still couldn't grab a hold. After two hours' effort, I gave up and called AAA asking for a big tow truck.

As I ended the call, one of the owners appeared at my driver's side window with a box of kitty litter.

"This might seem silly to you, but it usually works pretty good for me," he said sheepishly.

I said, "My Dad used to use kitty litter when we'd get stuck in snow." But Dad hadn't ever been dragging a 7-ton trailer with his Cadillac.

I poured the bag in front of my rear drive tire and slowly eased out onto the dry road bed, heading for the 4B Ranch in Melder, Louisiana.

I had cell service there and I checked in on Facebook. There was a personal message to me from a Gary Holt. He'd seen my posts on the Horse Trails and Camping Across America group page. Gary wrote that he was the host of an equestrian internet radio show and asked if I was open to being interviewed about my adventure on May 8th for a live broadcast? Gary didn't know the backstory of SHLEP and probably assumed I was a whole lot more experienced than I was. Did he mistake me for some free spirit adventurer that his listeners would be inspired by? Because they would probably be disappointed when I started talking.

But I was flattered so I quickly typed back, "Sure!" before I changed my mind. The more people following me on Facebook, the better. I had come to think of my Facebook friends as my real live social circle; they wrote supportive comments on my posts, encouraged me along and gave me advice about weather conditions along my route, horse care and different campgrounds.

I'd never heard of internet radio shows before. I grew up without calculators and competed with my siblings for the one phone in our house that was tethered to the wall. I sometimes felt like I'd landed on another more advanced planet. Gary's show was called Equestrian Legacy and was streamed live every Thursday at noon. My old iPhone 4 had horribly slow to nonexistent internet powers and I doubted I'd be able to listen in on one of his shows.

I hit "send" just as it occurred to me to wonder, where exactly was I gonna be on May 8th? And would I have cell service there?

It got very cold as the afternoon grew to a close, so I shut the door and windows and turned on the heat in the LQ. The day felt like a blur to me and I still didn't feel good because I had skipped lunch and had gotten low blood sugar. I was going to just go to bed early. But then I thought I should eat a hamburger—higher protein plan, and all. As I was flipping the burger, the grease in the pan caught fire and I panicked. I thought it would be better to just throw the pan and burger out the door than try and figure out how the fire extinguisher worked and make a big mess in the trailer. But in panic mode I couldn't get the damn door opened. There's the screen door latch, the door lock and the door handle. I couldn't remember which lever position was unlocked, and I kept grabbing the screen door latch which did nothing for opening the solid door part. In my other hand was the pan of fire and running between my legs was Jessie, who thought he was getting the flaming burger! Finally, I got the door open and the fire went out as the pan hit the dirt. No more frying burgers in the trailer for me! Especially when I wasn't feeling sharp.

As I crawled into my mummy bag, I wondered why I just kept plowing forward when my body obviously said to stop? I'd always been like that. I scratched at my armpit, which was hairy by now, and found two swollen ticks! Nothing grossed me out more than ticks. I quickly yanked them out and wiggled out of the bag. Rummaging under the sink I found the tick spray. I was naked now and began by spraying Jessie, since I knew he was probably covered with ticks and bringing them inside. He curled up, most likely terrified by my crazy behavior, right next to the CO_2 detector. The tick spray set off the high-pitched alarm and he started trembling. I didn't care, I was on a death to all ticks mission! I sprayed the rugs, the blanket, and the bench cushions. The fumes were so strong I started coughing and the damned CO_2 alarm wouldn't shut the fuck up! I threw open the door to air out the LQ and it was really cold outside! Why hadn't I just gone to bed?

The next morning, I had to laugh about it all.

I walked Jessie in the forest on Good Friday. I still didn't understand why Jesus had to be tortured and killed for our sins and why God felt it necessary; couldn't he have just killed all the bad guys himself? But for whatever the reason God had, I was still grateful that Jesus went along with His plan. I reached my arms to the sky and prayed out loud.

"Thank You Jesus, for Your suffering and death for my sins and the whole world's sins. Thank You for all that You've done for me so far. I can't believe I took so long to find You. I'm sorry. Please help my children in the struggles they are facing to find their way to You so they too can experience this wonderful feeling of being close to You. Amen."

I still marveled at how thanking God made me feel better. This time I felt an energy coursing inside my body, distributing life to all my cells, much like I'd experienced riding Dreamy. Being in the middle of the magnificent forest, which only God could have made, enhanced the magnitude of what I felt.

The physical sensation lasted for just a few minutes and I stood stock still, trying to hold onto it. This must be the joy that Christians told me about experiencing. When it ebbed and I stood in the afterglow, I felt a desperate urge for more. I could endure anything if I could summon this at will! I had no idea at the time, how much I would need it in the coming months.

Ebenezer Park camp sat on the southern edge of the largest lake in Texas. This part of Texas, near Jasper, was hilly and sandy with pine trees. Wildflowers were in bloom.

It was Easter weekend and the campground was full. I went for a walk with a fellow camper, Gina, who'd come over to greet me when I pulled in. She was a solo woman too, so I thought we might have a lot in common. We walked down to the beach with Jessie, who ran along the shoreline biting at the little waves. Gina lived about an hour away and came there often. She was single and usually camped solo. "So why are you solo?" she asked me.

I told her I was in the middle of a divorce and before I could go any further, she said she had been married eight times. I was visibly shocked and the only response I could come up with was, "Why did you get married again?"

She said, "And again and again." She just laughed and never really answered me.

On Easter, Jessie and I walked down to the lake to watch the sunrise. Jessie romped on the beach as the sun rose over the water. As it crested over the horizon, the sky lit up red and orange and melted over the water. It felt like I was watching Jesus rise from the dead and I was filled with awe. How had something so beautiful turned into a bunny bringing candy?

I thought of a picture mom had of me with the Easter bunny, I was all dressed up, hat, gloves and purse, those patent leather shoes. I wasn't looking at the bunny or the camera and I was scowling.

The campground host couple came over to my trailer and invited me to their Easter BBQ. Around 5:00 I moseyed over to their trailer. Piles of kids and grandkids were there. It was still strange for me to meet women much younger than myself who were grandparents already. I felt their love for each other the moment I got there. The little ones had an egg hunt going on once it was dark and I was so moved by watching them interact. There was no bickering amongst them; the older ones were helping the little ones, something I was never successful at getting my own kids to do. I talked for some time to one of the dads, who was a professional truck driver. We talked about highways, crappy drivers, speed limits and tire pressures. I was so moved by this family and I was sure that God was present in their lives, even though no one mentioned Him by name.

The next day I ran errands and fixed a leak in my grey water line. I pulled out my rasp and touched up my horses' feet, hobbled them and let them graze. Most of the campers had left and a woman from the last remaining trailer came over and introduced herself. Her name was Jennifer and she lived in Texas. As we were talking, Jessie grabbed Wildflower's lead rope off the ground and ran off with her trotting behind. I shouted "No" to Jessie and "Woah" to Wildflower, but they didn't listen to me. Jennifer and I chased them through the wildflowers and they finally stopped when Wildflower found a patch of grass that she was interested in. It was pretty funny and we had a good laugh. Jennifer then invited me to come have supper with her and her husband. We ate by a roaring fire and swapped stories. Their large yellow lab was curled up on a rug by the fire and I told them about losing Tucker.

In the morning, I saw the camp hosts mowing the grass and walked over to thank them for Easter supper and tell them that I loved their family. I shared that this had been my first meaningful Easter and that I had just recently gotten baptized. She smiled and said to her husband, "I knew God had a reason for us to be here!"

Jennifer came by and walked with me as I grazed my girls on lead lines. She handed me a gift bag. Inside was a red white and blue bandana with a card that had a picture of a cowgirl taking a bath in a horse trough while her horse stood by. She then told me a horrible story: Her husband had been driving their rig home from a camping trip they'd been on. A car swerved into their truck, hitting their bumper; he lost control of the rig and their trailer came unhitched! Adrenaline hit my blood stream. She kept talking; it left the pavement and somersaulted away. Her horse's leg was cut off in the wreck and she held his head as he was put down on the side of the road.

I was in shock and stood there staring at her with my eyes wide and my mouth open. It was my worst nightmare and I felt like I was living it.

Jennifer said, "I didn't mean to scare you; I just want you to be wary of crazy drivers."

This story stayed in my mind as I hauled to my next stop, the Fort Worth Stockyards. The highway sign read, "EXIT CLOSED." I slammed on the brakes as traffic abruptly slowed to a crawl. I took the next exit and wound my rig through downtown Fort Worth on narrow cobblestone streets during rush hour. It didn't help that my GPS was being stupid and changing its mind about how to get to the stockyards.

I finally pulled in, drove behind the big brick barn and parked alongside the arena. As I wandered around looking for someone to tell me where to put my horses, I saw a few long horn bulls and a camel in the outdoor pens. I wondered if the horses could smell them already and how they were reacting. I walked inside the barn and saw a baby camel and some more long horns. Where the heck are the horses? I found the office and a young woman checked my health papers and walked me and the horses to our stalls. Dreamy planted her feet at the gate and snorted her dragon noise. The girl said, "By the way, there is a reindeer in that next stall."

I unhitched the trailer and drove to Texas Christian University's campus to meet up with Emily, who had transferred there for Spring semester. She met me in the parking lot and seemed happy to see me. I was over the moon to see her. She gave me a tour of the campus including the arts building, which I thought was awesome compared to the art school I went to in Philadelphia. It warmed my heart to think of her spending time in those studios, making art, doing what I had always loved. I hoped that she was happy; she looked kind of sad though. I hadn't seen her since Valentine's Day, when I wanted to shoot myself; and I remembered that desperate night before she went to college. I never wanted her to see me as that pathetic person again.

"Do you wanna see my self-portrait?" she asked. Of course I did. She said, "It's not finished yet."

Emily pulled a canvas from the painting racks. It was stunning and I noticed she wasn't smiling in the painting; I thought it was interesting that she'd chosen a somber photo to work from. I thought of my first self-portrait from high school. It was very realistic and I looked very sad in it. I had never seen Emily's paintings before, just drawings. She had a very bold realistic style that reminded me of my college artwork. I'd had no idea she was so talented. "I love it Emily; you are so good!"

"Thanks mom! But you know this isn't my major,

right?"

That stung at first. But, yes, I thought, you're not like I was at your age at all. You're much smarter, stronger and you believe in God.

We drove back to the stockyards and I showed her my trailer and she met Jessie who, to my distress, lunged at her and barked his head off, so I locked him in the bathroom. We walked down the street together to a steakhouse. It felt so wonderful to be near her, but I wasn't sure she felt the same way. There were buffalo heads on the walls of the restaurant; it had leather booths and barstools made from saddles. I hadn't been to a steak house in years, except when Theresa took me to one in Boulder, and I tried not to worry about the cost. Emily got a stomach ache half way through the meal and stopped eating. Her skin lost its rosy tone and she looked miserable. She said she'd been under a lot of stress lately. Poor baby; she inherited my tendency to stress out over everything.

I drove her back to the dorm and she brought me up to see her room and meet her roommates. The room was luxurious for a dorm. I held her in my arms; she felt so fragile to me. Her silky hair brushed my cheek. I said good-bye and then sat in my truck in the parking lot. I started to cry but I didn't know why.

When I got back to the trailer there was a dead chicken right by my door. It was kind of creepy; had it just dropped dead there? Or had someone put it there? I didn't want to touch it, and trying to keep Jessie away from it was very difficult. In the morning, I used a dog poop bag to dispose of it.

As I was half way in the truck cab, a gust of wind slammed the door shut on my leg, just above my knee. It hurt so bad that I started crying.

I said out loud, "God help me!"

I'd never thought that before and certainly had never said it out loud. I looked around to see if anyone had heard me, but no one was there.

It was a windy haul all the way to Oklahoma. I discovered that if I kept a lighter touch on the steering wheel the truck didn't jerk around as much when the wind grabbed the trailer. This revelation kept me from overcorrecting and I thought about Emily for some reason. Maybe I should start letting go of her, stop worrying about her so much; she was going to be okay.

Jennifer's horse hauling accident continued to haunt me as I was driving, making me more tense than usual. I tried thanking God for all the things I was grateful for—my breath, my beating heart, my freedom. The severed horse leg was still in my head. I reached deeper, "Thank you for my body that works so well, thank you for my horses and their health, thank you for my children." The image dissolved. It came back several more times, but the prayer worked over and over again. I thought of the Jesus-take-the-wheel song. Thank you for my children!

Lake Carl Blackwell in Stillwell, Oklahoma was owned and run by the State University. The trail system was huge and was built around the lake. There was a big competitive trail ride that weekend but most of those campers were at a different camping section.

It got very hot the next day and I shed my normal camping clothes of jeans and long sleeve T-shirts and put on a pair of hiking shorts and a sports bra that made me look flat as a board. I must have looked ridiculous but I felt better. I walked the mares to a field, hobbled them and enjoyed the peace. I got a lot of good photos of them with a view of the lake in the distance. Wildflower figured out how to "run" with the hobbles on. It was more like hopping; she reared up onto her back legs then hopped forward.

We all went out for a long ride and were exhausted afterwards, mostly because of the heat. My thermostat said 90 degrees so I broke down and turned on the AC. I tried to nap but couldn't fall asleep. I checked my weather app to see if it was going to cool down while I was there and it said, "TORNADO WATCH!"

I got up and walked over to a group of five trailers and introduced myself; I wondered what they were going to do about the tornado watch. They were a fun-loving group of women with a couple of kids, and they were constantly cracking jokes about each other. They were from Oklahoma and not concerned about the tornado watch.

They had been at campgrounds before when tornedo sirens went off and the rangers told them to go to storm cellars. They were tracking the storm on their phones and assured me that they would come get me if we had to go seek shelter. All their horses were tied on picket lines for the storm. They had planned a pot-luck steak dinner and invited me to join them. One woman made the most delicious steak I'd ever had and I asked what kind of beef it was.

She said, "Well, it was my cow, that I named Husband #1. I cut off his horns and something else," slyly eyeing the horrified children's eyes, "then cooked him for supper!" The little girls looked as mortified as I was, but everyone else broke out laughing.

I decided to keep my mares in their corral with the power turned off in case they needed to run for safety. I painted my cell phone number on their hips with acrylic paint in case they did and relief workers found them.

The trailer was rocking and rolling with the wind. I checked my weather app again. The storm was predicted to be "the worst tornado potential of the season thus far" for Oklahoma City, which wasn't far from where I was. I posted my situation on the Facebook horse camping group. When I woke at 5:00 it was calm outside so I figured the storm had passed. I got up and decided to ride and fed the mares a little early. As I was eating my own breakfast, all hell broke loose outside.

Ethel, a Facebook friend in Kansas, was tracking the

storm and stayed in touch with me. She told me the center of the storm was 15 minutes away from me and it would last half an hour. I could barely see the horses from my window; they were braced together side by side, butts to the wind, Dreamy looked like she was having difficulty standing at times. The sun wasn't up yet or the clouds were too black to see well. It began to hail, thunder and lightning, and the trailer was rocking hard. But it was a very fast moving storm and was basically over in a half hour. No tornado landed near us, the siren never sounded and I breathed a sigh of relief. The horses didn't appear too freaked out but were shivering when I came out to rescue them from the slop they were standing in. I put them on the picket line, gave them dry hay and got working on moving the portable corral to a dry grass area, closer to the shoreline.

All the campers left quickly after the storm was over. The sun came out and it was 80 degrees. The wind remained, however; its constant blowing was really getting on my nerves. I could never live there with that wind. This was my first state where I didn't say, "I want to live here."

I stayed a couple of more days in Oklahoma by myself and thought about the storm a lot. While it was frightening, I hadn't panicked or felt confused. I wondered if that was because I now believed that God was in control, not me. Was this what they called faith in the storm? Would it be strong enough for my life storms?

The road approaching Blackhawk Horse Camp in Lyndon, Kansas was rough gravel and the vibration probably felt good to the horses' legs. I had to pee so bad by then and the vibration made it impossible not to pee in my pants. My back pain had been horrible on this haul and my right leg was numb by the time I pulled into camp. Susan, the owner was there to greet me as I hobbled out of the truck.

"I was worried about you; you're a little late and I'd heard there was a horse trailer accident on the highway."

She had a kind face and dark brown hair pulled back in a ponytail. She had on a thick, warm-looking jacket. It was pretty cold and looked like it was going to rain so I grabbed my jacket from the backseat. The pocket zipper was missing and the fabric was all wet in that area. Damn it, Jessie!

"Oh, I hope they're all right. Hey, I gotta pee so bad—"

"Ha-ha, that's always the first thing I gotta do when I get somewhere too! There's an outhouse over that way. You can park anywhere you'd like; no other campers are here."

I limped to the outhouse as fast as I could.

About an hour later it started raining so I retreated to the LQ with Jessie. Shortly after I sat down a pickup pulled in and Ethel, my Oklahoma storm watcher, knocked on my door. In her truck bed, she had eight bales of her own hay with sunflowers in it. I was flattered and invited her in the trailer where we talked for a couple of hours. Jessie sat under the table and drove me crazy trying to chew on my boots.

"I can't believe you really came; how far away do you live?"

"Just over an hour. It's my pleasure; I've been dying to meet you. I've followed your whole trip so far. It's so exciting. Can I take a selfie with you?"

I wondered how messed up my hair was and whether I had dirt on my face. Ethel slid next to me on the bench, snapped the selfie and showed it to me. "Nice." One eye was bigger than the other, my smile was crooked. Was my face always so asymmetrical? I remember Bob saying that Debra's was perfectly symmetrical, that it was an indicator of beauty; I'd never known that before.

Ethel told me she was a caretaker on someone's farm. In exchange for caring for the animals and property she got two bedrooms and a kitchen in the house and free board for her mules. I wondered if I could find an arrangement like that somewhere. My back hurt just thinking about the heavy labor involved.

The next day was Teddy's 21st birthday. I hadn't mailed his birthday card yet and felt bad about it. It had a sound chip of a dog barking the happy birthday song. I opened the card and Jessie started barking at it. I took a video and texted it to Teddy.

He replied, "Ha Ha, thanks, mom, love you."

I thought how kids often forget the "I" part of I love you, at least mine did.

When Bob and I were dating, I'd say, "I love you," first. He'd respond with, "I love (big pause) your eyes." Then my hair. He used this diversion for quite a while. He loved every part of my body apparently.

I texted back: "I love you too, Teddy."

It was windy, 45 degrees and raining, but I had an electric hook up and the trailer was warm. At dinnertime, I called Dad, and Yvonne answered the phone. When did Dad stopped answering the phone?

"We just got home from the hospital. Your dad needed a blood transfusion after his surgery."

And nobody called me?

She continued in her annoying authoritative voice. He'd had an ablation of a spot on his liver and the surgery took a lot out of him. He'd told me he was tired from the drugs and not to worry. She said they cancelled the next ablation for another spot because he was too weak for surgery. *So, they're gonna just let it stay there?* But before I could put some words together, I heard Dad say, "Jesus, Yvonne, give me the damn phone!"

"Hi, honey!" He sounded chipper. "Don't worry about me, I feel much better now and I have the utmost confidence in my doctor's decisions. And I've got Yvonne!"

He chuckled and I sighed. I didn't take the cancelled surgery as a good sign; it scared me. Did it mean that they were giving up on treating him?

We chatted for a bit longer and he asked if I'd spoken

to Liza lately. I said no, why?

"I think you should call her."

So I did.

Liza answered my call with, "Kath? I'm glad you called." Liza sounded uncharacteristically authoritative and serious, like a doctor. I wasn't sure it was her. "Mom isn't doing great; she's been complaining of intense back pain lately and she seems very confused at times." *I bet my back hurt worse than hers right now and she's always seemed confused to me.*

"Oh, that's not good," I said.

"I think she should move to an assisted living facility to get more attention."

I should have felt sympathetic, poor mom, but for some reason I didn't.

Liza said, "I can't come down here every day and I'm worried about her being alone."

I started breathing faster and faster but needed to speak calmly. I was the strong one, the survivor of mental illness in our sad family.

"Do you have any idea how much that will cost? Isn't she broke?" I felt panicky; I couldn't afford to pay for it.

"I don't know; I've looked into one that sounds nice. I think insurance may cover it?"

How'd she find that out? What a relief.

I remembered Mom had refused to move in with us years ago, saying she couldn't leave her friends and home. I'd been hurt by that, but it was partly my own fault. I'd paid off her mortgage.

I asked, "Do you think she'd actually agree to move?"

"I don't know."

"Do what you think is best, I'll support whatever you decide to do."

A memory flickered through, from when I was a teenager: finding Mom out cold, in bed, an empty orange prescription bottle was on the nightstand. Dad wasn't there.

Liza said, "When will you get here? I hate doing this alone."

I said, "About a month, I'll be there by June."

As soon as I hung up, Emily called. She sounded stressed out.

"Hi, honey, did you have a nice Easter break?" I knew that she had gone to Bob's new apartment for the week.

"No! I'm never staying with Dad again! And I hate Texas too! I'm coming home for summer. Why can't you just come home?" She was crying and it broke my heart. I heaved a sigh. I didn't want her to ever see me wanting to die again. I just couldn't come back till I was sure that was behind me.

"I can't afford to live there, Emily. I just can't. How about I ask Rose if you could stay with them?"

It was her turn to sigh. "I guess that would be okay. But I hardly know them anymore." She finally agreed to the idea and I emailed Rose offering to pay her for room and board.

It was harder to let go of these issues; the steering wheel had been much easier. I said out loud, "Let go and let God," but I was still riddled with guilt. I was not being a responsible parent or daughter. I wished I had the energy and strength that I used to have. I missed the old me; I would have just dealt with it and not freaked out, but I'd had lots of money and was emotionally stable then.

I started to really feel awful. I began questioning what the heck I was doing this journey for. It was a stupid idea and so hard on me and my animals and my kids.

I took Jessie for a romp on the trail. The footing was either packed slippery mud or rocky on the trail. but on the rough sides of the trail, grass held the ground in place. I could choose to focus my gaze down to where I was placing my feet or up at the trees, the lake or Jessie who ran ahead. This moment seemed to equate with my life somehow. Would I choose the easy path or the hard one? Where would I choose to focus?

It was so darned cold and still raining. I could see the corrals from the trailer's kitchen window. Wildflower was eating both my old hay and Ethel's hay, but Dreamy was eating neither, just staring at the trailer. She was resting her left front foot out in front, which meant that it hurt. It made me feel terrible but there wasn't much I could do about it.

I re-read the daily inspirational in *Jesus Calling*. The last sentence was "My Word is a lamp to your feet and a light for your path." Should I stop looking down at the messy path of my circumstances and just look up to God?

I spent the cold rainy day painting and finished two I was fairly happy with. I started thinking of all these paintings as just studies. They had little detail, since they were so small. My hands shook so much lately; when had that started? I decided I'd like to paint them in a larger format with oils once I settled down somewhere; that it would keep me busy for a long time. It could serve as a purpose, something to do. I had 17 of these small paintings so far. I'd never done such an extensive series before and could envision all 48 hung close together like tiles, filling a wall.

I went out to check on Dreamy. It was freezing outside and she was wet. The wind gusts were wicked. As I got closer I could see that she was shivering badly, which is their natural way to keep warm, but it scared me to see her in such distress. I took her out of her pen and led her to some tall green grass. She started gobbling it up. I'd never seen her eat so fast; it was like she was starving. After about 20 minutes she stopped shivering and relaxed. I thought how Jack always said that horses heat themselves from the inside.

I moved both horses to pens where the fierce wind was buffered by some thick evergreen trees and threw in a super generous portion of hay. They had just shed their winter coats a few weeks earlier in Florida when it started getting hot there. I worried about heading even further north next weekend.

I heard back from Rose and she was fine with having

Emily stay with them for the summer. I sent her a check for $3,000 to cover her room and groceries, even though Rose said that was too much. I thanked her and then God for helping me out on this one. I texted Emily and she seemed okay with the solution.

As I dozed off in the gooseneck I noticed how muddy Jessie's paws were. I threw my arm over his warm body. I thought about how four messy trials had reared up today; three of them were now in someone else's capable hands. Yvonne still gnawed at my gut.

Susan's husband, Dave, offered to go for a ride with me the following day. "I know all the trails around here and can show you where the eagle's nest is."

He went on to say that he couldn't go the day after tomorrow because they were taking their granddaughter down to Kansas City for the removal of her leg cast. Every couple of weeks they had to cut it off and put a new one on, in an attempt to make her leg muscles stretch more. She had been born three months early and had been so small that she'd fit in his hand. He extended his palm up towards me and I envisioned a miniature baby in the fetal position there. I thought of my aborted fetus; I'd had no idea that they could survive at six months. He continued talking; she had cerebral palsy so she didn't walk quite right and the kids at school made fun of her. The little girl and her mom lived in their old house, which he nodded toward on the next lot of land, and they had moved into the trailer next door at the campground to accommodate them.

He said all this very matter-of-factly, like it wasn't a hardship or an out of the ordinary solution. But his story shook me to the core. I thought my family had trials 'cuz my perfectly healthy daughter had to stay with friends in their luxurious home in La Canada for the summer? What tragic pampered world was I comparing my circumstances to? Then I thought about my parents; had they even considered helping to raise my baby when I was sixteen?

On my way into the shower that night, a country love song came on the radio. The singer sang how he "remembered where I was when I fell in love with her" on their first date, then again when his son is born he "remembered where I was when I fell in love with her" and then again, he remembers when she dies. It was about falling in love, about falling in love with the same woman over and over, like it was new and special every time. He cherished her. I was standing in the doorway between the kitchen and the bathroom, naked, the water was running in the shower. I couldn't breathe. I'd never felt cherished by a lover. I started sobbing in uncontrolled gasps and gulps.

I calmed down as I was toweling off but the pain deep inside my chest remained. Was I unlovable? Did I even love myself? I thought how I thrived on praise and admiration for my achievements or how I looked or how much money I made, the things Dad always praised me for too.

I hadn't gotten much in the way of praise from Bob. And I didn't react well to criticism; it made me shatter inside. I couldn't have found a more critical man to have married. No wonder I was such an emotional wreck.

Dave rode with me the next day as promised. He told me some of the history of the state-run "horse camp" that was located nearby and that he had helped build. He pointed out an owl's and an eagle's nests, and told me the names of local trees. The red bud trees were in bloom and so pretty with tiny red flowers on them. Then we talked about our lives and marriage, divorce and children.

I was on Wildflower and ponying Dreamy. Dreamy kept stopping to grab grass so I lost her rope a couple of times, once in a stream. The thick long cotton rope got very heavy once it was wet. Dave showed me a better way to handle my pony rope. He said to pull the pony rope under my thigh, then do one turn on the saddle horn. This freed up my right arm and my leg easily kept the rope from slipping out too quickly.

As we came upon a dirt road and turned onto it, I realized Jessie was no longer with us. I started to panic. He had been ahead of us and we must have taken a turn without him. According to Dave, he was most likely headed back toward camp when he realized he was separated. I used my super loud whistle and we backtracked a while, eventually finding him quite winded, his long pink tongue limply hanging out of his mouth.

"Thank God! Jessie, where were you??" I let out a sigh of relief. I was surprised how upset I'd gotten when he was missing.

Dave said, "If that ever happens again and you don't find him after backtracking, you should lay your jacket, or something with your scent on it, on the trail at the spot that you last saw him. Come back the next day and if he loves you, he'll be lying on your jacket waiting for you."

If he loves me, he'll wait for me. Would my kids do that too?

Dave also suggested putting a bell on Jessie's collar so I would notice when he strayed. I wouldn't have to remember to keep checking for him, I'd just know right away. This sounded like a great idea and I wrote "little bell" on my Tractor Supply shopping list.

Later that day Dave and Susan brought me along to their Bible study class. There were about 20 people seated around the tables arranged in a giant square, taking up the entire room. They were studying Revelations, which I knew nothing about. This was in the Bible? I'd never learned any of this in catechism, was I just a poor student? I tried to follow along with what they were talking about. I thought I'd like to read this alone when I could concentrate better, but I'd found the Bible very hard to understand. I needed an interpreter; didn't the priest do that?

When the meeting ended, we all wandered out to the

main hall for coffee and donuts. Susan introduced me to her pastor. He softly put his hand on my upper arm and showed us into his office, I guess for privacy?

He asked me where I was from, how long I'd been away from home, was I new to having faith?

"Well, new to me, sort of. I was raised Catholic and God was all about fear and guilt back then."

"Ahh, yes, I was raised Catholic as well. So true, such a shame."

That was shocking.

"Your study on Revelations was interesting, I don't know much about the Bible, I just got baptized last month."

He hugged me like a child and patted my back. I was surprised and didn't know how to react so I didn't move.

He pulled back and looked me eye to eye. I felt vulnerable. He said, "Welcome."

Welcome, like not just a formal thing someone says when you show up somewhere. I shivered. I felt it, deep in my soul. And it felt so safe and good.

We drove back to camp and Dave started a fire. The three of us roasted hot dogs and marshmallows for dinner. I also cooked a chicken breast that was about to go bad, using a marshmallow stake, but it looked too much like the skunk innards I had seen on the trail earlier, so I called Jessie over and he snatched it off the stake and swallowed it whole. I'd never seen a dog eat his food so fast and wondered if he'd ever get over starving on the streets of Palm Beach. I smiled; he'd never have to worry about that again.

Susan and Dave were still talking about Revelations and I felt comfortable enough to ask some elementary questions.

"You guys seem to know the Bible pretty well. I have some things that have bothered me for a long time. Do you know if a baby dies before he's been baptized does he really go to purgatory? I was taught that in Catechism and it sounds really unfair to me. I mean, it's not their fault; they're innocent babies, right?"

Susan quickly answered, "Oh, no, that's not true at all. In fact, the Bible says nothing about purgatory at all. That was made up in the Middle Ages by the Catholic Church, I think; right, Dave?

Dave nodded as he stared at the fire. *The Catholic Church just made it up?* I tried to hide my outrage.

"What about a person living in a remote jungle that's never been told about God or Jesus, what about them? Why do they go to Hell?

"They don't; they never rejected Christ," said Dave.

I asked, "Jews talk about Moses, right? So, what is it that differentiates their religion from what Christians believe?" I thought about my boyfriend, Richard's father; he'd threatened to cut Richard out of the family business if he married a shiksa. My offering to convert wasn't good enough for him.

Dave raised his eyebrows. "Well, Jews follow the Old Testament, the stories before Christ was born. You know, Jesus was born a Jew."

"Yeah, that's confusing to me too. So why did Jews end up crucifying him?"

I could see in their faces that this wasn't a simple question. How come I didn't know this stuff?

Susan said, "Well, Jews don't believe Jesus was the son of God, which is what the New Testament is all about."

A light bulb went off, kind of like how BC stands for before Christ? "I've tried reading the Bible, really I have; I went to a Bible study in Florida while I was there. I even have one in the trailer in fact, but it's confusing to me; I don't understand what they're talking about most of the time. I need an interpreter."

Dave said, "That's why we go to Bible study."

Susan added, "And we read the Bible together at home and then talk about it."

I couldn't picture Bob and I reading the Bible together. I remembered Brad's middle school friend, Brandon, whose family read the Bible together every night after supper. They were from Texas and were all blonde. They were renting a small house in La Canada while the dad was finishing his Masters at Fuller Seminary. When I went to pick Brad up after a playdate, I saw their monstrous old Bible opened on the dining room table. There were colored post it notes marking places between some of the pages. We didn't even own a Bible. I remember thinking that they must be religious fanatics.

I smiled, "What are your favorite parts to read? Like, I mean, where should I begin?"

Dave offered, "I kinda like Revelations; it gives me hope. That there's a better life to come for us."

Susan interjected, "I think you should start with John."

"Funny, my daughter told me that too."

I popped my burnt-on-the-outside, liquid-on-the-inside marshmallow in my mouth.

It reminded me of roasting marshmallows with the kids when they were little. We'd often camped out in the woods on our property back in Illinois and we'd always made a campfire because s'mores had been an important part of the experience in the kids' eyes. We'd had so much fun sleeping in the teepee together. Bob was so different then. He had a wonderful smile, he adored us all. I thought it would be the same but even better after I stopped working. He said we wouldn't change, that my income didn't matter; he'd build this company for us.

The next morning I was pretty tired. I saddled up and rode Dreamy to 110 Mile Park on the blue trail, and felt much better afterwards.

I had supper around the campfire again with the owners, their daughter, her husband and little Emma, whom I had met earlier before they left for Kansas City in the morning. Susan had brought her to my trailer; she said Emma loved to draw and wanted to see my paintings. I unwrapped them and showed them to her one by one, telling her the story of where I was and which horses were mine. She barely spoke but I could tell she was listening as she kept her eyes on the little panels I placed before her.

I watched Emma trudging through the dirt and leaves on the ground with her new cast; she wandered over to where her mom and dad were seated on a log and squeezed in between them. I said, "A whole year in the hospital, that must have been so hard on everyone."

Susan said, "Emma was never alone in the hospital. We all took turns being there."

I thought, *little Emma with the messed up leg, don't you worry, you'll be just fine. You are surrounded with love.*

The following morning Wildflower flat out refused to load into the trailer. Susan and Dave sat on a log and quietly watched as I tried bribing her with feed and carrots, sending her in from behind, loading Dreamy first as an incentive, using a dressage stick, but she still wouldn't load.

I was trying to contain my anger. I'd been through this with her before and getting mad never helped. So I tried something new, I put her in the round pen, loaded Dreamy and shut the doors.

"Bye, Wildflower," I shouted and I got in the truck and pulled out onto the road. She went nuts running circles and calling to Dreamy. I drove down the road a ways, made a U-turn and came back to try again. She still refused. I wanted to just leave her there.

Thankfully, Susan and Dave didn't say a word. I wanted to work this out on my own. I dug through my box of extra tack, pulled out an old leather halter and chain. I removed her rope halter, put on the leather one and strung the chain through the halter over her nose. I snapped my lead rope clip to the chain, snapped the rope once and clucked as I marched up the trailer ramp. She followed me right on.

What a brat! I can play by those rules if I have to.

Wildflower was a typical bully and took advantage of me when she thought I wasn't strong. That really pissed me off, I guess because it reminded me so much of Bob.

Chapter 8

I used the chain over Wildflower's nose again to load her the next morning. She again planted her feet at the edge of the ramp and I snapped the rope hard, I wasn't putting up with her crap anymore! Her head snapped up and her eyes widened, then she sighed and walked right like a perfect little lady. Why did she make me have to do this? I didn't like being mean.

After two uneventful days of hauling, I pulled into Turkey Creek Ranch in New Castle, Nebraska. Brenda, her husband John and their dog, Buddy, were at the campground to greet me when I arrived. When I'd made my reservation with Brenda, I'd told her how I was trying to ride in all the lower 48 states and she'd said she couldn't wait to meet me and hear some of my stories. She was super bubbly and I was drawn to her right away, even though I was again the only camper staying there.

I told Brenda about my upcoming radio interview. It seemed I wasn't getting cell service there.

"Here, use mine!" she said, handing me her phone.

"Thanks!" I said, "This won't take long." I called Gary to discuss the details.

"Okay," he said, "We won't record you live then in case we have connection problems. Can you use a landline to call me Tuesday? It'll take about a half hour and I'll record it for next week's show." I asked Brenda about using her landline and she said sure.

On my 60th birthday I got a message from Dad, singing Happy Birthday to me. I wondered if this would be my last one, which made me sad. All the kids texted me Happy Birthday and in the evening I even got a message from Bob, which felt kind of creepy. But nothing from my mother, the one person I'd thought would never forget my birthday. Mom had always sent a wrapped gift with a card and called me. This was very out of character and made me sad.

John and Brenda took me to a little fish & chips joint in town for my birthday dinner; Brenda had been reading my SHLEP blog, so she knew it was a "big birthday." It was a lovely evening, complete with a piece of key lime pie with a candle in it; Brenda and John sang happy birthday to me. Still, being 60 made me feel old.

The next day I loaded up a ton of laundry and headed to a laundromat. On the way out of camp, I found Jessie wandering in front of someone's house; Brenda had told me that someone named Earl lived there. She'd described him as an authentic old cowboy and a cowboy poet.

I introduced myself and put Jessie in the truck. I asked if Earl still had horses, he sadly looked off to his pasture and told me he had lost his 39-year-old horse recently.

I said, "Oh, I'm so sorry." I paused a bit, "But wow! 39? That's a real testament to your horse care. You should be so proud of that."

"Thanks." His expression didn't change and he stood staring at the empty pasture as I waved goodbye. It made me sad.

Tuesday morning, I drove up to Brenda & John's house to do the radio interview on their landline. John showed me to his lazy boy chair with the phone sitting on a small table next to it. I dialed the number and was eventually connected to Gary Holt. He gave me a little prep talk, which I needed, and his voice was calming to me somehow. "I'm going to start recording now, okay?"

He introduced me as "a woman who is on the horse adventure of a lifetime." I cringed. I'd told him that this wasn't an adventure to me. Maybe he was trying to keep it lighthearted and inspiring. Or maybe he was protecting me. Maybe he was one of those rare nice interviewers who sensed that this could be painful for me if he pried. He asked me all the usual questions I got about SHLEP and I relaxed some and answered as honestly as I could. I noticed that Gary had a smooth Southern accent that felt like velvet flowing over my skin.

He took three song breaks during the interview, playing "A Horse That Can Fly" and "Wishing You Wings" by Templeton Thompson and "Horses & Life" by Mary Ann Kennedy. I'd never heard any of them before and listened carefully to the lyrics to see why he chose them. Two lines hit home and made me catch my breath. I quickly jotted them down.

Gary said he'd sure like to talk with me again later in my SHLEP and I said, "Okay, that would be nice." I placed the phone in the charger stand and sighed; I was relieved that was over. I hadn't cried or rambled on too much. I did okay.

At 7:00 that night, Brenda picked me up to go to Earl and his wife, June's, for wine and cheese. We sat outside at their picnic table with a checked tablecloth and a pot of pansies as a centerpiece. June and Earl had been together forever and lived a simple life. I bet they were truly happy. June had the most genuine smile I'd ever seen. She brought out a plate of fresh asparagus from her garden with a mayo dip and Earl had made a cheese dish. We had a couple of glasses of wine and talked, nothing profound, just a nice easy normal conversation. They only asked a couple of SHLEP questions; I wasn't the center of curiosity in the conversation.

Before we left, they showed me the inside of their home. It was a small old clapboard typical Midwestern farm house. I love old houses. It reminded me of my old NJ farmhouse, where my wedding was held, the one I sold after I got married. I wished I still had it. In June and Earl's dining room hung a lovely painting that I stopped to admire. It depicted a cowboy standing next to a horse in a rural landscape. June came closer and quietly said, "That's Earl and his best horse, the one that just died." I turned to face her. Her blue eyes locked on mine and told me so much; this was obviously an epic loss for Earl and his pain was in her eyes. And then it was inside me. As we were walking out, Earl handed me a spiral bound book.

"Oh, is this your poetry?" I asked.

He nodded. I asked him to sign it but he said he already had.

As I lay in bed that night I started to read Earl's book. I read the last line of his dedication with tears filling my eyes, "and to June--she, like the country, is always there."

Oh, how I wished I'd had a love like that in my life.

Earl wrote about all the horses and cows that he'd worked with as a cowboy with intense love and compassion. It wasn't what I was expecting, but I guess I'd never read real cowboy poetry before. The poems made me feel so good I decided to only read one a night, so the book would last longer for me. I fell asleep with a smile on my face, expecting sweet dreams, maybe even a flying one.

In my dream that night, Bob and I were standing in the driveway outside our "little old house."

Bob was saying that the beams holding up our house were rotten, that we had never fixed them and I shouldn't let the kids play in the basement since the house could collapse on them. I was confused as to why playing on the upper floors wouldn't endanger them as well but I didn't say a word; I just listened to him. We then walked into a "secret" room that I had not known about before, and Bob nonchalantly said, "This is where you were exorcized."

My mind screamed. What the F---? Me exorcized? How did I not know about this? What happened in this room? I was frozen in fear.

I woke up shaking in a cold sweat. Jessie was lying on my chest. I got up and pulled on my boots. My song lyric note from the interview was on the dinette table and I glanced at it.

"I gotta get back to living before I forget how."

I couldn't stop thinking about my nightmare as I drove to Iowa. Exorcism was about driving out the Devil! And if Bob, my devil, was the one in charge of my exorcism, was he driving out God? What had happened in the little old house? I'd quit work; I was no longing raking in tons of cash. That's when everything changed; he'd married me for my money and when that was gone, I was dead weight!

I got so distracted I missed my turn. The roads were all gravel and I got hopelessly lost. I called the number I had for the camp and a nice woman talked me through the turns as I was driving. Eventually I pulled onto the pretty but deserted property of The Natural Gait in Minona, Iowa. I was the only one there.

Apparently, I was in this neck of the country a little too early for most campers. It was windy but a comfortable 74 degrees and drizzling. I heard thunder in the distance as I was settling in. I had no cell signal nor internet and couldn't pick up the campground Wi-Fi that I'd thought they had.

I scouted a bit and found that there were many acres of lush grass, but I couldn't find a fenced off area anywhere, so I hobble grazed the horses for an hour before putting them in their pens. An old truck pulled up while they were grazing and three guys in camouflage clothing headed out on the trail—hunters maybe? Jessie had on his new bell and I noticed that the jingle was moving away from me. I turned to see him charging towards the men and blew my yellow whistle. He stopped and came back.

The next morning I'd found a Wisconsin NPR station on the radio and started breakfast. The familiar voices made me feel at home. Over my morning coffee I read my daily devotional, which reiterated the admonition to "Let go, Let God."

I had cell service for a while and got a call from Mom. She said she was at the Jersey shore and had been arrested. Could I come bail her out?

Huh? She needed to be rescued? By me? She didn't sound drunk. Had Liza gotten her into a home already? That was impressive. I tried to tell her that I supported Liza's decisions, but she kept talking over me. She yelled something mean and angry that I couldn't make out, very unlike her, at least in front of other people, and I said, "What did you say?"

She said, "I thought someone was at the door. You haven't come to see me in years. You've never even seen my new place."

"Mom, I've seen your place. " I did visit, right? When was it, a year or two ago? My heart started racing for some reason.

Mom cried, "You never call me!"

I remembered years ago, I'd sent her a birthday card, promising that I'd start calling every Sunday. That lasted about a month. What's the matter with me?

"I'm sorry mom, I've been so preoccupied with my own hell lately."

She wailed, "You don't care about me!"

"I love you, Mom." Did I? My anxiety level was hitting the roof.

She was now angry and yelled, "I'm locked up! There are people drooling here!"

Drooling? Where was she anyway? This wasn't my problem, Liza was handling it. I stated my stance again, that I supported whatever Liza thought was best for her. I said I loved her. Then I just hung up. I'd never done that before and it was kind of satisfying. Then I felt guilty. I sat in a stupor at the dinette staring at my phone, a war in my mind of confusing rage and guilt. The phone dinged and I jerked.

It was Emily, texting that she had moved into Rose's house for her summer break. Rose is a wonderful mother; she and Warren get along well. Emily used to tell me that she wished our family was like theirs. She should be happy there.

I wondered if Bob felt abandoned. Although most of the

time I wished him paybacks, I now felt sorry for him and that felt really strange. Emily was his shining star; she'd had him wrapped around her little finger. It had to feel like betrayal to him. My pity didn't last long. A few seconds later, I felt like an idiot.

I called Dad to tell him about mom's distressing call. My rock. I didn't have a chance to say anything before he told me that he'd had chemo again. My rock was crumbling; my world would crumble along with him. How was I going to go on without him?

There was too much going on and it was happening way too fast for me. It was a bigger storm than I'd imagined, one I'd somehow known would be on the horizon. I'd been hoping I'd have stronger faith for it, enough to weather it with some peace. But I was failing the test. I didn't pray, I didn't even think about God or His will be done.

I was in free fall, in a deserted campground with a storm whipping up outside. That's when I lost cell service.

I slept fitfully, waking with every thunder strike to Jessie trembling beside me. Then the tapes of my brief connection to the outside world via cell signal played over in my head and I couldn't fall back asleep.

Mom was really messed up; was that dementia? There were different kinds, right? The most recent memories go first, which seemed odd to me. But maybe it's like the brain is full and just can't fit them in so they aren't embedded? She obviously didn't remember last summer, but then the visit was kind of fuzzy to me too. She probably doesn't remember what I'm doing right now, or that I left Bob. I wondered if she remembered me paying off her house. She obviously remembered my phone number or maybe it's programmed in her phone. Then I dozed off, but not for long.

I couldn't believe that Liza got mom to go to a home. My sister did have a way with words, making her sound rational and intelligent even during her crazy periods.

It was still windy and the sky was overcast the next time I opened my eyes. I was dead tired. I dragged myself outside; the mares looked okay and I threw them some hay. Jessie was chewing on an old plastic milk jug. I went inside the trailer, flipped on the radio for company and made coffee. There were country western songs and cattle prices on the radio. I felt so alone. Not just there, but my whole being felt separate from the universe, from normal people's lives. I'd set off on this trip saying that I wanted to be left alone; I wanted all my family's problems to solve themselves without me. That's not the same as wanting to be alone.

My devotional sat on the table in its usual place, where I sat drinking my coffee, I was so tired. I read it just because it was there, like it was just a cereal box. Today's message ended with "Trust Me, and watch to see what I will do." I think it meant what good things I will do, but that was hard to believe. None of this was going to end well for me. Or dad, or mom.

I put the horses in a fenced pasture I found. Boy, were they happy. As I headed out for a hike with Jessie, I met a young woman who managed the campground. She told me that no other campers were coming in and that a group of twelve had just cancelled due to a horse virus scare. I had heard some horses had died from it in Iowa and had called before I came to be sure the campground wasn't going to shut down because of it. She then said she wouldn't be around all weekend either, but I could do whatever I wanted, including using the pasture my horses were already in. Great, I'll just go crazy here all by myself.

I got a call from Liza. Yes, she'd gotten mom to willingly go to an assisted living facility the day before. I congratulated her. Apparently, this is where Mom called me from, which explained a lot about my conversation with her. Then Mom fell walking to the bathroom. They took her to the ER and found that she had broken her hip and needed surgery. The pre-surgery lab results showed that Mom was in kidney failure.

They ran the test again and got the same results. They said she was not a candidate for dialysis; Liza wasn't sure why, but they told her that sometimes the kidneys healed themselves. I'd never heard that before.

She continued the medical report like she'd written it herself. "They can't perform hip surgery until her kidneys are functioning." She paused. "Another doctor said he wanted to discuss the ethical question of dialysis."

"What's that mean?"

"If it's the ethical thing to do, for Mom's sake."

"Why wouldn't fixing her kidney's be the right thing to do?"

"I'm not sure, I made an appointment for when you get here—June, right? I still have a lot of questions myself; the specialists are consulting with her regular internist today, I'll get back to you when I know more."

She sounded really on top of things; I had no idea what most of what she was saying meant. How'd she get all that info and keep it straight? Thank God someone could. Who would have thought my crazy baby sister was so capable under pressure? Who would have thought that Kathy Burns would crack up?

"Watch to see what I will do," He said. It sounded ominous now.

"I support whatever you decide to do, Liza." This time I meant it not because I couldn't handle it or didn't want to, but because she was the sane sister now.

"Thanks, that means a lot to me, Kathy. Can you call Dad and tell him? I gotta get some sleep."

Why was Mom in kidney failure? I thought Diabetes caused that. How had she not known she was that sick; weren't there serious symptoms? Does dialysis heal the kidneys? I thought it was just a treatment. Kidneys can heal on their own? I needed the internet, but my phone wouldn't connect. But I did have a cell signal still. I called Dad.

He started crying like a baby; I hadn't expected this. They had been divorced for over forty years. Did he still love her? I bet Bob wouldn't cry about me being in kidney failure.

I felt so bad. Mom and I used to be closer. We went to the theater together, out to dinner; she loved being with the grandkids and going on vacation with us. I think she loved the kids more than me. She was proud of me, always telling me how she bragged to her friends about my success, telling me how beautiful I was. How strong. But I don't remember having intimate conversations; at least I didn't get intimate. She'd cry about that guy she loved who wouldn't commit. She told me about all her friends and her singing group. But I never let down the façade of strong-successful-beautiful. Until I started complaining about Bob. In the last few years I hadn't been there for her when she needed me. I hadn't been there for anyone really, including my kids. I had been trying to keep my head above water in my lousy marriage and had let most of my family and friends drift away. I felt like shit.

I said, "Let go, Let God." It didn't help.

Off and on, I tried to start my Nebraska painting. I loved the photograph but I couldn't seem to get going. I really didn't want to get depressed again. I needed to remember: eat, sleep, ride, walk, paint, do something, move. I felt frozen in place. Hold God's hand. Let go, let God. One step at a time. I tried all the mantras.

I ended up working on the painting most of the day. I had trouble with it, but it was a good distraction and I finished it. I used a shot from a grassy hilltop with the mares looking off to a tractor working on the next hillside. It was difficult because of the perspective and because Dreamy was blending into a tree line. Brenda's adorable pink cabin looked awkward.

I had less and less energy as the day progressed. My cell phone signal had disappeared again. I reset my phone's network settings three times and now it said that I had three bars but nothing worked! I was panicking that Liza was trying to reach me about my mother's condition. I didn't know what to do about it. I could barely walk and I was having trouble focusing my eyes. I hated my phone and Straight Talk. I started to think that Mom was dying. I'd been getting used to the idea of Dad dying for the past two years but this was pulling the rug out from under me. I thought about me dying and wondered if my kids would be there for me. I had set a bad example.

I threw up after dinner and went straight to bed. I didn't even check on the horses. Jessie threw up on the bed twice and I let him out of the trailer.

Upon waking the next morning, I remembered that I could send and receive messages with my inReach, so I sent Liza a text: "No cell service, reply to this and let me know what's going on with Mom, please."

I saddled up Wildflower and ponied Dreamy around the trails. We rode down through the woods, alongside the winding Yellow River, around corn fields, through a prairie and a pine forest; there were some good hills on our return. Jessie came along and behaved until he took flight after a deer. I hoped he'd find his way back to camp. I got tired of holding Dreamy's lead rope and just draped it over her back. I had never done this before but was pretty sure that Dreamy would just follow us and she did.

A couple of hours later I rode back into camp. Jessie was sacked out under the trailer. I put the girls in the pasture for the afternoon and drove to Prairie Du Chien, Wisconsin to try and fix my phone or just get a new one. I found a Walgreens and bought a no contract Verizon "burner". I called Liza from the parking lot to give her my new number. She gave me an update.

"Mom is starting dialysis after all, and she will be having hip surgery next week after her kidneys improve. She keeps saying that she just wants to go home, even though she can't walk with a broken hip and is seriously ill. She's blaming me for taking her to assisted living, saying that she wouldn't have fallen and broken her hip if she had been at her own home."

Thank God for Liza! I was relieved that she was apparently handling the crisis with compassion and a cool head. Neither of which I was able to muster when it came to mom lately. If I ever had. There'd be no possibility for a serious heart to heart now, no opportunity to air my grievances and try to resolve this shit I felt. Then I felt guilty for thinking that. Poor Mom was so confused, I should be loving on her now like a child; she was in need and at a very scary time in life. She could be dying. I should drive straight to her side, forget about my journey for a while.

Then I got resentful; I was always putting my life on hold for other people, I was sick of it. End of life is just awful and it wasn't even my death I was dealing with; I hoped I'd get lucky and get hit by a Mack truck when it was my time to go. Mom used to say that.

I called Emily to tell her about Grandma getting sick and told her to tell Brad and Teddy. She'd been sleeping and it was one of those teenager half-awake conversations. I remembered that she was at Rose's house and pictured her in Nick's bedroom. Oh God, my life, my family.

The next day was Mother's Day. Great timing I thought. I used to love Mother's Day. Mom was there for my first one, when I was pregnant with Brad. We showed her the house we'd just bought. We went out to dinner. Bob gave me roses. Eventually Mother's day got rolled into my birthday celebration for a family dinner out. I always resented that. I'd wanted to roll Father's day into Bob's birthday but they were three months apart.

I had a wonderful ride on Dreamy, except for the fact that Jessie took off after a deer again, showing up totally exhausted back at camp much later. This problem needed to be addressed but I didn't know how.

I called Mom to wish her a Happy Mother's Day. She

sounded glad to hear from me. There was no mention of being in jail at the Jersey shore nor angry accusations about me being a negligent daughter. Did dementia come and go that quickly? But I was grateful about it; it's so stressful talking to a crazy person. I wondered if I sounded like that to my kids.

Then I got a text from Emily, "Happy Mother's Day! I love you."

I thought, "Oh, my baby girl, I'm sorry. I'm a horrible mother. I'm such a mess."

I texted back, "I love you too."

One thing I like about texting, it's easier to fake that you're doing better than you really are.

A few days later I was on my way to High Knob Ranch in the Shawnee National Forest in Equality, Illinois. The last 50 miles hauling to the Shawnee area was agonizing; my lower back and sciatica were killing me. I limped into the lodge to check in. Jo Jo, the camp owner, checked me in and got a guy to park my rig by the barn. He said, "No big deal, you don't look so good right now." I hoped he was referring to my limp.

Back in December I'd read a Facebook post on the Horse Trails and Camping across America group that was posted by Jo Jo's daughter asking for prayers for her mom, whom everyone on Facebook seemed to know and love. She'd had a horrible wreck while riding her mule on the trail and had to be air lifted out of camp. I guessed those prayers had worked, 'cuz here she was and she looked fine to me. She had long blonde hair in a ponytail and bright blue eyes. I didn't notice any parts of her body not moving normally. We stood on the porch as my trailer was being parked and waited for a squall to pass. I asked her what a squall was.

"It's a quick rainstorm," she said. She told me that they had shavings and propane for sale, a shower house, and fresh brewed coffee in the office every morning at 7:30, adding that a neighbor sold hay if I needed it. Then she asked why I was doing SHLEP. I told her I was running away from my divorce. She didn't say anything and just looked at me very intently. Her eyes looked kind, so I took a deep breath said, "He was emotionally abusive."

"Oh, we have a lot in common," she said, and I relaxed a bit. "I left my husband, kids and a big house 20 years ago. I lived in my horse trailer on 15 acres that I bought here in Shawnee for several years."

I was speechless. Someone else had been through this exact same walk and survived, and they were standing right in front of me. I was in awe and wanted to hear more. But I couldn't find any appropriate words and just looked into her sparkling blue eyes. Mom had eyes like that.

When I woke the next morning it was still raining. I vaguely recalled Nancy in Missouri telling me not to go to Shawnee in the spring because it rained so much. Heck, I'd lived in Illinois for the first 11 years of my marriage; I should have remembered that it rained a lot in the spring. I stayed in my sleeping bag a while, the raindrops pinging on the metal roof of the trailer.

> *We bought a house in Barrington Hills just before Brad was born and I started renovating it a year later. The bathroom was now finished. The floor was oak. Everything else was white; there was a bidet, a giant whirlpool, a steam room and two sinks. Bob was shaving at one of them. I was eight months pregnant with Teddy and in the shower, I shut the water off. I'd gained a lot of weight being on doctor-ordered bedrest and eating Mint Milano cookies for the past five months. Teddy was going to be a big baby; when they induced him three months later, he was already ten pounds. My belly was enormous. Brad was two and with the nanny downstairs eating breakfast. I wished I was giving him breakfast instead of getting ready for work. But Bob had said it wasn't a good time for him; he said that a lot after we got married, and*

besides, how could I walk away from that kind of money? I guess he was right, because his business had just folded. I'd thought he was so successful when we got married; he'd said that we were the same, that our egos were our drive for success. I almost broke up with him because I thought I was much more than that.

Self-conscious of my pregnant body, I stepped out of the shower and reached for a big thick bath towel to cover myself. Bob saw me in the wall of mirrors. He slowly turned and puffed up his cheeks like balloons. His pursed lips looked like the rubber ruffles of a balloon opening. He raised his bushy brows. That's all he did. A silent, mocking gesture. Just under the radar, for just a few seconds. Like a bully on the playground trying to incite a fight without getting caught by the monitor. He didn't laugh nor kiss my belly to defuse what he'd done; he just turned and went back to shaving. I noticed that his puckered lips hadn't changed, like he was blowing himself kisses in the mirror. I couldn't believe he was making fun of me, but he definitely was. And by leaving out the words, "You're fat," or worse, he made it impossible for me to explain to myself why it hurt so much. But being thin and beautiful was very important to Bob. He had always admired my body and told me he loved this or that part, that it was perfect. My hurt turned to anger. I'm carrying your baby for Christ's sake. Cut me some slack. I didn't say anything and acted like nothing had happened.

Is that where I went wrong—I stuffed my anger? What would have been better? Ignore him? Would another woman have cried or laughed, or made the face back, or gone over to rub their belly on his butt, or danced around flaunting their body like a stripper? Should I have prayed for him?

I now know what the experts say to do; the best way to deal with this is to cut them out of your life. It only gets worse if you stay. By staying, you're giving them the message that it's okay.

Bob's fat-face expression seared itself in my mind. Many years later, I painted it from memory. The painting shows the meanness in his face. I stabbed his forehead with a dart and hung it in my studio. It wasn't the only portrait that he found offensive.

> *When he saw the other one on my easel, he filed a restraining order and I got a copy of his filing. Eventually it was turned down by the judge, but I thought what I received was a court order. I'd already filed for divorce and stopped hiding the canvas; we were still in the same house. It was four weeks of hell times a million. That "violent painting" is now called, "The Narcissist, someone who uses words as fists." It started out as my anger-therapy, just-throw-paint-at–the-canvas. I used to keep it hidden, but over the course of about ten years, it morphed into Bob's face. His full lips and cleft chin emerged from the swirling paint, then those gangster black sunglasses and black ball cap appeared; gold started dripping between his huge teeth. After our first court date, I tossed red paint at it and left it on my easel. Fuck him.*
>
> *The restraining order arrived about a week later. It called for me to destroy or remove from the family home any paintings depicting Bob. As I read it my blood boiled.*
>
> *I chose "destroy" and had just the right knife for the job in my back pocket. I slashed out his face and shredded it into strips. I wove them together and pasted them back in the hole. I cut up the restraining order and pasted them around his face like a halo. I cut up several paintings that ugly day; any that had his face in it was fair game. One hung in the dining room and I put it back up after I'd destroyed it.*
>
> *Emily followed me from room to room, crying, begging me to stop. I heard her; I knew I should stop, but I*

couldn't. Rage is powerful and I was already labeled dangerous anyway. Bob was very good at making people crazy. He was a master at turning the tables. It's a good thing he wasn't home.

I sound like a monster. I sound like a psychopath. I felt like one. What exactly did this to me? How is it possible that words could do this to me? Could repeatedly telling me that I was unstable or crazy make me crazy? Could calling me names turn me into those names? Could lying to me make me snap like this? Is that really abuse? Or was it my fault because I believed what he said about me, or thought that he loved me, or because I stayed?

I'd been asking myself and therapists these questions for the last fifteen years. I still didn't have the answer. This digging for the clues to my destruction, this racking my brain for memories I'd obviously blocked out, or someone somehow wiped out, was not healthy or constructive. I'd searched every email, every scrap of paper, every journal, every calendar. I'd saved everything. It all sat in a big wooden box that I named Pandora's Box, just in case I need it during the divorce.

I don't know how long I sat there staring into space in the horse trailer, but I finally snapped out of the trance I was in. I got dressed and walked over to the free coffee gathering in the office. There were about ten men hanging out drinking coffee but I steered clear of them.

I sat and talked with JoJo. She told me a little about her bad marriage, how he was controlling, a word I'd never given much weight to but did now, and how she ended up buying the campground and getting remarried. It must not have been as bad as my situation; there's no way I could ever let a man into my life again. I said little and just listened.

It was still raining and I had cell service so I did some route planning. I got in touch with several of my planned June camps. I wasn't intending to stay in New Jersey very long and I planned all of New England. I was a bit nervous about the Connecticut camp, which was primitive, meaning no water or electric hook up, and "walk up only." I had three other primitive ones planned too. New England had a bunch of states that were difficult to find horse camps in. I could only find a "horse B&B" in New Jersey where Kate, the owner, said, "Don't expect a secluded mountain top; it's in suburbia." But it was the only option I could find within an hour and a half drive of the hospital mom was in.

I went on a couple of rides with Sue and her husband who were also camping there. They knew the trails well and took me to see some beautiful waterfalls and rock formations. It rained almost every day.

Liza's son graduated college and she posted a photo of the two of them on the streets of NYC on Facebook. Tracy towered over my sister in his cap and gown. Liza looked so happy. I thought how nice it was for her to have successfully launched her child. How did she do that? *She must have been an awesome mother, that's how!* Doug was an alcoholic, she was bi-polar and Tracy had Asperger's. He was the same age as Teddy, who I thought was still classified as a freshman. Tracy had a job already and lived in Brooklyn. Totally independent. I was so proud of my sister.

Jo Jo's mare and baby mule arrived that night. I just love babies and he was so adorable. I loved how he followed his Mom around. It made me feel good just watching them. The mother/baby bond was so amazing to me. When I had Brad, I was physically flooded with some endorphin; there's no other explanation for the dramatic change in my priorities. Brad had to have me in his sight or he'd cry. When he cried, tornado sirens filled my mind, knotted my stomach and sent adrenaline through my veins. It was physically impossible to not attend to him. It happened with each baby. What a marvelous method God came up with for survival of the offspring, the survival of a species, the continuation of life itself. I just wish the sirens would quiet down some as the kids got older.

So, how had my mother ignored my cries? Was she simply missing some chemical inside?

The next morning as I was getting ready to leave, I got a call from Liza. "I hope you're not driving."

I sat down at a picnic table. "No."

She said that it now looked like Mom had cancer of the blood, something called Multiple Myeloma. Neither of us had ever heard of this, but Liza said it was very serious. She'd call me back when she'd learned more but thought I should know this now.

My mother was going to die. The ground came out from under me. My mind and body were short circuiting; they couldn't keep up. I couldn't breathe. I was going to lose both my parents soon. I'd be an orphan, a motherless child, wandering the earth alone.

God said, "Just wait and see what I will do!" Are you fucking kidding me?

I wandered around camp in a stupor trying to decide what to do. Like that homeless woman I'd seen in Pasadena. I told Jo-Jo and Sue what Liza said. I felt their hugs; I saw them in front of me. Their words sounded compassionate but I couldn't really hear them. Nothing inside me was working right. They were crying; why wasn't I?

They looked concerned that I still planned to leave. I had no time for delays in my schedule; she could be dead by the time I got there.

Jo Jo grabbed me hard by the shoulders and looked into my eyes. I blinked.

She spoke slowly, as if talking to a child. I could hear her. "Promise me two things: That you will drive safely. And that you contact my sister in Michigan and tell her that I said to take care of you."

"What do you mean?"

"She will take care of your animals if you need to get on

a plane."

"A plane?"

"Yes. Here's her number; call her."

She put a piece of paper in my hand and I looked at it. She shook my shoulders. I looked at her.

"Put it in your pocket."

I did. *Is Michigan between here and New Jersey?*

My GPS started talking as I pulled out; I must have already set the destination. Thank God for GPS. I forgot which state I was going to.

If I look on a map now, I can see I must have driven through Indiana, even camped there, but I scarcely remember it. I did the things I had to do—stay conscious of driving the trailer, take care of the horses and Jessie—as if on autopilot. A few days later I found myself in Pedro, Ohio at the Elkins Creek Camp. Somehow it was Memorial Day weekend and the place was packed.

I woke up early to a beautiful pink sky, fed everyone and walked over to the lodge office where I found Jill sitting on the front porch. Jill was married to Rick, the owner. She did massages there and I needed one badly. I sat with her and we talked a while.

She told me that her mother lived upstairs in the lodge, that Rick had built a room up there for her when Jill moved in with him. Her mom had late stage Alzheimer's and had been bedridden for the last ten years. Earlier, Rick had told me about her and, "that poor woman was a vegetable and would be dead by now if not for Jill's unwavering love." Jill said she'd been caring for her mom without help. She read to her and massaged her with special lotions.

Jill told me that she'd prayed for years for a good man and that Rick was the answer to her prayers. She said that she was in a perfect place now, and that I would be there someday too. She said that the camp was a magical place and I'd feel that way after I'd been there a while too.

I booked my massage and she lent me four books to read. As I walked away I thought how I felt like I'd known Jill my whole life.

When I got to the arena where the horses were, I saw they were caked in mud. I walked over to them and started knocking it off and picking off ticks. There were some manure piles in there with tons of yellow butterflies hovering around them. They were so pretty and I wondered why people killed them just to collect them. They reminded me of a creepy book about a butterfly collector called *The Collector* that my psychiatrist had me read in the early 90's.

> *Brad was maybe two and still an only child. Bob's company had gone under and he was depressed. I was too, I wanted to quit working to stay home with Brad, but I was now the primary provider for our little family.*
>
> *The doctor told me to find and read a book called, The Collector, so I did. The main character has recently won a lot of money and he collects butterflies. He abducts a well-to-do young art student and keeps her locked in his basement. He doesn't rape or beat her; he basically takes decent care of her, but he keeps her locked up and she never sees the sun. She tries numerous ways of escaping—surprise attacking the guy, seducing him, digging her way out. When she finally escapes, he chases her and brings her back. That was a very frightening scene to me. In her isolation she journals about loving art and her mentor and her family that she misses; she yearns to see the sun. Then she gets pneumonia and he doesn't get her medicine or a doctor and she just dies. In the last scene, he's stalking his next victim. The book scared the crap out of me but the shrink wouldn't explain why he'd had me read it.*

I finished the Indiana painting, which I liked. I thought

the picture might help me remember being there, but it didn't. It was a scene of my mares loose and grazing in camp after all the other campers had left. It was the kind of life that I hoped to provide for them one day, freedom to roam and graze like God intended them to live.

After that I lay down and picked up one of the books Jill lent me. Right away it hit home. It was spiritual and psychological, God with the science of psychiatry together. A couple of lines snared my attention:

"Our guilt of not living up to our imprinted idea of perfection makes us feel unworthy and "bad." We will tolerate a partner's abuse to the same degree as we feel we are deficient. When the abuse exceeds our own guilt for ourselves we are ready to leave the relationship."

I wondered if I had really started my marriage feeling as deficient as my mistreatment ended up being? If I felt that worthless, why had I thought I was Super Woman, had the world by the tail, young-successful-beautiful? Was that just a superficial confidence? I'd had so much therapy by then; I thought I was all better.

I finally got my massage from Jill and it was the best I'd ever had. She knew all of my story by then, so I felt very trusting of her. She took me to a small massage room. Incense and candles were burning and soft music was playing. She took a very long time working on my aching body. It felt like compassion was coming into me through her fingertips. Something changed inside me. I felt so different afterwards. Wonderful, actually happy, at peace. She ended the massage by placing warm stones on my back, told me to stay there as long as I liked and left the room.

I wanted to stay at this campground forever. I couldn't explain why—it was everything, the people, the trails and most importantly the spiritual energy there. Jill had hinted at this in our first conversation; now I understood what she meant.

In that moment, I wasn't worried about where I was

going to live, what I was going to do, could I afford this or that, what was going to happen with my parents' health, my kid's futures, my future. I remembered Pastor Steve had promised me, "Everything is gonna be all right!" My smile came from within as I prayed, "Thanks be to God, you truly are a great God." I had learned so much about myself on this trip. I didn't know if I could ever go back to a "normal" life again.

I'd met Ron and Penny last November in South Carolina. I remembered how I'd made a fool of myself, saying if I can't ride just shoot me. That was before Penny told me about Ron's MS. But they'd invited me to stay with them anyway, at JK Quarterhorses in Ivanhoe, Virginia

Chris, whom I'd also met in South Carolina, was there too; she came by my trailer to see my paintings. She was kind of quiet when I'd met her back in November. She had chin length blonde hair, which I'd noticed matched her Palomino's mane.

As I unwrapped the paintings, she told me a frightening story of when she had been home alone and pregnant; an intruder broke in and assaulted her. I didn't ask what he'd done to her and she didn't offer details. A man who hurt a woman in any way, no less one that's carrying a child in her belly or her arms, was a predator and a bully. I remembered how Bob's ex-wife called me right after we'd moved into our first house.

Bob asked, "What did she say?"

"She said, 'I just want you to know that Bob is an abusive man. You should be careful.' I told her to stop calling me and I hung up."

Bob shook his head in disgust and said, "She's unstable; don't listen to her. What happened was I pushed her. She was holding Alex, and she fell onto the sofa. She said that I was being abusive and is now going to a support group for battered women. Jeeez."

Bob and Debra had split up before Alex was one, so he was a baby when this happened! Why did he think that was okay? Why did I accept that as excusable? Because he'd said that she was unstable? He said I was unstable too.

Later in the day I was hanging out by the river under the covered deck. Penny came by on one of her souped-up golf carts with her two dogs, Socks and Bullet.

"Let's take the dogs to Cripple Creek! Grab a cart!"

I got into another cart and Jessie hopped in for his first golf cart ride. He'd been wanting one for a long time! He jumped off in a pasture of tall grass that was over his head. He ran full out alongside my cart, crashing through the grass. It felt so good to see him so happy and free that I almost started crying. We drove to a secluded spot along the Cripple Creek to let the dogs splash and play in the water. I'd never seen Jessie play with other dogs before; it was like watching a child get over being shy, and I thought about my heart breaking as I watched Brad all by himself on the playground after we moved to California. He had a stick that he dragged along the chain link fence as he walked back and forth while all the other children were playing.

Penny wanted to show me her "special place" to see her favorite vista. We got back in our carts and I followed her.

We climbed a grassy rise, and stopped under a big shade tree next to a very old barn that was falling down. We got out of our carts and walked to the crest of the hill. I could see rolling hills covered in thick woods interspersed with the patchwork quilt of cleared fields and dotted with farmhouses and barns. The New River cut through the landscape and the long wooden railroad trestle was visible. There were cows and their babies in the fields below us. It was breathtaking.

Penny said, "I don't see how anyone could ever live in a place like NYC and not be able to see this view every day, to be in nature and to walk in the dirt."

I got a chill. “I used to live in NYC. If you never experienced this kind of place, or felt the peace here for yourself, you’d never miss it.”

We stood there, side by side, soaking it in. How can you possibly deny that God existed when you saw something like this?

I’d read reports about the crazy-scary road going into EJ’s Cottages in Dunmore, West Virginia on the Horse Camping Across America Facebook group’s page. But many said that EJ’s was so lovely it was worth the drive. It was raining so hard at times I had to slow down just to see the road in front of me. The final leg of the route was on 92, a stunning two-lane that skirted the edge of a valley surrounded by mountains, like a bowl. I made a couple of turns into the mountain and took a firmer grip on the wheel. I had to swing completely off the pavement on numerous curves, which appeared one right after the other. I forced myself not to look in my right-hand mirror to check that my back wheels were still on the road; otherwise the next curve would catch me off guard.

The blacktop was exactly as wide as my trailer, but there was gravel laid down on the outside of the curves for swinging wide. I wondered what you were supposed to do if there was oncoming traffic, but thankfully, that didn’t happen. It was only four miles like that, then over a skinny bridge that crossed a beautiful rushing stream and one last crazy hairpin turn and up a very steep hill. I felt like a professional truck driver as I pulled into camp; no big deal at all.

It was early June when I got to Misty Manor, a horse rescue in Marriotsville, Maryland, where I was going to meet up with Joanie. Joanie and I had been friends since the late 70’s when we were in a running club, The Amazing Feet. Our logo was a running turtle. We ran and partied together almost every day back then until our relationships both fell apart simultaneously. We grieved and celebrated by driving down to the Jersey shore for a wild weekend of getting drunk and picking up total strangers in a bar. After that, we moved in separate directions, me to NYC and Joanie to Maryland. I hadn't seen her since my wedding day.

I stopped twice on the way there, once to go to Tractor Supply to stock up on animal supplies and my second stop was for gas. As I waited for the diesel pump to be free, I watched the car parked in front of me with its three young occupants for at least 20 minutes. They were oblivious to the fact that I was waiting. They were all pierced up and the girl was either missing her front teeth or they had been filed down. They were back and forth to the car looking for loose coins, back to the store, going to the bathroom and messing with the pump. I figured it must be their first road trip and it made me think of my children. As far as I knew, none of my kids had tattoos, filed down teeth or strange piercings, and they all had their Dad's credit card and nice cars. They were pretty normal and well off compared to these kids. So why did I feel so negligent? Wasn't "abandoned" a little harsh? I wanted strangers to be patient and kind to my children and that changed how I was looking at this little traveling trio. I put on my God glasses and just waited for them to get out of my way.

The Maryland I saw was lush and charming. Everything was very old, including the narrow roads. Misty Manor was on 80 acres and had over 80 rescue horses there. Judy, the owner, said she had saved over 100,000 horses. There were rescued goats, at least 100 cats and a few dogs too of course. When I arrived, there were 30 children from a camp. They had been there all day with the horses and were having a blast. Judy had a young volunteer help me get settled in next to the dilapidated barn. She had a thriving business doing trail rides but didn't spend her money on the barn or fencing apparently. Instead her funds supported all her animal rescue efforts and helping elderly people in the area. "Pay it forward," was her favorite saying. I had no idea what that really meant.

I put the horses in the arena and unhitched the trailer, then drove to meet Joanie at her antique shop in historic Ellicott City. I parked on the main street, a skinny, steep, twisted, old road. Quaint shops lined the street, which was a popular tourist attraction. I walked to Joanie's shop. The windows were beautifully arranged with treasured old items. The front door was glass and had painted on it:

Open Almost Every Day
Hours Vary!!
Opening sometimes at 10:00, 10:30; 11:00
(or thereafter)
Closing sometimes at
5:00, 5:30, 6:00
(or thereafter)
Thank You!

"Kathy!" Joanie squealed with delight and wrapped her arms around me. We faced each other and held hands just looking at each other for a while.

"It's so good to see you Joanie."

She looked wonderful; she hadn't changed much at all. A huge headful of snow white curls surrounded her face. Her smile was slightly asymmetrical from some rare disease she'd had when she was young but it just made her more beautiful to me. I remembered her jogging with me, encouraging me to keep jogging when my smoker's lungs felt like they were on fire.

"It's been too long," she said, "so how are you doing?"

"It's been kind of tough actually."

She made a sad face, and it made me laugh. Joanie was the most upbeat person I've ever known. It was hard to be sad around her.

"Let's go get dinner." she said

"Wait, I want to see your store first! It's so cool, by the

way I love your hours painted on the front door."

She was so proud of her store and her collection, and walked around showing me her favorite pieces. I oohed and ahhed at everything. I was proud of her; she'd left the guy she was married to when we first met and now she was leaving this one. Her little kids were grown and she had grandchildren. She'd had some tough times but was doing real well.

We went out for dinner, where Joanie announced to the hostess, the waiter, the wine steward and several friends she encountered, "This is my dear old friend Kathy who's riding her horses in 48 states! And she's writing a book about it!"

I didn't feel nearly as accomplished as she was making me out to be. I remembered she was the loudest cheering spectator at the road races; she hadn't changed one bit.

We drank wine and tried to speed-tell each other what had happened in the last 30 years. Joanie was on her third marriage and told me that she was moving out of their house that week because she couldn't tolerate her husband's 35-year-old daughter who had emotional problems and was living with them. She said it was going to be okay; she loved her life and seemed excited about it. Her son was a successful professional poker player and had bought her a condo. I had no idea that poker players made enough money to have their own plane, but apparently, they did. She asked me what had happened with Bob and I had to relive the slow decay of my relationship with her.

"It was storybook in the beginning, well sort of; his company folded and he didn't take it too well, but then he got this one in California and I thought it would be like the early days again. Until I quit my job. I'm starting to think he married me for my money and it's hard to accept."

We'd ordered a bottle of wine and I took a long drink from my glass. I didn't want to continue, but she said, "Go on."

"By the time we moved to California it was really bad. I'd had a couple therapist advise me not to go, but I thought I was strong enough and that it would be better than a divorce for the kids."

"I can relate to falling into that trap," she grimaced in sympathy. "As if kids like to be around unhappy parents."

I nodded. "I used to feel so independent, but with Bob I felt like an indentured servant and he treated me like one. I loved being a stay at home mom, but not having an income made me feel trapped. He kept everything in his name and all the finances were kept secret."

I went to take another sip of wine, but my glass was empty. Joanie filled it from the bottle. "And the constant fighting, like loud screaming and stuff. I felt like I had to walk on eggshells around him. I was so tense all the time, waiting for the next outburst; after a while I started to think I'd gone crazy."

I could feel my heart racing. I hated telling this story. I must seem like such a drag. Joanie was giving me one hundred percent of her attention; her expression was kind. "After I left I just fell apart. I had panic attacks and it was awful. Nothing's happened with the divorce. Bob thinks I shouldn't get anything and he's dragging his heels as usual. He's probably got it all hidden in Switzerland by now. I can't get a job; no one is willing to hire me. I hope I can write this book, or sell my paintings; otherwise I'm gonna be broke. My kids think I've abandoned them, but I'm so fucked up and worried about going broke, there's nothing I can do to help them now."

Then she asked how my parents were.

"Oh Joanie, Dad's dying, I just spent four months with him. And Mom might be dying too; I'm on my way there now. I'm in no shape to be dealing with this now. I'm just overwhelmed. Some days I'm okay and others I just fall apart."

Joanie's eyes got a fierce look in them. "Listen to me, Kathy. I know who you are; you're invincible! Look at what you're doing right now! It's an incredible undertaking! You can do anything! You stop this right now!"

I laughed. "You always were the best cheerleader, remember how hoarse you were the day after a race?" I felt grateful to have known her all these years.

The next morning, I took Jessie for an hour-long hike, then spent the rest of the day basically comatose. It was hot, and that didn't help me gather up any energy. I napped, painted, talked to Judy a few times, took a lot of photos of the rescue horses, and dragged myself around without enthusiasm.

Judy was around most of the time and told me so many bizarre stories, it was hard to believe them all after a while. They just keep pouring out of her. Her Mom had thrown her out of the house when she was 16 with no shoes on her feet; she'd worked for a carnival jumping a six-legged horse; she broke horses and slept in the woods; she had her arm almost torn off by a race horse; her ex-husband had a contract out on her; and she'd worked with every kind of animal you could imagine, including big cats like tigers.

Who could make all this stuff up? Then there were the horrifying stories of the animals she had rescued there. One cat was used for pit bull bait and set on fire; there was a pregnant two-year old horse, and on and on. In between answering calls from people booking trail rides, and giving a banamine shot to a horse that was colicking, and taking delivery of grain, she told me stories about crazy people showing up to ride in totally inappropriate clothing—busty women in tube tops and thong shorts, shirtless guys with flip-flops on. She had so much chaos and hardship in her head and it was just overflowing. It was exhausting being around her.

There was a rescue dog that spent the entire day trying to hump Jessie. Judy said she was getting him fixed but hadn't done it before because he came to her in such poor shape and she didn't want to traumatize him anymore. She said she had never seen such a badly abused dog. When I returned to the trailer after feeding the horses, a very large pig, who didn't appear to have any eyes and whose teeth were curled up alongside his cheeks, was licking Jessie's bowl clean and the "mean" dog was still loose. And boy, was he mean; he went for Jessie again, but someone yelled at him from the house and he quit quickly. He had also pooped and peed on Jessie's towel that I left outside our door. I wasn't clear who actually lived in that house; there were quite a few people coming and going.

There was another half-built, two-story house on the property, smack in the middle of a horse pasture. It appeared to be the shell of a house with the windows installed, but no front door. Judy said that her ex built it over a weekend. And another very strange story began. One day he announced that God told him not to work anymore and all he did from then on was sit in his truck and stare at everyone. He said that his brother was God, and the brother thought that he was God. These crazy tales were starting to get to me. And I felt unsettled amongst the many unwanted and previously abused animals.

Judy's chaos made me feel even more chaotic. Contagious chaos, I thought. I couldn't relate to all the details, but I related to what all this had done to her. I wondered if I'd ever feel sane in the midst of chaos; I needed to have peace and quiet and no stress if this PTSD didn't go away.

I rode with two boarders, Howard and Braddy, to the Woodstock Inn, which was a bar/restaurant along the train tracks in the rural town of Woodstock. Howard was pretty quiet and Braddy was not. Braddy was long and lanky with a ponytail and didn't seem to have a care in the world. It took me some time to figure out that everything he said was a joke of some kind. He said we took a wrong turn, that we were lost, stuff like that, trying to scare me. Then he'd laugh and it made me laugh too. How do people end up like that?

As far as I could tell, the Woodstock Inn was the only thing in Woodstock. It sat on the edge of the state park, which was a lot bigger than I had originally thought. We tied up at the hitching post across the street right alongside the railroad tracks and we went in for a beer.

On our way back, a slow train came along. The track ran parallel to the trail for a while. The engineer kept blowing his whistle; it must have gone off 30 times and it was traveling the same direction as we were. Wildflower and Dreamy thought it was following us and kept turning around to check it out and trying to run off. Then the lead horse galloped off. There was no way I was going to let Wildflower run the way she was behaving. We did a collected trot the whole way back, stopping occasionally for a few spins to shut her down. That was it! I was getting a shank bit for her, and probably not ponying off her any more. She required my full attention and both hands. She really knew how to blow a good day.

The following day, I rode Dreamy first, just wandering around in the woods for two hours, but it was pretty. There was so much horse traffic in and out of the property that the horse's hoofs made a washboard effect in the mud. It looked like a tractor tread had created it, kind of like scooped out muddy steps. Coming back, we ended up entering Misty Manor through a broken fence back by the arena where Wildflower was.

Then I went out on Wildflower trying a tom thumb bit that Judy lent me. I tagged along on one of their trail rides led by a young blonde girl named Bridgett. I made Wildflower follow like the trail horses were expected to do—no passing or cutting off each other. We went to the Liberty Dam. A ton of water was thundering over it, it was so loud! Wildflower had at least one ear turned back to me the whole ride, which meant that she was paying attention to me for a change. I was so impressed with the difference using this bit.

Later, I called Liza. She said that Mom was often delirious and had a lot of pain. On top of everything else, she now had a heart fibrillation too. Liza said she couldn't wait for me to get there; she was overwhelmed. Mom's quality of life really sucked, and I wasn't sure if she could be cured or ever return home. I guessed I would stay there for a month. My chaos was going to hang around for a while. And then there'd be the divorce to deal with. I hoped that my coping skills improved with time.

Judy gave me a similar bit and a headstall with long split reins. I loaded up my truck with hay from her barn. She wouldn't tell me how much I owed; all she would say was, "Pay it forward." She started talking about going to the kill pens and buying horses to bring them back, rehab them from their trauma and getting them adopted.

Then I couldn't stop thinking about the kill pens. I'd never seen them but her description was haunting me. How could human beings do these things? God, please help the poor animals. A song popped into my head, "God, why don't you do something? He said, I did, I created you!"

I'd told Judy that Wildflower was a PMU baby. She said that since PMU foals are pulled off their mothers early; they are like orphaned foals, with no mom to teach them horse social skills, so it was very important that you be the alpha with them. Charni had told me this too. I knew that when I felt in charge, Wildflower listened; it's just that often, I still felt like a doormat. And you can't fake this stuff with a horse, they see right through it. Dreamy accepted me as leader no matter how crappy I felt; I guess that's why I loved her so much.

Judy again refused my check and said, "Pay it forward." I knew what the words meant now, but how did I do it? When Judy was off somewhere else, I put my check in the storage shed that served as her office and pulled out.

It only took three hours to get to Lum's Pond in Bear, Delaware. The state park is located in a more developed area than I was used to, but it was the only horse camp I could find in Delaware. There were just four horse sites, all primitive with one water spigot to share. I was the only horse camper there. The rest of the campground was filled with RVs. I set up the electric corral in one of the empty sites next to me, put the mares in it and took off on a walk around the pond with Jessie. The sun was out and it was warm. The woman at check-in had told me that the Swamp Trail was an eight-mile loop, but it took us four hours, so something was clearly wrong.

As I approached my site I saw that a young family had moved into the horse site across from me. They had two cars, two tents, two toddlers and a baby, but no horses. The Dad asked me to put Jessie on a leash when we were about 100' away. Ugh. I was trying to keep an open mind, but really, what were they doing in the horse area? The kids were crying and there was a lullaby music box playing non-stop for the baby. The road traffic noise was getting on my nerves too.

I cancelled the rest of my June camp reservations in anticipation of needing to stay in New Jersey for a while. I got a very accommodating response from my New Jersey "camp," which was a horse bed & breakfast.

I talked to my neighbors, the ones with the cars and kids. Dad had been a ranger in Yosemite and so had his wife. Then he became a ranger in Delaware, quite a switch I guessed. Now he was a cop. This explained his abrupt approach when telling me to leash Jessie. He apologized and tried to explain it away, saying that he looked like a puppy. Jessie didn't help change his opinion any; he lunged and barked at the man the entire time he was over by us.

The children kept trying to come over to my trailer to "see the doggie," but the ranger/cop kept bringing them back. This was good, because I could just see them wandering into the horse corral and getting shocked by the electric tape or stepped on by the horses. The baby wasn't crying for a change, thank God. Something about a baby crying set off air raid like alarms inside me.

It was too hot to cook dinner so I had peanut butter out of the jar. Protein and carbs. Then I notice that there were millions of lightning bugs out! I hadn't seen so many since I was a kid and sat outside to enjoy them!

The following day, I noticed that the baby had been crying a long time again. Dad had taken the toddlers fishing and I thought Mom might need a break, so I headed over to their camp. It turned out they were all there and they were just letting her cry. The baby was only ten weeks old. I said to the Mom that she was a brave girl and that I couldn't have gone camping with an infant, but I wasn't a park ranger either. Little Ben told me that he was "almost seven" and that his sister was five. The kids wanted to pet my horses and dog so we all went over to my site. I took Dreamy out of the corral and let them pet her. The Dad went to get carrots so the kids could feed them to her. Ben got Dreamy to "smile" a couple of times after I showed him how to ask for it and the kids seemed delighted by this. I showed them Wildflower's "Grab It!" trick. I tossed my hat on the ground, she picked it up in her mouth and trotted over to me. I took the hat from her and gave her a small carrot.

Ben said that his Mom lived in California. Oh, another broken family! My heart flip flopped. He asked if he could get up on Dreamy and I said sure. Dreamy had a lot of experience with tiny kids sitting on her back. I walked him around for a while, then the little girl wanted to do it too, so we switched riders.

I learned a lesson from all this. I knew that my initial knee jerk negative reaction to the dad, just because he had asked me to tie up Jessie, was not good. I didn't like being angry; it was an uncomfortable feeling. But when I opened my heart to them, it all went away. And I got to expose two more little people to a life with horses and the magic that it could bring.

As I packed up the next day, the ranger family was breaking down camp also. The baby cried for hours. I felt bad for the Mom, but she seemed oblivious to it, calmly going about packing up and minding the other two kids. The little girl was crying too. I heard the boy say, "What else can I do to help

Dad?" Bob and I would have been screaming at each other under those circumstances.

Next stop—New Jersey, my mom, sickness and despair. I was filled with dread; there was no getting out of it. I heaved a heavy sigh and put the truck in gear. *Dear God, please stay with me.*

Chapter 9

I took a slightly longer route through Pennsylvania's rolling countryside and crossed the Delaware River into northern New Jersey. I got onto I-78 and headed east, eventually passing my old exit for Schooley Mountain. I just wanted to see the exit again, as if it could answer the question, "How did I get so lost?" For a year before I got married, I'd taken that exit, driving from Manhattan. Bob's son from his first marriage used to call my place "Fantasyland," because that's how he felt driving down the gravel driveway canopied by the surrounding woods. Dad used to come over to just watch me working, because he said it was so peaceful there.

Two hours later, I got off the highway in rural Augusta. In a few miles, I turned into Celtic Farms, a seven acre farmette, near where the Appalachian Trail cut through the northwest corner of the state. Its owner, Kate, was my age; she had short blonde hair and sported a mischievous grin. Her distinctive Jersey accent reminded me of when I'd lived there as a teen. She was excited to hear about SHLEP and compassionate about what I was facing with my mother, offering to take care of my animals whenever I needed.

My mares had a huge pasture all to themselves with a cute run-in shed. It was exactly what I wanted, because I probably wouldn't get to ride much there; they could just run around and graze all day. Kate had three older horses in an adjacent pasture and another at a training barn nearby. She showed me around and handed me eggs out of her chicken coop. I had never seen such pretty chickens; they were all different sizes and colors. She told me to help myself when I ran out.

I left Jessie tied to the trailer. Kate offered to bring him into the apartment in her basement if there was a thunderstorm or if it got too hot. Driving down took about 45 minutes and I used the time to prepare myself. I felt so vulnerable, it was critical I didn't step on a land mine.

Unless they have mental illness in their own family, most people might not understand the mental prep I did before I visited my mom, sister or brother. As a self-protecting measure, I needed to avoid certain subjects and remind myself of a few things about them. If I didn't, I often got hurt. I tried to remember what they were touchy about and steer clear of those topics. I tried to remember what behaviors signaled their depression and anger. I reminded myself that their words and behavior weren't necessarily aimed at me or even coming from the person, but from their disease. They probably did the same things to get ready to see me too, even though I'd not ever been diagnosed with a mental disease. But I had been in therapy most of my adult life, so I knew I was far from perfect.

I hadn't seen Liza since she'd come to Dad's about six months earlier and before that I hadn't really ever been close to her. She was diagnosed as bi-polar sometime after her divorce, around the same time that I was going through Teddy's OCD/Diabetes diagnosis on the opposite coast. My parents had kept me informed about her trials; Doug's drinking and her divorce, about her painful spinal fusion, her numerous psych-hospitalizations, two suicide attempts and her resurfaced repressed memory of being sexually abused by a neighbor when she was only eight. But we had never been very involved in each other's lives and I didn't reach out to her like a normal sister would have done during any of these crisis's. I didn't know anything about bi-polar symptoms, meds or therapy. All I knew was that Liza experienced bouts of serious depression and occasionally got manic, when she'd get very focused and enthusiastic about stuff and spend a lot of money. I wasn't sure if her meds were helping with all this or not. At one point, I think she'd gotten involved with AA, thinking that she had a drinking problem too.

I really didn't know Liza at all.

At Dad's, she'd been drinking wine so I figured that

drinking wasn't an issue any more. We'd talked about how we both hated Yvonne. We'd gone to the clubhouse gym together, she swam and I used the gym. She'd blow-dried her hair, I didn't. When Dad went over his Will with us, she'd asked tactful questions with regard to Yvonne and his Will. She was quiet and so was I. Add Dad to that mix and there wasn't much conversation at all. But it hadn't been tense; quiet can feel good when in the right company. Liza hadn't said anything crazy-sounding or directed any hostility toward me. She hadn't seemed terribly depressed or manic. Maybe things would be okay between us.

I pulled into the parking lot of Mom's nursing home in Berkley Heights. Liza was in her car there and got out when she saw my truck. She had on black culottes and a bright blue tee shirt. The sun reflected off her snow-white hair. Lucky Liza, she got Dad's gorgeous hair. She seemed to be standing up straighter than I remembered. We hugged and she said she was so glad to see me.

Liza led the way to Mom's room, she was awake but she didn't speak. She was in bed and didn't move the entire time I was there. When I hugged her she seemed very frail, soft and warm, like a baby. I had been worried I'd be afraid to touch her; I'd never touched a sick old person before, but it felt completely natural and good. I held her hand; it felt bony and the skin was practically transparent. I could see her veins popping out, much like on my own hands. A few times she squeezed mine. Liza and I stayed a couple of hours, then said goodbye. The nursing home was not as depressing as I'd pictured it, but I hadn't ever been in one before so I don't know what I was referencing.

We then went to see Dr. Solomon. He repeated what he'd already told Liza, that we wouldn't be questioned if we refused chemo and dialysis, in light of Mom's poor prospects for a quality life. In fact, he thought the ethical thing to do would be to withhold treatment.

Boy, this guy was frank. I was too stunned to ask questions. I'd realized before that Mom was going to die, but somehow, I kept talking myself out of it. Each time I'd get reminded by Liza's texts, I'd be floored all over again. Somehow the words coming from Dr. Solomon made it official for me. Liza was asking the questions and taking notes and she'd been here taking care of everything all along. Why had I still thought I was any more stable than she was?

We drove to Liza's apartment in Scotch Plains. We passed the high school I'd graduated from; I'd only gone there for my Senior year. No kids were there; it looked gloomy. I tried not to remember my second abortion, but passing the high school made it impossible.

When I moved back to New Jersey after Georgia, none of my old preppy friends would talk to me so I made new ones in a wilder crowd. I wore my hair long and hid behind it. I wore a long navy blue wool cape most of the time. I smoked pot and cut school a lot with my new buddy, Lisa. My parents bought me a car and flew in Kevin, my Georgia boyfriend, for Christmas break, all in an effort to cheer me up. But they did nothing about getting me on the pill and I got pregnant again.

Once more, mom took full control. This abortion was performed in a doctor's office in a seedy neighborhood of Brooklyn. I was fully awake this time. The doctor and nurse talked about the recent Yankee's game as he worked between my legs. I felt humiliated and was in pain. When he was done, he pushed his stool back and said, "It was a boy," the only words he'd said to me the entire time.

I was allowed to recover on a cot for one hour. I was bent in half with severe cramps and my whole body ached as if I had a fever. I was forced to walk out, leaning heavily on my mother. I didn't tell anyone but Kevin, the father. I called him and some girl answered. Loud music and party sounds were in the background as she went to get Kevin, who then shouted, "Shut the fuck up; it's the chick I knocked up," before saying, "Hi, is it over?" I stayed in bed for days, rolling around in agony.

I couldn't believe I was back here. The mix of guilt and sorrow hung around till we got to Liza's. I'd never seen this place before. In fact, I hadn't visited her home since she was married, had I? How long ago was that? Maybe ten years?

Now she lived in a two-bedroom with a tiny balcony. There were about six cats living with her, all fed at different stations. Two were feral and immediately hid as I walked in the kitchen. I recognized the oversized furniture she'd had in her house with Doug. It looked out of place. Tracy's room, where I would sleep, was crammed with lights, wires and computers. He'd been working in the film industry doing lighting while in college and apparently stored a lot of his equipment there. I remembered reading that women take two steps down the economic ladder when they get divorced; most men might take one.

Liza made tacos and we talked about the feasibility of bringing Mom back to her home in Pennsylvania. Mom repeatedly requested this so she could be at home with her cat, Dana, whom she asked about often. Dana sat on top of Liza's fridge and watched us.

I told Liza, "I thought maybe I could take care of Mom at her house if you helped some, but it depends on how long it would be." I don't know why I said that. I must have been feeling guilty about taking so long to get there.

Liza made a crooked smile and cocked her head in question, kind of like a therapist I used to have. "I don't know about that, Kath."

When I left to head back to my trailer, I saw that Mom had called me twice and I listened to her messages before I started the truck.

"Kathy, hi honey, I'm in terrible trouble. I'm at the Jersey shore in some motel here. I ran out of money; can you send me some, please?"

I tapped: call back.

"Oh good you got my message, I need some cash. I've run out and I'm at a motel at the Jersey shore; can you wire some money to me?"

"Mom, you're not at the shore."

"Yes I am! My foot's not working so I'm at this place learning how to walk."

"Mom, you're in Berkley Heights."

"No, the shore, and I just walked up and down the hall, I'm all better now, so I need some money for a taxi."

"You walked??"

"I walked in a wheelchair, oh, why won't you help me?" She started sobbing.

"Mom, I was there today, don't you remember?"

In her cheerful voice she said, "Of course I remember you, you're my oldest daughter!"

It pissed me off how Mom used her tears to make me feel like shit. I wanted to say, well then what's my name, but I didn't. Her mind was gone and so was the person. She went from mom that I love/hated to a baby-old person, whom I had no idea how to relate to. I wasn't going to have any more meaningful conversations with her. This was very depressing.

"I'll see you tomorrow mom, I love you."

I hung up and started crying.

The next day I went to see Mom at the dialysis center. I was nervous about going. When Teddy was a teenager, his blood sugar was out of control and his urologist had said, "Do you want to have to do dialysis three times a week by the time you are 30?" That had sounded scary to me, but it had little effect on Teddy.

This facility didn't look so scary; it was clean and high tech-looking. Mom had been delivered there on stretcher by ambulance. God only knew what that cost and if Medicare or Medicaid or whatever it was called was covering it. Liza had said that mom had been going to dialysis for four-hours, three-times-a-week.

"I'm overwhelmed," I said.

Liza said, "Me too."

"Yeah, but I just got here. I read online that kidney failure can cause dementia; maybe her mind will come back after some dialysis?"

"Really? Sometimes she is lucid," Liza said.

"Really? Maybe we should wait and see?"

"Maybe. Doesn't she have to make the decision anyway?"

"I don't know; how can she if she's got dementia. Don't you have medical power or whatever it's called?"

"I have power of attorney; that's for finances."

"Oh, it's not the same?"

"I don't know."

Most of the patients looked alert and comfortable, but not Mom. She was lying under blankets; her eyes were closed and she was shivering, sometimes grimacing, sometimes snoring.

"Is this her blanket?" I asked, as I touched a velvet soft grey blanket that mom was fingering.

"Yes, I gave it to her for Christmas, she loves it."

Did I send Mom something for Christmas?

Liza went to the rest room and I leaned over the bedrail to hug Mom. I whispered a prayer into the soft grey blanket.

"God, give my Mom peace. Do not let her suffer; take her into your loving arms." I repeated it over and over and I started crying.

I pleaded silently, "Don't make us have to make this decision; please, it will crush us. We won't be able to; you gotta do this, please."

Mom hadn't stirred and I went to the bathroom to compose myself; I hated crying in front of people. We stayed about an hour. Mom never woke or responded to us. To me, she looked like she was dying, although I had never seen anyone die before.

I had supper at Liza's and drove back to Augusta. My back was in spasms even though I had taken two Aleve earlier. I lay on my bed with a bag of frozen peas on my back and hugged Jessie for a long time. I loved him so; I hated leaving him alone like that all day. I was pretty sure he had been abandoned as a pup and I hated to think he worried that I had abandoned him as well.

When I was in Augusta, I hung out with Kate. Kate had some pot, which I had really missed. Kate had owned an ambulance service and mentioned a TV news story she'd seen about Medicare not wanting to cover ambulance transport to dialysis and doctor's offices.

I said, "What? How are they supposed to get there?"

She smirked and shrugged her shoulders. "Dialysis is Medicare's single largest cost now. There's a ton of people on dialysis now. Most of 'em aren't ever gonna get a kidney, though. They just stay on dialysis till it stops working."

"It stops working?"

Kate nodded.

I asked, "Why isn't it available in nursing homes? That's where all the sick people are."

"Most of the folks in nursing homes are old, they'll never get a kidney. The machines are real expensive; it's become a big business. They're all private companies; most of 'em are chains. And the patients gotta get there to stay alive, so the ambulance business is booming too."

I spent some time on the internet and learned that the United States used to require a dialysis candidate to be under age 65, but there were no restrictions any more. There's a long waiting list for kidneys, and they go to the young and healthy first. Mom was 81 and had cancer; she'd never get one.

On another visit to mom, we stopped in to see Connell, the nursing home's social worker. I asked, "Are our mother's ambulance bills being covered by insurance? Liza got a bill and we're not sure if we should pay it or not."

Liza showed him the bill. He said, "Yes they should be, let me straighten this out for you."

"Thanks. If we wanted to, can we move mom to hospice care somewhere else?" I didn't know then that hospice care meant discontinuing treatment.

Connell said, "Yes, that's probably a good idea."

"Could we bring her back to her home?"

He paused, "Yes, if you hired professional help to come in; she'd need a nurse."

Liza took over, "We met with Dr. Solomon." I couldn't ask, can we let mom just die, but when Liza spoke, it didn't sound like that at all.

Connell, nodded as she talked and said, "Yes, I agree with Dr. Solomon."

I said, "I find it odd that only one of mom's doctors has brought this up to Liza so far."

Connell explained, "It's a difficult subject to broach. So, I'll explain it to you. Your Mom has dementia and two progressive fatal diseases, cancer and kidney failure. She will not recover from either, no matter what you do. And you shouldn't second-guess your decision after you make it. Or feel guilty."

Liza and I just looked at each other. I knew that last part was going to be hard advice to follow, for me at least. It wasn't like putting down Tucker. She was my mother; what if someone thinks we did this because we didn't want to be bothered with her illness or didn't love her or were just evil people? Some of which might be true, at least for me.

As we left Connell's office, my phone rang. It was Mom and she was crying, "I've wet the bed!"

"Hold on mom, we'll be right there."

When we got into her room I noticed her inflatable bed, which prevented bedsores, was deflated; it had come unplugged. Wasn't someone checking on her regularly?

Mom said, "I'm so embarrassed." Liza went to get a nurse. Mom kept crying, "I'm so embarrassed," over and over.

I told her not to be, after all she'd changed our diapers. She stopped crying and smiled sweetly. I was surprised at how appropriately I thought I was acting. She'd told me that dad did all my baby care; she'd thought I was too fragile, or she was filled with shame or she was too young or something that should have pissed me off, but that all that flew out the window of my brain.

I said, "You look good, Mom."

She perked up and said, "Well I do feel great! I'm not tired at all," and then promptly closed her eyes and was out, as if she'd just gotten a shot of morphine.

Her roommate wandered in sobbing, "What am I doing here?" again and again. She then shut off the air conditioning, opened the window and turned on the TV full volume. Liza pulled the dividing curtain between her and Mom, but it was just a thin curtain. I felt awful for the woman, but I felt even more sorry for Mom having her as a roommate. I looked at Liza, in disbelief, or shock or outrage or I don't know what my face actually said.

Liza said, "She does this all the time, usually repeating, 'I'm so nervous,' or 'What should I do?' And crying, always crying."

What should I do? Just like I had often asked myself over the last two years, just like the homeless woman in the Pasadena park had asked me, just like I felt at that very moment.

I said, "Can't Mom get a private room here?"

Liza said, "I don't think so; she doesn't seem to mind."

A couple of days later I left to head down to Liza's. Liza had told me that she was bringing Mom's cat, Dana, around 1:00.

"I think it would be good for us to establish this as a

regular visit time, so Mom has something to look forward to," she said.

I'd asked, "Do you think she even notices what time we come?"

Liza said, "Probably not, but maybe it would be better for us."

On the long drive down I thought how Mom needed to be told about stopping treatment—that she was going to die and what hospice care was—whether she understood it or not. I didn't want to do anything behind her back. Not just that it seemed morally wrong to me, but also because Mom would get furious and that was still hard for me to handle.

I then thought about her dementia. Most of the time mom didn't think there was anything wrong with her. She thought that she'd broken her leg or foot, insisting it wasn't her hip, saying, "I saw the x-ray, I'm not an idiot!" The other day she'd said, "Oh, everyone my age has cancer," with the wave of her hand, as if it were no big deal. And she didn't understand the seriousness of her dementia, saying, "I know that I sometimes forget little things," which I took to mean I'm okay, I'm normal. And don't infer that I am not!

When I got to the nursing home, Liza was already in the Garden Room with Dana who was in a plastic carrier on top of the table. Mom was in a wheelchair. Liza opened the carrier's door and Dana stepped out. Mom didn't reach out to touch her. I watched mom's face; it was how you would look at your baby, full of adoration. I'd seen that expression when she looked at me. She must have loved me.

Liza said, "She's on Oxycodone now."

I asked, "Is she in pain?"

Liza said, "The nurse said that she'd been crying about bedsore pain."

"Bedsores?!"

Mom always had a low threshold for discomfort, so she always had a stash of prescription bottles for pain. And anxiety, insomnia and depression.

Once I left, I realized that I'd never brought up the question of discontinuing treatment. Mom's confusion was making me more confused, as if it was contagious.

On another visit, Mom asked me if Bob still wanted me to go to "all those society or whatever-it's-called gala things." I assumed she meant Scientology.

I said, "No, I left him."

"Oh that's right," she replied. "Why am I in Puerto Rico to learn how to walk?"

I was still reeling from her bringing up the Scientology galas and didn't respond.

She said that Dad had come to visit her; stuff like that was interspersed with our general conversation. She was easily distracted and would get concerned about every little noise. The nursing home was a very noisy place. The intercom on the phone on the wall kept spitting out calls for nurses and aides; the air conditioning system grunted and started blowing; other patients wheeled up and down the hallway in wheelchairs, making odd noises and talking to themselves, and aides were talking in the hall. I thought all these noise distractions made her feel chaotic, as if she were a part of everything that was going on. The environment was doing that to me too.

In one of my more lucid moments, I asked, "Do you know why you're going to dialysis?

She looked at me with childlike innocence, her bright blue eyes piercing my heart. She was still so beautiful, I thought.

She quietly said, "No."

I said,"To clean your blood."

She said "Oh, yeah."

But I couldn't get any further with the conversation.

"What am I doing in this rebate place?"

I wanted to ask if she understood each of her physical

issues but couldn't bring myself to; it felt too invasive and confrontational.

Before I pulled out of the parking lot, I sat in my truck and cried a while. When I got back to the trailer, I sat down and sobbed again. I wanted so much to get Mom's lucid input on the decision about stopping treatment. Maybe we were wrong; maybe she could recover. I tried to remember the latest medical report; didn't it say that Multiple Myeloma caused her kidney failure? I had thought they were two different issues. The first round of chemo hadn't improved her kidney function. Her progressing confusion or dementia could be related to or made worse by the cancer.

I kept asking myself, were either of these conditions reversible if the cancer was put into remission by chemo? Because if not, then what was the point of treatment? Her quality of life would suck, her mind was gone and she could not be independent at all. All the information sounded like chaos in my head.

A week went by like that, and then we went to see Peggy's House, a nursing home that Liza had found near her apartment. As we pulled in I realized it was where The Sleepy Hollow restaurant had been; I had waitressed there during the summers while I was in college. I remember waiting on Mom one night in the bar and her laughing loudly that I was the highest educated waitress there. I hadn't thought it was very funny.

They gave us a tour of the luxurious new facility. There was no comparing it to the place in Berkley Heights. Everyone had a private room and you could bring stuff from home to decorate it; there were living rooms and a beauty salon and libraries to read in. They had a 4-to-1 patient to nurse ratio, a dining hall and walking paths outside with geese wandering around and fountains.

Liza told her that we needed to discuss it so we went

back to my truck.

"Can she afford it?" I asked.

"Medicare covers it."

"Then what's not to like?"

"I think it'll be good, and it will be a lot less driving for me. Should I go give them a deposit?"

"Do they take credit cards?"

"I've got mom's check book."

After paying the deposit we headed straight down to Mom's townhouse in Yardley, Pennsylvania, to get stuff for her room. We had dinner at a Mexican restaurant and slept over.

Jessie slept between us in Mom's bed. I thought how Liza and I used to share a bedroom when we were little. We got our own rooms when we moved to Connecticut, starting a 57-year void in our sisterhood. Maybe now that would change.

In the morning, we picked out things to make Mom's new room homey. We packed some framed paintings, her bedding and towels, more clothes and an old photo album into Liza's Subaru. At Trader Joe's we got some two-buck-chuck that Liza said mom liked and fresh flowers. Back at Peggy's House we decorated the new room. Mom's ambulance arrived that afternoon. I was into magical thinking by then and thought we could fool mom into thinking she was at home so she'd stop bringing it up.

They wheeled Mom on a stretcher into her room and she turned her head to look around. She smiled and asked, "When can I go home?"

I exhaled and sighed. We had hung a picture across from her bed that she'd had in her bedroom, thinking that she must like seeing it when she woke up. Mom looked it and said, "If I have to look at that picture one more time I'll vomit!"

I sighed again and took it off the wall.

She seemed lucid, sort of. Not perfect, but better than any time since I'd arrived. She kept asking, "Why can't I go home and have an aide?"

Each time it hit me in the gut and I heard, You should take her home, you should be her aide! And I felt worse and worse; I knew that I wasn't capable of doing it. I was just a bad daughter. I felt so ashamed.

I said, "You can't walk, your house has stairs, you need a 24-hour aide and you will run out of money." It sucked having to say it. But it was true. And somehow I got it out.

"Why can't I go home?"

Liza said, "If you go home, you will die, Mom."

Mom looked me straight in the eye, her stern face and said, "I choose suicide." Normally I'd do whatever she said when she shot me that look.

I gulped and said, "That's not legal."

She said, "I don't give a shit! I have the pills at home. Phenobarbital; go get them."

I was horrified. Is that why she wanted to go home? I'd looked for the bottle when we were down there because she'd asked for it a few times already, saying, "I just like having them in my pocket, you know."

I said, "I looked already, I couldn't find it." Thank God, I thought.

Mom went in and out of lucidity as the day progressed, but I thought that she finally understood how close to death she was. I needed confirmation of that and that she didn't want to live in her current condition for a long time. That recovery and return to her previous life would not happen. Somehow Liza had said it.

I knew I couldn't be a caregiver. I had never been one and had no medical training. Until then all I had really done for Mom was try to entertain her and keep her company and say that I loved her. I'd read to her sometimes, watch Downton Abbey with her, rub lotion on her hands and get her fresh ice water. But being around her with all my unresolved shit was making me crazy.

A few days later, as I was driving down to Peggy's

House, I got a call from the director. Mom had refused to go to dialysis and they'd sent the ambulance away. I said that it was okay with me. When Liza and I arrived, the director told us that Mom was lucid. Now would be a good time to discuss discontinuing treatment. She walked us to mom's room and led the conversation with Mom. She started with how mom had refused to go to dialysis today.

Mom said she just wanted to get it over with. To just go to sleep and not wake up in the morning. The director told her it could take up to six weeks. Mom said okay. The director confirmed that mom wanted to stop chemo and dialysis treatment and start hospice/comfort care. Mom said, "Yes," and Liza signed the papers. It was done, I thought. The worst part was over, and I sighed. I felt like I'd been through a war inside.

A couple of hours later, Mom said, "You can't take everything I say literally," as she waved her hand and cocked her head.

One of Mom's friends, Bobbi, was texting Liza things like, "You should not give up on your Mom!" Liza was stressing out about it.

I said, "Liza, if she wants to step up to the plate and take over that would be one thing, but Monday morning quarterbacks drive me crazy. Bob used to do that to me."

Liza said people who started their sentences with "You should" were trying to control you. Bob often started his sentences with you should.

Liza's 20-year-old son, Tracy came to visit Mom. What a nice young man, I thought. Liza did that.

After he left, I Skyped Emily for mom. I watched the laptop screen. I knew that Emily had ambivalent feelings about her Grandma, but she was pretty good at feigning affection. I'd heard the boys recently saying how much they loved Grandma and Emily had chimed in, "I thought Grandma was mean."

Then I Skyped Brad's phone for her. He was on a beach

in Spain and he and Mom chatted. Mom kept getting distracted by what was going on at the beach and it didn't help that Brad kept walking around. It made me kind of dizzy watching him. Brad clearly loved his Grandma, I could see it in his eyes. And I saw it in Mom's eyes too; they lit up.

I remember mom lovingly peering into the tiny bundle I was holding when I opened our front door. She pleaded, "Let me see him, let me see him!" barely acknowledging me. I'd felt a flash of jealousy, but dismissed it, "It's her first grandchild, I'd be excited too."

When we were staying at her townhouse and Brad was maybe 3 or 4, he had been looking forward to planting her potted tree outside with her, and he'd wandered into the living room with his sandbox shovel and started shoveling the dirt out of the tree's big pot and dumping little piles of soil on her tan and pink custom upholstered furniture.

I thought Mom would go ballistic when she saw the mess, but I heard her laugh! "Oh dear sweet Brad, you just can't wait to plant the tree with Grandma, can you?" I saw her scooped him up in his arms and kiss him. "Let's go get you cleaned up now, okay?"

Liza and I were with each other 24/7 now and we alternated sleeping in the trailer with staying at her apartment. Jessie liked this arrangement much better. I rode the horses once in a while. I felt like I was just floating along on a river with Mom on this bizarre journey of losing your mind and dying.

One night we went to Peggy's House to take Mom's phone away for the night, something they'd asked us to do because she'd called 911 again with a kidnapping story. As we entered her room she barked at us, "Turn off the light and go!" It felt refreshing somehow, sort of normal.

Another day we went to visit in the morning and watched her sleep till noon so we finally just left. The doctor said she would be sleeping more and more.

Liza was good about calling and texting back Mom's many friends and keeping them posted on her condition. Thank God they didn't have my number. She often sat in a chair at the foot of mom's bed for hours like that, her reading glasses on, telling the story and answering the same questions over and over. I was impressed with how patient she was.

We were just waiting now. Mom seemed at peace and because of that it wasn't as difficult for us. She wasn't spiritual; she never talked about God or heaven, but she didn't seem afraid or anxious about dying. She'd lost all track of time during this phase. She'd shut her eyes for a moment then opened them, saying, "Why is it taking so long?" I told her it would take about three more weeks and she started to cry.

Liza and I went for a short hike up to Sunrise Mountain in the state park on the Appalachian trail with Jessie. The view was pretty but a bit obscured by the overcast weather. Afterwards we stopped at Gyp's for an early supper, where I had two beers, which was a lot for me. It was an old biker's bar with a porch out back on the lake and a pool table inside where they played music from the 60's and 70's. They welcomed hikers since the Appalachian Trail passed nearby. We met a group of three hikers out on the porch where they were charging their phones, eating and rolling cigarettes. They had started the Appalachian Trail in Georgia in March and planned on getting to Maine by August. They had done something like 1,300 miles so far. One was probably my age, the other two were young bucks. One of the young bucks sat with us for a while. He told us that he was from South Dakota, that he wanted to hike in the California mountains, that his home state was ugly and boring and that he really liked the trail there in New Jersey. I told him I hadn't been to South Dakota yet.

As we ate our burgers we watched a cute family of little ducks out on the lake. Liza and I had stayed in Augusta for two nights, which meant we hadn't seen Mom at all for one whole day. We didn't talk much, we were decompressing I think. We both needed a break.

Signing into the guest book when we came back to Peggy's House the next day, Liza said, "Look how many friends have come to see mom; she never even mentions them to us."

She sure was popular. "Everybody loves mom," I said.

Liza said, "Of course they do, she's vivacious."

That was a good word for her I thought. "Remember when she sent us to Actualizations?"

In the 80's there was a branch of EST called Actualizations. Mom went and thought it was life-changing and talked both of us into going. It was a three-day weekend of psychological revelations that they manipulated out of you. I'd nearly had a nervous breakdown while there and they wouldn't let me leave; they actually locked us in.

"How could I forget?" Liza said.

"I was complaining about mom being controlling and cold and the facilitator chewed me out, said he knew her and I was lying."

Liza started down the hall towards mom's wing and I stuck with her.

"So, I confronted mom about it and I went off on all sorts of stuff, landing back at the whole love-child, not-picking-me-up-much thing. Mom was crying and said, 'I did the best I could. I was only 19, Kathy, and Dad was much better at taking care of you anyway.'"

Liza heaved a heavy sigh. "Mom's complicated."

Mom's friend Barb came by. She reminded me of the TV character, Colombo, who never outright accused anyone, just nagged, nagged, nagged till he drove everyone nuts and they confessed. Barb wanted to talk to me alone. Oh shit, I thought.

As is often then case when I get angry, I couldn't remember exactly who said what and when. But I remember I was trying to say, "At least get accurate medical information. Anyone can Google that stuff. Don't tell me what a relative or friend of a friend had to say about a disease someone they knew had; there are many kinds of cancer and don't you know that dialysis isn't a cure but a treatment? Dementia doesn't reverse itself. Broken hips take six to eight weeks to heal in a young healthy person, much longer—if ever—if you're old and have cancer and no kidney function. Multiple Myeloma is treated differently if you're young; they can use stem cell therapy. Dark blotches on her skin are from the cancer; they aren't bruises from being roughly handled. You can't turn a person in bed every two hours with a broken hip, and mom turns herself back to lie flat when you leave the room. I can't monitor Mom's care 24/7; I have to trust the staff. Dementia is very complicated; lucidity changes by the hour, by the minute. My Mom is in very bad shape, this is not living!"

I thought we were done and Barb said, "Why can't she go home? I will drive her down there myself."

The idea of me personally doing mom's care 24/7 felt self-destructive. But thanks to Barb, I felt guilty about it all over again. Not one of the medical team had tried to dissuade us from stopping treatment, so why did I doubt myself because one friend questioned it?

I suddenly realized why Bob's accusations had bothered me so much. Deep down, I must have felt what he was saying was true. I had too much self-doubt. I thought this might be a clue to answering those two big nagging questions: How did he tear me down and why did I stay so long?

I worried about having the stamina to continue my SHLEP after this was all over, whenever that would be. I was getting anxious about that time. So was Liza. One day she said, "I want to follow you when you leave."

I thought how I hadn't really known her before, but this painful time together had turned us into sisters. Pretty dysfunctional ones, but sisters nonetheless.

I said, "Why don't you come along, do New England with me and see the fall colors?"

In addition to wanting to have a sister, I now knew I

wanted to live near my children as I got older. I didn't want to have the divide with my own kids I'd felt with mom. I thought about the last time I'd seen the boys when I visited after New Year's. I saw their smiles and their eyes twinkle. I felt their embraces. But something was broken still. It was tearing me up that I wasn't a part of their lives anymore; I had to fix this and go back.

Every other day I was back and forth to Augusta. Liza came up with me most of the time. We went with Kate to a Ribs and Rock concert at the fairgrounds to see the Outlaws and George Thoroughgood. It was a good distraction but I wasn't really into the music. There were a lot of people there, mostly older folks like us. We pulled Kate's little camper and set up chairs and a tiki umbrella, but eventually made our way over to the concert area, thinking it would be more fun with the crowd, food stands and bands.

Liza and Kate ogled a hot guy in jeans standing nearby. "Come on, Kath, you gotta admit he's hot," Liza said. I agreed that he was but I found their interest foreign to me. I felt sexually dead.

Another time Liza and I went to a small country Catholic church that had the stations of the cross outside. A family had started this project around their home a long time ago. Along the grassy paths were large stones marking the stations of the cross and they looked a bit like large grave stones to me. There was a chapel set in the woods too. I forgot the name of the place, but Mary was in it. That's mom's name.

When I was with Mom, I kept wanting to leave, especially if I was just watching her sleep, which was most of the time now. Talking with her was usually depressing; she was too confused. She didn't know where we were most of the time and she'd ask if I was ready to go to the show, or out to dinner, or back home. One day it was about our flight plans. I had seen my Mom more this past month than I had in the last 40 years. When I was at Liza's apartment I didn't have much to do and I'd think about leaving for Augusta. When I was in Augusta, I'd think I should be down seeing Mom. I was starting to get seriously depressed.

One day Mom asked me if I wore anything besides those ugly shorts. "No, Mom, I only have a few things with me in the trailer."

She said, "Oh it's good to travel light. Does Dad know you're homeless?"

She could still find my buttons: my clothes aren't good enough and I'm homeless. I couldn't even get mad about it anymore.

The next few days I never saw Mom awake. She was now on morphine. I didn't think she was eating or drinking anymore. She took two ice chips to suck on. This was awful to watch.

On July 7, my younger brother finally got on a train and came down from Connecticut to see Mom. Johnny is paranoid schizophrenic. I know it took tremendous courage for him to get there. Even so, I couldn't stand to see or talk to him anymore and neither could Liza; all he ever talked about was how bad he felt and his therapy. Liza wanted him to stay in a hotel, which kind of shocked me. He arrived in the afternoon. His hair was now grey and to his shoulders and he was very stooped over. I thought how his illness had aged him dramatically and felt sorry for him. He'd always called mom and dad several times a day; who was he going to call now? Not me, I hoped. He still thought he'd get better one day, but I knew that was unlikely. He never smiled. His hands shook out of control, a side effect of his meds. He'd been like this for the last 37 years. I wondered how God could be so cruel.

Johnny had always been mom's favorite. She'd waited for him. Shortly after midnight, Mom took her last breath as I held her hand. All three of us were there. I think I saw a misty spirit rise and leave her body, but maybe I hallucinated it. I broke down sobbing on her shoulder, surprised at my reaction.

Nurses quickly came into the room. I felt out of control. Liza called Dad but I couldn't speak. Eventually I calmed down enough to dial my children but I lost control again speaking the words, "Grandma died."

I'd thought it would be a relief to see her go. An end to her suffering. And mine at having to witness it. I wasn't sure I really loved her anyway; why was I crying? I pitied her, I resented her, I had an obligation to her. It was so complicated; she was complicated. Maybe I got so upset because I harbored an unresolved longing for her love. And guilt that I hadn't been able to love her enough when I was a baby to make her love me. I hadn't even tried to talk to her about this stuff; she was already gone when I'd arrived.

I missed my children so much it formed a deep ache inside me. I wanted to go home, but I didn't have a home. The effort to produce a home seemed monumental, just breathing required so much effort now. I couldn't settle far away from them. And I must be in a state that allowed assisted suicide. I couldn't put my children through what we had just gone through. And what we'd be facing again soon with Dad.

I thought that Mom was the lucky one; she was in heaven, her pain was gone, her mind was back. I wished I could take her place. Life was too hard down here. My life was too fucking hard.

I was surprised at how much there was to do after someone died. Liza and I discussed how we thought all these activities were designed to keep the survivors busy so they didn't go insane with grief. But I didn't think what I was feeling was grief.

A week later Liza and I took my mother's things back to her townhouse in Pennsylvania. We were going through her belongings, looking for important papers. In her sweater drawer, I found a newer Will than the one we'd been going by, her birth certificate and an eight-page typed diary covering 1967 to 1993. I saw the words, Kathy got pregnant again, on page one. I folded it and stuck it in my purse.

"Liza, look at this birth certificate, she was born in 1932; she was 22 when she had me. Why did she lie to me?"

Liza looked at the paper and shrugged her shoulders. "Is that a new Will? Where's it from?"

"It says Bucks County Elder Law."

It said I was trustee to settle the estate. I had no idea how to do that.

We drove across the street to his office. The lawyer said that Mom had made a $105,000 bequest to me, repaying me for paying off her mortgage years ago. Mom had promised me this but I was surprised to learn that she'd have enough money after the townhouse sold to do so. A Special Needs Trust was set up for my brother and Liza was trustee, for which I was grateful.

Mom was cremated and we picked up her ashes. They brought us a wooden box smaller than a shoebox. Liza said, "It's so small." I told her how Teddy's horse, Ty's, ashes were just a half trash bag full. She gave me a weird look, as if to say it was wrong to compare mom's death to a horse's, but I loved that horse. I cried for weeks. That was grief! I remembered placing the bag of Ty's ashes in a freshly dug hole in our front yard and then placing on top a Pink-Lady apple-tree that a friend had given us as a condolence gift.

First Ty died, then Teddy went to Los Encinas, then he got diabetes— a six-month time period, now welded together in my mind in one nanosecond feeling of despair.

I bought plane tickets for Teddy and Emily and they flew in. Bob took them to the airport and had them tell me that he'd send flowers, but he didn't; I wasn't surprised. Brad said that he couldn't come in from Spain. Tracy flew down from New York City. Forty of Mom's friends came to the memorial lunch at one of Mom's favorite restaurants overlooking the Delaware River. Liza arranged everything. There was no church service because Liza said that Mom was agnostic.

Mom's small wooden box of ashes sat on a table next to a vase of peonies, my favorite flowers. We'd had tons of them along the driveway in the big old house. And at my wedding.

The Copper Penny Players, Mom's beloved singing group, sang some of her favorite old songs; we ate lunch and drank wine. People stood and said lovely things about Mom, how loving she was, how she made people feel special, how much fun she was, how pretty she was, what a nice singing voice she had. One black man talked about dating her. I leaned over to Liza and asked who he was. She shrugged her shoulders. I stood and said a few words but ended up crying, which I didn't want to do in front of everybody. I barely knew most of them. Teddy hugged me till I was done. We all stayed at Mom's townhouse and played board games and went through her old photos.

The next morning, I opened my eyes feeling euphoric because Teddy and Emily were sleeping in the next room! They both slept late and I went down to make some coffee. We played a game that Liza had brought, Rummikub. We went through mom's photo albums and some memorabilia she'd kept from my grandma's youth. Emily was fascinated with her dance cards from school dances. We ordered pizza. My children were kind to each other and to me and it seemed genuine. Liza and Tracy meshed with my family seamlessly, although we'd always lived on opposite coasts. The boys laughed with each other. I missed spending a whole regular day at home like that with them and then I thought, how long had it been since I had a peaceful family day, maybe ten years?

After they all flew home, I put Mom's ashes in the trailer and planned to bury them when I got to Wisconsin, next to her mother and father.

I spent the next three days at Liza's hunched over my laptop planning the last 20 states for SHLEP. I'd be on a three-night-per-state schedule and it would take three more months till I was home. One and a half months longer than I had originally planned. I would be finished before winter hit the Northeast. I couldn't wait to be with my kids again, even if it meant living in California.

It didn't matter if I spent every penny of my half of the house equity, mom's bequest and whatever I was able to keep from my IRA after Bob was done with me. I figured it would roughly cost me $300,000 for three years in L.A., long enough for Teddy to graduate and the remaining college tuitions. My attorney's payment could come out of my settlement, if I ever got one. I didn't know what I'd do after the money ran out, but I didn't care anymore. I had to be with my kids. And I had to make sure they all had a degree so they didn't go work for Bob.

Chapter 10

I really hadn't thought that Liza would say yes when I'd suggested she come along on SHLEP with me. But here she was sitting in the passenger seat of my truck, heading toward the Lost Silvermine Horse Camp in Natchaung State Forest in Eastford, Connecticut. Liza knew that I was a mess, but she still wanted to come along with me. She said she'd do all the housework, the stuff that I hated doing, like grocery shopping, cooking, dishes and laundry, all the stuff Mom called "shit work" after Women's Lib. Liza agreed to split the grocery bills too. She didn't know anything about horses or hauling a trailer; in fact she couldn't drive her car very long or her eyes wouldn't focus. I suggested that all her meds were causing that, but she didn't agree. She said that she might ride Dreamy a little bit too. She agreed to sleep on the dinette bed despite her bad back.

Having Liza along in the truck was easier for me than I'd thought it would be; I'd worried it might make me more tense, but it didn't. She was very quiet and calm, almost subdued. I hoped that she wasn't depressed, but she didn't offer her emotions to me and I didn't want to pry. I wasn't sure if she was looking forward to the adventurous part of SHLEP, the healing part or just looking for a way out of her depressing life in New Jersey. It was comforting having another human body near me. I thought of Frankie talking about the bubbles around us in his truck and how sometimes they touch. Liza's and my bubbles barely touched. Neither of us talked much, and we were both fine with silence. Mom and Johnny were the only ones in our family that made silence feel like you were getting electrocuted.

I asked if she minded listening to Christian Rock and was grateful when she said no. "Our God" came on. Liza laughed and said, "Whenever I hear this song I think," then sang, "Our dog is greater, our dog is stronger—'" She turned and ruffled Jessie's head in the back seat. My Catholic guilt zipped through me, was it sacrilegious to turn God to dog? How do you uninstall those guilt buttons?

I laughed, "You're so funny!" Jessie panted in agreement; he was nuts about Liza. She was more demonstrative with him than I was and he liked it a lot.

An hour later she asked, "When are you stopping?"

"In a couple hours."

"I need to eat."

"Get something out of the snack bag."

"I want to eat lunch, though."

"I don't usually stop for lunch. I stop for fuel after three hours."

"I won't make it that long."

Seriously? Are you going to faint? I said, "Okay, as soon as I see a place I can stop." I passed a few exits.

"How long do you think it will be?"

"I can't just pull in anywhere, as soon as I see a place I can get in and out of."

Eventually I found a rest area and we had peanut butter and jelly sandwiches in the trailer.

An hour later she said, "I'm sorry, but I gotta pee."

"Okay." I took a deep breath. I passed a few exits that didn't say there were facilities.

"How long do you think it will be," she took a swig of water.

"I don't know, I'm looking for a place." I thought, stop drinking so much in the truck. Pack a lunch. I have a hauling routine; it's not like we're on a car trip, this trailer is fucking huge and I hate stopping all the time.

Luckily the next exit sign had a truck stop.

After five hours, as we neared our exit, I asked, "Can you read these directions to me?" I handed her the camp's papers all stapled together.

She opened her eyes wide and started flipping through the pages. Then she found her glasses from her purse and put them on. I was on the exit ramp by then.

"Umm, where are we, what's this highway?"

"Just read what I wrote in the corner."

"1st L Gen Lion Rd. then, see cemetery go 1m Pilfershire Rd L?"

As I pulled into the thickly forested camp, I got nervous about hitting a tree with my trailer. I didn't think that I could maneuver into a site and so I just parked in the middle of the dirt road and got out.

Liza said, "You going to just leave it here?"

I said, "I'll figure it out later."

There was one other group there with a bunch of kids and horses. As I was setting up a picket line to tie the horses to, two women from the other group came over. I said that I hoped I wasn't blocking anyone's path by parking where I had and that I was nervous about getting into a site. They said no, it wasn't a problem for them. One of them said that her boyfriend was a truck driver and that he could get it done for me when he arrived that evening. The other one told me where the trail head was and said to be careful when I rode out, that the trails weren't marked well and that she always got lost.

Liza emerged from the outhouse, "I don't recommend using that, it's full of spiders and webs, gross!"

"We have time for a ride; do you want to ride Dreamy?"

She wasn't sure, she didn't have boots.

"You can wear my old boots, you can wear my helmet too, it'll be fun."

She said okay, so I got the horses ready. It started raining as I finished up.

We mounted and rode out anyway. The trail markers were terrible and my GPS inReach batteries died half way out. I replaced them and it started a new "track" so I couldn't see my original one to follow back to camp. I forgot to put my paper trail map in a plastic sleeve and it was like wet toilet paper by then. The bugs were horrendous. There was a swarm around Wildflower's head most of the time and she was going nuts trying to shake them out of her ears and eyes. I had a general idea where camp was but was getting nervous about Liza.

"Do you know where we are?"

"I'm trying to figure that out, I think the turn is up here."

"Oh my God, we're lost!"

"Not really; we should have seen a trail off to the left. Let's turn around, I must have missed it."

"We're doomed!"

"No we're not, we're close to camp."

"I'm getting off."

"Why?"

"I'm sore, I want to walk back."

I took a deep breath and took Dreamy's rope. "Ok, follow me then."

But she walked very slowly. "Liza, stay on this trail; I'll trot down there to see if the trail is there."

I rode back and forth to Liza, ponying Dreamy, trying to find the right trail that would lead us back to camp. Liza seemed more scared every time I came back to her; she thought we were in danger, and she started crying. It continued to rain. Eventually I dug deep to feign some authority and told Liza that she had to remount, that it wasn't safe being separated as we'd been doing. With tears streaming down her cheeks she complied. We found a dirt road and followed it. We saw a remote farmhouse and stopped for directions. We ended up doing a few more miles on a dirt and gravel road and the horses started getting ouchy without their boots on.

When we got back in camp, Liza said, "That was a terrible experience for me. I'm not riding any more on the trip."

"I'm sorry," I said.

She went inside the trailer. As I untacked the horses I

beat myself up. I should have rested the horses as I usually did on the first day. I should have taken the first ride out alone to scout out an easy short trail for my sister.

But on the other hand, she was being a big baby and made the ride horrible for me too! How could I figure out how to get back to camp when I had to keep backtracking to her because she got off Dreamy? And how can you get sore just walking anyway? Doomed? Kind of dramatic, no? I'll have more fun riding by myself anyway; I was trying to make it fun for her. I shouldn't have talked her into riding in the first place.

The next morning five horses were running around camp when I went to throw mine some hay. I went and woke the tent campers, who then rounded them up. One said that one of their horses knew how to pull out the stakes of their portable electric fence with his teeth without getting shocked. "Clever horse," I said. A while later they came by to tell me that a big thunderstorm with hail was on its way, so they were going home and left us a bunch of firewood over at their site.

I was hesitant to leave my horses tied to the picket line during a storm. I still worried about Wildflower getting hogtied. This had happened to her a couple of years ago and it was not only terrifying getting her untied, but a horse can seriously hurt themselves in their panic reaction to it. So, I set up my electric corral, but when I touched it to test it, the tape wasn't hot. I fiddled with all the connections, and there was still no zap. I put the horses in it anyways and hoped that they didn't figure it out too quickly. Maybe I'd gotten out of the swing of SHLEPing.

It didn't stop storming until the following day, so we sat in the LQ and played cards and Scrabble all day. Liza was a great Scrabble player and always won. I usually didn't know the words she laid down though. She smiled a lot that day in the trailer, I noticed. I hated being stuck in the trailer on rainy days, but she didn't seem to mind at all. The next day the sky cleared but it was very muggy and the mosquitos came out in force.

I unhitched the trailer and set off to Tractor Supply to replace my solar fence charger and Liza took a nap. She'd been taking a nap every morning around 10 and I wondered how you could get tired right after you got up. Either she was depressed or it was her meds. She took pills by the clock, several times a day. I had no idea what they all were.

The salesman tested my solar charger and said that it simply wasn't charged enough to make the fence hot and that it had to sit in direct sun. Aside from it being overcast, the whole campground was under a heavy tree canopy. The original box had said that it held a charge for rainy days, but I guess they lied. I ended up buying a marine battery, a fence charger and a separate charger to recharge the marine battery. The salesperson said it had to remain dry so I got a plastic box to store everything.

When I returned to camp, I set it up. I sat down in the trailer to paint and turned on the generator to charge the house batteries and it shut off almost immediately. Liza was sitting at the dinette with me and said, "Is that supposed to happen?"

I groaned and plunked my head on the table. "Nothing that is happening is supposed to happen." I was making a terrible impression on my sister.

The generator control panel was blinking three times which I figured was an error code. I dug through my papers and found the owner's manual. Three blinking lights meant, "Call an authorized Onan dealer." I found a dealer that was willing to send someone to our camp and then waited for him to show up.

My phone rang; it was someone from Quad Graphics, a huge printer that I used to compete against, about a sales job for their Huntington Beach, California facility. I thought I was dreaming. I rambled on that I was in the forest horse camping and that my generator was broken and I was waiting for a repair man and that I had kind of given up my job search to finish this journey that I was on.

I took a breath and gained some composure; she must have thought I was nuts already. I said, "But what exactly is the job?"

She said, "Wow, that's so cool!" I couldn't tell if she was being sarcastic or not. Then she explained the job to me. It wasn't in the catalogue market, where I had sold; it was for signage and point of purchase products like those you see in grocery stores. She set up a phone interview for next Monday, when I would be in Acadia, Maine. I hoped I'd be feeling more confident by then. I hoped I'd have cell service. If this turned into a real potential opportunity I had to accept it. Welcome it, even if it meant cutting my trip short.

I told Liza everything the woman had said. Liza had been in the printing business too and knew a little about Quad.

"Doug worked in that plant," she said, "I'll pray for you to get the job." I didn't know that Liza prayed.

"Kathy, you know the industry has changed a lot in the last 15 years."

"I know, but I really need a job."

"A sales person has to also be their own customer service and production person now too."

Why was she so negative? "I'll just have to try anyway. This would be so awesome, it's in Huntington Beach! I love that town, and it's on the ocean too, Emily loves the beach!"

Liza said, "You know how impossible it is to get a job after turning 50, right?"

"I know." I was 60 now. And I had a long unemployment gap on my resume. But I was hopeful anyway. I started Googling Huntington Beach rentals.

"Oh, I needed this so bad," I said.

Kevin, the Cummins Onan troubleshooter, showed up in camp around 4:00 and I watched as he crawled under my trailer. He said he smelled a short and found it in the conduit that ran under the trailer from the generator to the house plug. I told him that this had just been rewired in Florida to the tune of $1,500. I was pissed. Kevin said that they hadn't done it the best way possible and that it had gotten pinched under the trailer. He spliced and patched the torn wire and told me to buy rubber hosing and zip ties and showed me how to protect the conduit until I could get the line replaced by an electrician. The bill was over $700 with travel and overtime.

I went back in the trailer and vented to Liza; she was still sitting at the dinette. "I'm sick of primitive camping. Leg 3 isn't starting off too good. This is not indicative of what you should expect." I felt like crying. "It's so frustrating when mechanical things go wrong. I don't know how to fix this stuff. The generator, the wiring, the electric fence not working, getting lost in the woods with you getting scared and all, the pouring rain, the constant money pouring out for stupid stuff like this, the biting flies and mosquitoes here." My heart was pounding in my chest and I felt a panic attack coming on.

Liza listened and nodded her head, just like one of my therapists would have.

Silently I said my thank-you prayer to myself to stop the panic and try to put it all in perspective. "Thank you, God, for this breath, my beating heart, my children, my animals, my sanity, for the beauty in nature, my sister." I said it again. And again.

Liza just looked at me and didn't say anything. She picked up her phone and called Dad. She asked how he was and told him that we were in Connecticut. I pictured Dad writing on the large USA map pinned to his office wall where he'd been tracking my trip. She told him about the generator breaking and the repair bill. They chatted some more, then she said she loved him and good bye.

After she hung up she told me that Dad was transferring $700 to her account. What? I was stunned, the panic vanished. We both simultaneously said, "Our hero!" and laughed.

I thought of all the times that Dad had saved the day for me and I'm sure Liza was doing the same. It wasn't just financial either; he'd physically rescue you from the bad guys or the mistakes we'd made.

"Do you remember when Dad and his buddies went into a heroin den in Bedford Stuyvesant to rescue Aunt Judy?"

The next day I could see the sun peeking through the dense tree canopy when I got up. It had finally stopped raining. Liza made breakfast as I checked my email. After several months, Brian, my divorce lawyer, finally responded to my numerous requests for an update. He said that Bob still hadn't produced any financial disclosure documents and had dismissed the forensic accountant, saying that he was too invasive. Nothing at all had happened. He said he had a plan and was going to address it soon. I remembered Dad saying that I needed a new lawyer. Another good reason to go back.

Liza put a plate in front of me and smiled. She really liked cooking, I thought, how odd.

I got a text from Brad; he said that Bob hadn't sent him his rent money. He was behind; could I send him some?

"Bob!! I'm paying the tuition, can't he at least pick up the rent? How can he just leave a kid stranded in a foreign country like that?"

"You're paying the tuition?"

"I'm paying all their tuitions. I don't know why that wasn't in the separation deal."

I was beginning to see that anything was possible when it came to Bob; none of us could count on him. That wasn't going to change.

I got the horses ready and talked Liza into trying another ride, "We can do an out and back so we can't possibly get lost."

At 45 minutes out, we turned around and when we got back to camp, I helped Liza dismount.

She said, "That was perfect." It made me feel good.

"And the bugs weren't so bad for the horses too," I added. It was a sunny day and I felt good again.

I touched up the horse's feet, then crawled under the trailer to zip tie rubber hose over the generator conduit. I then went to a bank to deposit my inherited portion of Mom's IRA and transferred money to Brad's account. Then I did all the things I was supposed to remember to do before hauling: I got the tire pressures checked and adjusted, dumped the trash, wrapped the hay and filled the tank.

The following day as we pulled out, I asked, "I've never been to Rhode Island, have you?"

"I don't think so. So, what did you decide about Breck?"

I'd lived with Breck in NYC back in the 80's, just before I met Bob. He'd messaged me on Facebook last summer thanking me for saving his life. I had no idea what he was talking about at first. He'd been following my SHLEP and asked about meeting with me when I was in Connecticut. Today he'd texted asking when he could come and I'd told him that I was leaving for Rhode Island. Well, these are all pretty small states and that didn't deter him, I guess, 'cuz he then asked for the camp's address.

"I said okay. It'll be okay I guess. It's probably something to do with the 12 Steps."

We passed the primitive LeGrande Horseman's camp where I had originally planned to stay—I was done with primitive camps—and not much further down the road, pulled into Stepping Stones Ranch in Arcadia Park in Escoheag, Rhode Island. On our second day there, Liza and I went out for a short hour-and-a-half ride. On the way back we passed a very old graveyard in the middle of the woods. I couldn't help but think of Mom's ashes under the dinette in the trailer; it was as if she was on SHLEP too. But I didn't feel sad and I thought how I hadn't cried since the memorial luncheon. I wondered if Liza was sad about losing Mom; she never brought it up. She didn't bring up much of anything, though.

Our ride the next day was with a local rider, Sue. She took us on a beautiful ride for about two hours. We rode to the stepping stones falls from which the stable got its name. The water tumbled over very large flat boulders that looked like oversized skipping stones. I got a bunch of good photos there to use for a painting. I said, "This is so cool, thanks for bringing us here. I never would have found it without you!"

Liza said, "Yeah, thanks Sue, I don't do well with kind'a lost." Then she laughed. I just looked at her; had I said that when we got lost in Connecticut?

On the way back, I rode behind Liza. I admired my mare's big butt, which is a compliment in Quarterhorse circles. I missed riding on Dreamy's beautiful big butt.

The next day, my back was killing me again, probably from loading hay the day before. I broke down and took half of my last pain pill, left over from my kidney stones. It lifted my back pain dramatically and I felt so much better about everything. I needed to get more somehow. Alleve and frozen peas weren't working anymore.

Liza was in the gooseneck, taking her morning nap with Jessie. I said, "I'm going up to the road. Breck's on his way now."

"Good luck."

She never did like Breck. I remembered her saying to me, "Breck sure likes spending your money." Why does she say shit like that to me?

As I trudged up the hill, I thought back to how Breck and I had met.

> *I was in a SoHo bar waiting for a blind date that never showed up. Breck kept checking me out and I notice that he was cute in a preppy sort of way. After about 30 minutes, he came over and said hi. He was a few years younger than me and kind of sexy. He said that he was a*

building contractor. I slept with him that night. He had some coke and I tried it. I loved the high; it made me feel invincible.

In a of couple weeks, Breck moved into my Hoboken apartment and then he found us a loft to rent in Manhattan. A few months later, I bought the place and Breck put up a few walls. He helped me decorate; actually he picked everything out and I just paid for it. We threw huge parties with lobster, champagne and coke. We frequented all the hot clubs and hung out with his preppy trust fund friends. I thought I was having fun.

One night after doing coke and champagne till dawn, Breck took some valium to get some sleep. As I crawled into bed I noticed how still he was. I didn't think he was breathing. I don't recall getting panicky or questioning what I should do; I just called 911. Paramedics crowded into my bedroom and, unable to revive Breck, strapped him onto a stretcher and left. Breck's mother met me at the emergency room. While the doctors worked on reviving Breck, I had to tell everyone that we'd been doing coke all night. That night I realized that I was hooked on a dangerous drug.

I called Dad and he took me to rehab, where I immediately felt trapped and feared losing my job. I got out in three days and the Rehab doctor told me that the only way I'd be successful quitting without his help was to break all ties with other users and start going to Narcotics Anonymous (NA). I told Breck to move out before I returned home. I went to meetings at least once a day, whether I was in NYC or at the plant in Chicago. I experienced intense anxiety for a year. Dad checked up on me a lot and listened to my struggles. "You got this, Kiddo!"

I never touched it again, and I was proud of that.

I sat on a boulder by the road and saw that Breck had texted me, "Took a rong turn, b there in 5 min." I thought how hard texting must be for him; he wouldn't leave me notes or add items to the grocery list because of his dyslexia.

I remembered Bob had seen my coke addiction and recovery as something I should be ashamed of. He told me never to tell the kids about it.

After Teddy had been diagnosed with diabetes, I started to worry about the teen drinking problem in La Canada's high school. Drinking with diabetes could be deadly, so I told Teddy that if he was going to partake in partying, it was safer if he smoked pot and I told Bob too.

Bob was furious. "What's the matter with you?"

I said, "Nothing," and explained the science of a fast sugar, such as alcohol, and the risk of a diabetic dying if they pass out while they're drunk. I reminded him that the cops had found Teddy passed out drunk in his car once already. Bob didn't understand diabetes and I felt like I was like talking to a brick wall.

Bob said, "Who are you to advise Teddy about drugs, with your history?!"

I thought, had he been so drunk that he'd forgotten that he'd told me that he'd once shot heroin?

I saw a cloud of dust down the road and sighed. Breck pulled up and got out of the small car. He looked the same to me, kind of preppy and boyish but a little older and a little rounder. I wondered what he thought about how horribly I'd aged, the fact I no longer had fake boobs and was living in a trailer. I felt self-conscious standing there listening to him. He asked how my parents were and I told him that Mom had just died and Dad had stage 4 cancer. He was sorry to hear that. He was sorry to hear about my divorce. I said thanks, but it was long overdue and I was doing okay. I didn't mention that I wasn't actually divorced yet.

He said, "I'm sorry how I treated you at the end."

The end? I'd thought his ninth step was going to be about getting me into coke. I had forgotten about him jerking me around. We had gotten back together once he got in recovery, but he was also into someone else. We went back and forth a few times; it broke my heart each time. I was such an idiot, in such a vulnerable state of mind; I kept taking him back. Oh, wait, maybe he means when he cheated on me when we were still living together. Had I always been such a doormat?

Breck said, "I often tell the story about you saving my life, hoping to inspire others."

Somehow those words sounded too heroic for dialing 911. I said, "Thanks."

"I know you didn't have to call 911, involve the police, our parents and possibly threaten your career. I want you to know how grateful I am."

I stood a bit straighter. I said again. "Thank you."

There was nothing more to say so we gave each other a quick hug and then he got in his car and drove off. I felt like I'd been in a time warp and walked back down to the trailer.

Liza was sitting at the dinette doing something on her phone as usual. Her reading glasses were perched at the end of her nose and the sun lit up her beautiful white hair.

Liza raised her brow and tilted her head down as if inspecting me like a therapist does and asked, "Are you okay?"

I forced a smile. "I'm just happy it's over with."

I went out to feed the horses and started listing all my boyfriends in my head: Referred to me as the chick he knocked up, cheater and drunk, cheater, cheater, wouldn't marry me because I wasn't Jewish, cheater. Oh my God, they all were so awful to me, how did I not see this before? And I always took them back anyway! What the fuck was the matter with me? What made me think I would be any different with Bob?

We only stayed in Rhode Island for three nights

because of the extra miles and overnight needed to switch our next stop to further north. Acadia in Maine was a park that Liza really wanted to see, so I'd agreed. I loaded the horses and we headed north.

From our overnight in Bath, Maine it was a backbreaking six-hour haul to the Wildwood Stables in Acadia National Park, in Mount Desert Island, Maine. Sitting somehow irritated whatever was wrong with my spine. I pulled through the Acadia Park gates and The Park Loop Road wound through the forest; big rocks lined the edges that they referred to as Roosevelt's teeth, but they looked like tombstones to me.

Liza pulled out our camp chairs and our loose things that were stowed inside the trailer during the haul. I was happy she'd started helping me more and thanked her. I put the mares in stalls that were roomy, with rubber mats and shavings. Most of the horses in the barn were carriage driving horses owned by a few groups that were there. None of them were camping though; they had homes to stay in, and hired help cared for their horses and carriages. These people obviously had a lot of money. The owners didn't mingle with the campers. They hung out in a field by the barns where their trailers were parked. Some were horse trailers, some special trailers for carriages and one apparently was for entertaining. That one had a serving window and wine goblets were set out on a table under the awning. That wasn't my group anymore, and I wondered if any of them were happy, or how many of them were being cheated on or being used for their money.

Liza and I took Jessie for a long walk along Jordon Creek, which was one of the most scenic hikes I had ever been on. The creek ran through the woods and under graceful arched stone bridges. It was a hiking only trail; the branches would have been too low to ride a horse on it. Jessie had a grand time charging through the creek every opportunity he got. Liza laughed every time. I was glad she was happy; it made the extra drive worth it. We followed the rocky creek past small waterfalls. There were quite a few of these bridges there. We passed through a rock walled carriage gate complete with a house that was called "the gate lodge" on my map. The amount of labor that must have gone into developing this park was impressive.

Jessie wouldn't be able to ride with us there. The rangers were all over the place and enforced their leash rule. Not to mention all the bicycles, hikers and horse carriages. Keeping him on a leash and using his shock collar was not terribly effective at getting it through his thick head to stay out of their way.

We'd just gotten settled in when it was time for my phone interview with Quad. I felt nervous but hopeful about it; this could be the job to get me back to my kids! Liza wished me luck and I drove down to North East Harbor for a cell signal. The interviewer told me that the job would require a six-month to a yearlong training period. The pay was base plus incentive and she said the incentive was too complicated to explain to me. My interviewer said they would contact me in two weeks if they "wanted to go forward with the interview process." My phone told me the call lasted seventeen minutes, which seemed short to me. She hadn't given me any feedback either. It felt like a rejection and it hurt.

There were only a few other campers in the park. We went for a two-hour ride at a walk on the carriage trails, which were made of crushed granite and as wide as a two-lane road. The scenery was lovely to look at, mostly wooded with a few open meadows. The carriage roads were well marked and the map was easy to follow. Liza said it was perfect. I thought it was boring but didn't say that. Back in camp we ate dinner as the sun went down. Someone was outside playing a saxophone. Liza said that she really liked Acadia and I agreed it was really pretty. Liza announced that she wanted to learn how to trot and I said that I'd teach her.

On our ride the next day I showed Liza how to post,

going up and down with control so that your weight isn't banging on the horse's back. Liza tried for a few strides, then quit. I thought about the rod in her back, watching her bouncing in the saddle and worrying about Dreamy's back too. I encouraged her to keep trying to post or she could try doing a two point, which is basically standing up in your stirrups and gripping with your lower leg.

She said, "I can't do it." It pissed me off that she didn't even try.

I knew she wouldn't be able to do a seated trot; that had taken me a long time to learn and Dreamy would have to round up her back and collect her body. That had taken me even longer to master. Dreamy could handle a beginner bouncing around a little bit; she'd put up with me learning how to ride. But she was older now and I worried about arthritis causing her pain. Liza was a good 50 pounds heavier than I was.

I told Liza that she had to keep trying and work at it and that she'd get stronger. She still wouldn't even try.

I said, "Then you can't trot; you'll have to just walk."

When we got back to camp Liza slid off and grumbled, "I'm really mad, but not at you." She handed me the reins like I was her groom and stomped off into the trailer. I untacked both horses, put them in their stalls and fed them as I got madder and madder. She said she wasn't mad at me, so why was I mad? Did she think caring for the horses after a ride was shit work?

In the morning, we made Liza's bed back into the dinette and sat there drinking coffee. We hadn't spoken since she'd stormed off to the trailer yesterday.

Liza looked into her cup. "I'm depressed about the black hole of my life. I just want to be your housewife. I miss my bed and my cats at home. I want to drive to do some sightseeing. I miss going out to eat."

Black hole? Was she getting depressed? I couldn't

address the wanting to be my housewife; maybe she meant something else? Like a partnership of sisters? Did she want to go home? If she was depressed, that probably wasn't such a good idea. But she was fucking up my journey; I didn't even want to come to Acadia and now she's depressed anyway? Maybe she should go home. I'm not working on healing. I wondered if she'd stopped taking her meds, but thought she'd probably get mad if I asked that. I latched onto the sightseeing and eating out part.

I swallowed hard and said, "You know, going out to eat and sightseeing isn't what this trip is about."

She didn't respond.

I asked, "Do you want to go out to dinner tonight?"

I'd hoped she'd say no but she didn't. We went to a restaurant inside the park. I couldn't hide my displeasure. I ordered a salad and water. Liza had a couple of glasses of wine and a complete dinner; I noticed she looked happy. I moped, just as I used to do at those expensive Beverly Hills steak houses when Bob wanted to go out for a family dinner and I was a vegetarian.

I wanted to say, "Ya' know, Liza, I don't like going out to eat, it reminds me of working. I'm just not that into food. Family dinners at home were so stressful; you remember that, right? And going out with Bob, it was similar." But I didn't.

The next day Liza drove with Jessie to the top of one of the mountains for a hike and then to town to fill the gas tank for our departure. I hoped this excursion would satisfy her desire to go out and explore. I went to the barn to feed the horses dinner a little early. While I was there the skies opened up and it poured hard for a long time. I sat on a bale of hay and was soothed in the cozy atmosphere of the barn with the sound of the rain hitting the metal roof. I loved the sweet organic smell of horses and hearing them munching peacefully. I relaxed there for at least an hour.

I remembered Dr. Lasarow telling me to spend at least

an hour a day at the barn. I should live in a barn. It was still pouring so I put an empty plastic bag from the shavings over my head, cut a hole in it with my pocket knife for my face and walked back to the trailer. It kept me completely dry in the downpour and I thought about the money I'd wasted on an Armani raincoat.

On our last night there, a trail riding club pulled in. In the site next to us was now parked a truck with junk piled up high in the bed. They stabbed a plastic pink flamingo in the ground nearby. It really changed the atmosphere and I was even happier about leaving the next morning.

Having Liza along was changing my whole experience. I wasn't getting invited to campfires or dinners. Campers had either felt sorry me being alone or intrigued by my journey and they went out of their way to include me. I missed the social interaction of getting to know new people.

I dreaded the haul coming up; my back had been killing me. I wished that Liza could do some of the driving and mucking, both of which were hard on my lower back, but she said that she couldn't because of her own back pain and her eyes "going out of focus." How could she not consider that being on pain meds was doing that; how could she not see that taking a morning nap an hour after she'd swallowed a handful of pills was related. And just as Mom's depression bugged me, Liza's did too. It made me feel like it was my fault or I was a bad person because I couldn't fix it.

I stripped the stalls as my back spasmed and a stabbing nerve pain developed in my right hip. I loaded the horses then grabbed a bag of frozen peas from the freezer, stuck it in my jeans and got behind the wheel.

Buck N Horse Campground in Groton, New Hampshire was at the top of the mountain, surrounded by other smaller ones. I felt like I was in the sky instead of looking up at it. It was breezy, and light puffy clouds were moving swiftly overhead. I walked Jessie down the dirt road and back, then cleaned the LQ and the horse stalls in the trailer. I dragged out the dinette table to paint outside as Liza drove off to do our laundry and get groceries. Did we really need groceries, or did she just like going to the store?

The horses were roaming around camp with cowbells on and their lead ropes dangling so they could graze. Wildflower sauntered over to me and sniffed at my paints. The entire camp was covered in green grass punctuated with shade trees. Down the hill was a dog pond with a canoe on the shore. Across the way, I saw a covered lodge area with a giant fireplace they called the "people pen."

When Liza got back, we walked Jessie down to the dog pond. Liza got in the canoe and paddled out. She called to Jessie, trying to get him to swim to her, but he wouldn't. I felt bad that he wouldn't jump in for her but I understood he was afraid the canoe would tip over. As the canoe neared shore Jessie finally jumped in and Liza cheered.

She had a strong bond with Jessie and he loved the attention. She'd started letting him sleep in her bed and had said, "He's better than cuddling with a man," which made me laugh. I missed sleeping with him in the gooseneck.

I got invited for a ride with Dave, the owner, and two other campers, Kathy and Larry, the following day. They said that it was going to be long, fast and on rough trails. Dave was leading and knew some great trails, they said. "Oh, that will be too hard for my sister, she's a beginner."

Kathy said she would take us on a short easy loop the following day, one that Liza could handle, so I said yes, I'd love a good hard ride.

I met Dave a few hours later when he stopped by the trailer to introduce himself. He was an attractive guy and I wondered if he was married or had a girlfriend. The chat turned into an hour-long rambling monologue. I wondered if it was just me that had trouble following him; I felt like I was talking to Bob.

After he left, Liza came out of the LQ with a bag of trash and Jessie followed her. "I didn't want to interrupt you," she laughed.

I groaned. She went off with Jessie looking for a dumpster.

A while later, I heard Liza scream and a minute or two later, she jogged up the grass hill with Jessie wagging his tail in delight. She was out of breath. "A dog went after Jessie and he scooted in front of Larry's truck as he was driving by. His leg was pinned under the truck's front tire!"

Jessie stood next to her his tongue hanging out and panting. I probed around his hip and legs with my fingers and he didn't react.

"Nothing hurts, he's not limping, he's okay. He needs to learn to stay away from trucks; he's been chasing trucks and golf carts and four-wheelers since I got him. He even tried to attack a truck speeding by us on the road! Maybe this will finally teach him."

Liza looked at me like I was crazy, but I knew that I wasn't.

Kathy invited us to the "people pen" for dinner that night. Larry had cooked up a delicious meal of pork chops, two kinds of potatoes and grilled veggies. Kathy made drinks of vodka, pomegranate juice and Fresca, which sounded awful.

Liza said, "It's called the BuckNBeverage!" She made me try it and it was pretty tasty. I didn't finish it, though; I really don't like to drink much.

We all played Scrabble on a picnic table until one of their dogs jumped up and scattered the tiles on the board. There was a roaring fire in the fireplace. Liza was laughing and talking with everyone; she looked so happy. And that made me smile. She deserved to be happy.

Kathy, Larry, Dave and I rode out in the morning, Larry ponying another horse. I rode Wildflower. The trail was supposedly marked with ribbons but I didn't think I could have followed it. Once we were in the woods and hit the first hill, Dave took off at a canter through belly high brush without telling us, which I thought wasn't good trail etiquette. Wildflower tried like heck to run off with him, but I won the battle. She lost a boot and I had to stop and as I put it back on she kneed me in the cheekbone, giving me a black eye the next day.

There were some great vista views and I got a good photo of Dave and his gray horse on a rock ledge to use for a painting. During our lunch break Wildflower kicked another horse even though she was hobbled. She kicked out at Kathy's dog who obviously was too close to her feet. She jigged and rushed most of the ride, even though I was using a shank bit, which should have given me more control. On the way back, Larry let his pony horse loose without warning me. Wildflower was in season, and the loose horse kept getting too close behind her. I was nervous that he might try to mount her and I'd get crunched. A lot of the trail was heavily overgrown and I couldn't see the actual ground much of the time. The hills were tough and we crossed many streams. Everyone else seemed to be riding a calm horse but me. Wildflower was in a full sweat and breathing hard. Her legs were quivering towards the end and I decided to walk her the rest of the way back. Kathy stayed back with me and I thanked her for doing this. A horse left behind usually gets very fearful.

I finished the Maine painting in the afternoon. It showed Liza riding Dreamy down one of the carriage trails. There was dappled light on the ground from where the sun made its way through the tree canopy. When Liza got back and peered over my shoulder she said, "Is that me?!"

I said, "Yes, it is. Doesn't it look like you?"

She said, "Wow, I'm honored."

I smiled and felt good inside. It was my way of showing her that I cared about her. I hoped she got it.

The following day, Kathy took Liza and me out for the very easy ride she had promised us. We rode on mowed grass trails in the woods for part of the ride. Then we went through a logging area to an old mica mine. Mica was on the ground all over the place and it sparkled in the sun. When Wildflower noticed the glittery ground she planted her feet and looked around bewildered. I got off and picked up a pocketful of the stuff. It was transparent, yet reflective, and it was compressed sheets that I could easily peel apart. Wildflower watched what I was doing and got over her fear.

Kathy was kind and considerate of Liza, encouraging her along. I should be more like that. Kathy got Liza to do a brief canter up a hill. I asked her how she liked it.

She said, "Kind of scary, but it was fun!"

We packed up and left the next day. During our short haul to Vermont, Liza said that she wanted to finish SHLEP with me.

I almost choked, but I swallowed hard and took a slow breath. "Really? That's great!"

What else could I say? Liza's emotional rollercoaster was crazier than mine.

"Wow, Vermont is so beautiful, even from the Interstate!" I said.

"Doug was from Vermont you know. They have strict laws protecting their natural beauty and there are no billboards in the entire state," Liza said.

New Discovery State Park in Marshfield, Vermont had a big campground and a smaller separate, but very pretty, area for those coming with horses. We had it all to ourselves. The entire area was mowed grass and each site had a stone BBQ fire pit. I got very cold setting up camp and I headed to the shower house where they had ten minutes of hot water for 50 cents. It felt so good I put in two more quarters.

There were practically no bugs at all, probably too cold.

We could hear other non-horse campers but they were nowhere near us and hidden from our view by the thick woods. In the afternoon, Liza and I went for a hike with Jessie, but the map sucked, which was exactly what the ranger had said as he handed it to me when I'd checked in.

When I woke the next morning, Liza was putting her boots on and said she was going to feed the horses for me. Now that's the spirit! Maybe this will be okay after all.

After breakfast, I set up my paints on a picnic table in the sun. I finished my painting and we decided to ride even though it was technically a rest day. Liza and I set off together on a nice dirt trail. We'd planned to ride the rail trail but Liza wanted to head back early into the ride and we never made it there.

Over dinner I brought up that I wanted to ride Dreamy and I wanted to do longer harder rides. I asked her if she'd be okay to just ride every other day and suggested that she could hike on the days that she didn't ride. She said that was fine with her.

The next day we hiked to the top of Owl Head trail for a spectacular view of the mountains and two brilliant blue lakes. It was about three miles roundtrip. It was drizzling on the way out but started raining hard on our way back. My rain gear had started leaking lately, so I was a little concerned about my phone getting wet, but it was okay. Liza walked very slow so I kept turning around to be sure she was still there and then I waited for her to catch up. When we finally got back, I asked how she was.

She answered, "Miserable. I hate being wet."

I had been thinking what a nice little hike it had been, but I remembered feeling like she did in the beginning of my trip. When you're depressed, which it looked like was happening to Liza again, every little comfort, like being dry, is important. I got used to it; I'd thought that she would too.

The next day it was still drizzling and the horses looked

miserable in their muddy pen. I pulled them out to graze for a while and practiced my amateur roping skills, trying to rope the water spigot. Camping in the rain was not much fun. We played cards in the trailer. We had no cell or internet so I couldn't play on Facebook nor could Liza use the online Scrabble games that she was addicted to. Liza crawled up into my bed in the goose neck and cuddled with Jessie in the afternoon. They looked cozy but I worried about Liza sleeping so much.

I went out to check on the horses. It was raining hard and the temperature had dropped. I felt horrible when I saw my mares shivering. I worried that I was changing climates too quickly for them to acclimate. I undid the electric tape to the pen and they rushed out and ate grass in a frenzy. They stopped shivering almost immediately. It was going to get even colder at night and the rain didn't look like it was going to let up. I walked over to the ranger station and said that the horse pens were a muddy mess and that my horses were shivering and needed grass to graze on. "Can I set up a portable corral somewhere?" The park was so beautifully landscaped I'd doubted they'd allow me to but as Dad says, nothing ventured, nothing gained.

The ranger said, "Sure, you can use the horse overflow area, which is on grass." The ranger pointed to it on the map. I thanked him and then set up a gigantic corral with my electric tape and step in posts. It felt like nesting.

As I was walking the horses to the new area, a few youngsters came over to see what I was doing. One boy helped me fill their water bucket and asked a lot of horse questions. Two younger ones came by on their bikes. A little boy ate some pieces of hay and was asking questions about what horses ate. When I said that I couldn't believe he was eating hay he replied proudly, "I'm a redneck!" It made me wanna be a redneck; it sounded like so much fun. He announced a few times that, "We're having homemade French fries tonight and the last time

I had 'em they were delicious!" I loved this kid. I wondered what made these kids so carefree and happy; was it growing up in the country or was it that they had happy families?

I walked with two of them through the woods to see a small graveyard they'd discovered. There were three weathered headstones from the 1800's. I couldn't make out the names etched in the stones, I wondered if any of their descendants ever visited the site. I thought about mom getting buried when I got to Wisconsin; would anyone ever visit her grave? What's the point of visiting a grave anyway?

Another group of about 10 adolescents were camping there with their parents, who'd periodically haul them around the park roads in an open trailer, the kind you'd use to perhaps haul firewood or an all-terrain vehicle. They went speeding around the dirt roads with the kids screaming at the top of their lungs. Liza nicknamed them the bucket o' kids, which made me laugh. They were over by the horses in the morning when I went to feed. Three of them announced to me, "We got shocked by the fence!" I asked if they had all done it at the same time.

"No."

I said, "So I guess you were doing it for fun?"

"Yes!" they shouted at once.

One girl added, "I liked it!"

I loved being around these kids. I remembered how much fun it was playing with my own when they were little. Bob hardly ever played with the kids. I remember how he yelled at Dad when he was playing Crazy School with the boys in the pool.

While up at the ranger station I saw other campers using laptops and asked if they had Wi-Fi up there. I went to tell Liza that they had Wi-Fi! We sent a message to Dad and Yvonne separately, asking how Dad was doing. Yvonne replied, "Dad is fine." But Dad didn't reply.

"That's disconcerting, don't you think?" Liza said.

"Yes; she wouldn't lie to us just to get that camera bag of cash in Dad's closet?"

Liza said, "For $30,000? That's not enough money to risk going to jail for."

"Do you think she'll try to change his will? Is that possible?"

Liza said, "I think Zochowski has it locked up pretty tight."

"I guess." I said. I had a sour taste in my mouth though.

It stopped raining the next day, and I rode Dreamy and ponied Wildflower. Our new riding plan was working out better for me. It still wasn't as much real riding as I wanted but it was a definite improvement. Over dinner, Liza told me that she'd changed her mind about finishing the trip with me. She wanted to be dropped off at the airport in Albany, NY to go home. Something hurt inside my chest. I felt rejected, but I tried to hide it.

Then she said, "I might meet back up with you for the Northwestern states though, I've always wanted to see Washington and Oregon." Her mood swings were getting to me.

Next stop was the Wagon Wheel Campground in Warwick, Massachusetts. I started singing that "Rock me mamma like a wagon wheel" country western song as we pulled in. It was such a happy song!

Saturday I painted the Vermont painting. It was a nice day and I dragged the picnic table under my duct tape-patched awning for some shade. There was a huge patch of black-eyed-susans in the foreground and giant evergreens in the background. I liked it; it looked happy with all those colorful flowers in it.

Liza was reading in a camping chair nearby.

She said, "My ankle's really bothering me, I'm not going to hike for a while. My back's been bothering me too." We discussed how her transition to an active lifestyle had probably been too abrupt.

She was going back home in a couple of days, and I would be solo again. I got a pang of anxiety every time I thought about it. Having a travel partner had made it easier on me; it took the focus off me.

I made my second camp fire on SHLEP using a fire starter brick that Nancy had given me back in Missouri. I put my grill over the fire and cooked a chicken breast for Jessie that needed to be cooked or it was going to go bad. He intently watched me unwrap it and put it on the grill, full of anticipation. I asked Liza how long she thought it would take to cook.

"Jessie thinks it's just fine now; he likes it rare."

I laughed. Jessie didn't take his eyes off the chicken as it cooked. When I finally gave it to him, he swallowed it whole and was wagging his tail like crazy. It made the effort so satisfying to me.

I said, "Maybe if my kids had been this appreciative of my cooking, I wouldn't have stopped making dinner."

Liza laughed, "It definitely would have helped, I had to make three different dinners to get Doug and Tracy to sit down together."

It rained overnight. At breakfast, Liza said she needed to rest her ankle again and she'd try riding the next day. My back was killing me so I took my last half of a pain pill and thought how I needed to find a pain clinic. Or call my spine specialist in California.

Liza fed the horses for me again in the morning. It was our last day there and it was freezing outside. We headed out for a short ride, our last one together. She'd be flying home the next day. Everything was going well; I took her to a meadow that I'd let the horses graze in the day before. I was leading on our way back to camp and crossed a stream, then trotted up the next hill.

I heard Liza shout, "Woah!"

We had successfully crossed water a few times already and I thought Liza had it down so I hadn't waited for her as I should have. I turned and saw Dreamy jump the creek and start cantering up the hill. Liza lost her balance on the jump and fell off on the other side of the creek, slamming into a tree on her way down. She got the wind knocked out of her and was clutching her chest. I grabbed Dreamy's reins as she ran by me and walked down to where Liza sat crying.

Liza shouted at me, "I know what you are going to say and I am not getting back on her." She sobbed, "You said no one ever fell off Dreamy. You promised me that she'd never hurt me." Tears were streaming down her pretty cheeks. She was covered in mud. I felt like shit.

I sighed and said, "I'm sorry, but you have to get back on. It's too long of a walk on foot."

Liza pulled herself together and I helped her get back in the saddle. We walked slowly the rest of the way back to camp, practicing "Woah" a lot along the way. I'd hoped it would help Liza regain her confidence.

The next day I pulled the rig into the Albany airport. As Liza got out of the truck, I asked if she had learned anything about herself in the past three weeks.

She looked at me for a few seconds then said, "I learned that I hate pain." She sounded just like mom. What a depressing thought.

She walked into the airport and I started crying. I couldn't fix her, I wasn't good enough.

Chapter 11

A big sign with the Statue of Liberty painted on it was posted at the state border. As I got closer I could read "Welcome to New York, the Empire State."

When I lived in Manhattan, I could see the Empire State art deco spire from my window. Mom used to work in that building designing sweaters. She never visited me in my loft, though, saying that my neighborhood was too dangerous.

I was selling for Alden Press back then and I was their only New York City rep so I worked from my 13th floor loft. Every day at the crack of dawn, I ran up to Central Park and around the reservoir to burn off my anxiety and stay thin, grab a coffee and roll at the deli across the street, and then sit at my desk for most of the day on the phone. I'd dine with clients in fancy restaurants and see Broadway shows at night. And fly to Chicago for color okay's and more fancy restaurants and expensive hotels. Clubs on the weekend with Breck and coke. I got fake boobs, a mink coat and a BMW. I'd thought I was on top of the world up there in that Hell's Kitchen loft.

It didn't sound so fun now. Had I really been that shallow? That gave me something to chew on for the next couple of hours.

Emily and Teddy both texted me that their tuition payments were overdue. I had emailed Bob warning him that all the money I had saved for their tuition had now been spent and that the rest was up to him. I reminded him that he'd promised to split it with me when I'd retired and moved to California with him. Bob never did respond. If he ignored it, it might as well not even exist. Why was I still surprised? It was his stall-till-they-drop tactic.

Then I remembered that Bob had said that his contribution to the children's college tuition was the house equity! Did he think that the $200,000 I was awarded after it sold was his college tuition contribution?? Fuck you, Bob!

During my stay at Manestay Stables in Glenfield, New York, I got very depressed. My back was killing me and I worried about everything in my fucked up life. I reworked my camp schedule for the rest of SHLEP, shortening my stays at camps and adding a couple of overnights on the hauls exceeding 300 miles because driving made my back even worse. Then I called all the camps and the upcoming overnights, giving them new dates. Some of my camp contact notes were in an app on my iPhone, some were on spread sheets, others on scraps of paper. It seemed like an overwhelming task but I managed to get it done.

In the process, I stumbled on an old note on my iPhone labeled, "I want to die 11/11/12." I clicked on it. It started out pretty black about my new apartment and my support, dad's loans, car problems, horse supplies, starting an antidepressant that made me sick, our dog Blue dying, Rachel getting into Point Loma, Bill losing a big contract, considering reconciling with him, job search ideas. I remembered going through all of it and it seemed so far away now. The last entry wasn't familiar, I read the words and thought who wrote this? Me?

June 2013 I am not disposable!!!!!!!!!!

Mom said: I've often wondered if putting you up for adoption would have been better for all of us. I was filled with shame.

This explains a lot.

She said: You are so officious.

Looked it up...I hate her

June 2013? Last summer? I did visit her! Right before I left on SHLEP. The memory slowly surfaced. We were in her kitchen; I was seated, she was standing. I was so anxious, she'd given me a valium. Wasn't Liza there, or had she left?

How could I have erased this memory? Was my mind that fucked up? Or just overloaded?

Mom still *wondered* about this; she never stopped

thinking this. She didn't want me, even after 59 years, everything I'd become, overcome, all I'd done for her or tried to do. Why did she choose this low point of my life to tell me this? What a bitch! Fuck you, Mom.

I cried myself to sleep and woke up feeling like shit.

I used my TENS unit and headed towards Pennsylvania. I got through the drive with very little pain which was a huge relief.

I'd stayed at countless overnights so far; they were usually like staying at a highway motel on a long road trip—stop, stretch your legs, eat, sleep and leave right after breakfast. Most of them were uneventful, except for Jane's place in Colby, Kansas and Donameer Farm in Hammondsport, New York.

I happened to arrive the night that Cynthia and Niel and some of their neighbors were getting together for their annual dinner party. Neil invited me to join them once I got settled in. As I walked up to their house, I passed the huge grass paddocks where my mares were making quite a ruckus. The flies buzzing around them looked more like New York City cockroaches. There were drips of blood on Wildflower's white legs. I sprayed them with DEET, trying not to get kicked in the process, and their rodeo antics quieted down.

The lodge house was a very old wooden farmhouse that had been renovated. The floors were wide planks that reminded me of my 200-year-old house in Schooley Mountain, New Jersey. The one I wished I still had. Something about all that thick wood surrounding me, with low ceilings and wood burning stoves made me feel solid, stable, safe. There were about ten guests there, most of them around my age or a bit younger. Neil was Italian and since he loved to cook, he was the party chef. The extra-long pine dining table was crowded with an array of dishes including deviled eggs, eggplant, lasagna, homemade pies, cream puffs and black garlic. Lots of conversations were going on and eventually I'd been introduced to everyone; they were all very friendly. They were all passing around plates of food, eating and talking all at the same time. I guess that's typical of a big Italian family dinner. Cynthia gave me suggestions of what to try next and Neil went back and forth to the kitchen bringing out more and more platters, announcing what it was on each one before setting it down. I tried black garlic for the first time, and was surprised at how sweet it was. "Wow, Cynthia, this is amazing! How did you make this?"

"Oh, it's easy, you steam it, I grow it myself, but you steam it for 25 days."

That didn't sound easy to me, but maybe she had a crock pot kind of steamer thing? Then dessert and coffee was served in the kitchen, where at least 15 pies and pastries were on display. And some of the richest best smelling coffee I'd ever had.

Around 10:00 I thanked them and said I'd a wonderful time. Walking back to the trailer, I noticed that negative screaming in my head was gone.

As I lay in the gooseneck, I thought about the transformation I'd experienced. What was it about breaking bread with people that cared about others, whether they lived next door or had wandered in like me?

I thought how our nice family dinners had died long before I quit cooking the year before I'd left. And my childhood supper memories weren't so great either. Someone once told me, "If Mom's not happy, no one in the family is happy."

While I was camping in Pennsylvania, Liza called. I asked how she was recovering from her fall off Dreamy.

"Well, I was having a lot of pain in my chest, so I went to see my doctor and he took some x-rays. I've got three broken ribs."

"Oh man, that sucks, they hurt like hell."

She said, "The pain's diminishing. I'm going to buy a

jumping vest and some rain gear. I think I'll join up with you in Wisconsin."

I took a deep breath and said, "That's wonderful that you're coming, I really can't wait. But I don't want you to get hurt again and I don't want to be responsible if you do. I have enough to feel guilty about. If you want to learn to ride, you should take lessons from a professional, and do it in an arena."

I hated being firm, I hated saying no, even when I really wanted to. I rarely ever did it with my kids either. I wondered if she'd still come. I wondered if I wanted her to.

At my next overnight, as I crawled into my sleeping bag, my phone dinged. Teddy texted a long rant about not being able to tolerate living with Bob anymore and Liza texted about where and when she would join up with me again. I guess my saying no to riding hadn't changed her mind about coming and I felt relieved.

She kept texting with changing her arrival details. Then she said she didn't want to complicate my plans.

I texted, "It won't."

She replied, "I just want it to be fun and relaxing."

I texted back, "I can't guarantee that."

It was neither of those things for me and her ability to have fun or relax was out of my control anyway.

She texted, "Ha ha!"

I smiled, I wasn't trying to be funny.

When I got to Michigan, I stayed with JoJo's sister, Sherrie. She said that they'd just gone on a week-long ride together in South Dakota. I thought how cool it was that they had this common interest and dynamic sisterhood. I wished that I had a sisterhood like theirs with Liza.

I called Dad while I was there too. He answered in such a chipper voice, I wasn't sure if it was him. He said he had some good days and some bad. He told me that a new woman, Pauline, was now staying there at night, so he had round-the-clock attention if he needed it. Somehow this news made me feel better; perhaps Pauline was a good person and I didn't have to worry about Yvonne being the only one around the house with him now. He said it wasn't so bad *yet*.

I didn't like the way he emphasized "yet." Did that mean that he was accepting the fact that he was going to die soon? I'd known for two years that this cancer was going to kill him, I accepted that. Everyone dies. I remembered two etched cocktail glasses that my parents had. I did the dishes, so I washed them almost every day. One said, "My mother loved me, but she died" and the other said, "Life sucks and then you die." I used to wonder why they had those glasses. I now wonder if Mom bought them. That made me sad. She was so unhappy.

Heading towards Wisconsin, I stopped at an overnight in Indiana. I pulled out my art supplies and started my Michigan painting of Wildflower in the wildflowers. I was just beginning to get my painting groove back. I had gotten kind of stiff in the last ten years I thought; my style used to be much more about the sensual feel of paint and it was coming back some. The earlier ones looked stiff, self-conscious and overworked to me now. I took this as an indication that I was getting better. An artist's style can tell you a lot about the artist.

The crickets were chirping and I heard trains sounding their horns in the distance, the sun had just set on the last day in August. I turned my calendar page to September. I'd been gone a year. Eleven more states to go. You got this, kiddo!

On September 3, I was headed towards Shawano, my mom's hometown. Wisconsin was full of dairy farms, cows grazing on rolling green hills and big old red barns.

A green highway sign read, "Neenah, next exit" and caught me off guard, I was born there! Mom had said that we didn't actually live there though. I wondered where we did live.

I was about an hour away from Shawano. I wondered why they drove an hour to this hospital; was it the closest one? Or was it to hide the birth from everyone she'd grown up with?

She resented her situation; she'd told me that when I was 16. She gave up her dreams at 19 or 22, it didn't really matter; she was a young woman with dreams, and her life took a sharp turn.

I remembered, "I was filled with shame." I hadn't given that statement much thought; I was too hurt from, "I've often thought of putting you up for adoption."

Can you bond with a baby if you are filled with shame and need to hide your pregnancy and birth? And lie for the rest of your life about your age or the year you got married? Could I? I couldn't imagine how she felt. I could never fully put myself in her shoes.

I was filled with shame. What a profound statement. It's as if Mom knew her mind was going and she wanted to leave me a clue. I'd been in therapy most of my life trying to figure out why I felt so insecure despite my outward appearance; strong-successessful-beautiful. What an awful place for Mom to be. Suddenly I felt grateful that she was finally able to utter those sad honest words to me.

Life is too complicated to blame anyone for being a lousy mother. Mom had said, "I did the best I could." What more could I ask for?

An hour later I pulled up to the cemetery gates and realized that my hay rack wasn't going to clear the metal entrance arch. Dana, with whom I'd been speaking on the phone, pulled up in a truck and led me to a different entrance. I parked the rig by the quaint old stone chapel. Dana said I could let the horses off if I wanted to. I said thanks, but no; I could just picture them tearing up the manicured lawn. I opened the horse's windows and gave them water buckets. I crawled under the dinette and dug out the small wooden box of Mom's ashes from the cabinet under the seat where it had been for the last six weeks. I noted again how small it seemed. Dana walked me over to my Mom's headstone where a small hole had already been dug. There were three matching headstones in a row; the other two belonged to Grandma and Aunt Judy, who was still living. Where was Grandpa's grave?

I thought of Aunt Judy; I hadn't seen her since her heroin den rescue. I was her trustee now that mom was gone. Her life wasted away due to schizophrenia, she now lingered in a nursing home not far from where I stood. Poor Grandma, two such unhappy daughters. She must have died from a broken heart. I placed the wooden box of ashes in the hole and Dana covered it with dirt. I thought of Brad with his little shovel digging up Grandma's tree. Dana lay some pieces of turf on top and discretely walked away.

I felt a slight breeze on my neck. "Good-bye mom. I'm sorry you suffered at the end. I wish I could have eased your pain or helped you end it sooner. I'm sorry you were so lonely and I failed to comfort you during those last few years. I was in hell; I didn't see anything but my own pain and suffering and it was real. I'm not making this up; he made me seriously crazy. I know that's not a good excuse, but it's true. I hope you understand; you deserved a better daughter. I'm sorry I destroyed your dreams. Thank you for keeping me anyway. That was very brave of you, I see that now. I hope you're enjoying heaven, I bet it's really wonderful. Better than down here."

I thought of a performance of Mom's that I took Emily to when she was little. Mom sang the whole song to Emily, locking eyes with her in the first row. What was the name of that song? *Wait till you see her*, I think.

I looked up at the sky. It's not just a color I thought; it's infinite. There are little sparkles floating around and a million shades of blue. Just like mom's eyes. The chapel bells were chiming, and I started to softly cry. So this is grief, I thought. It's not what I expected it to be.

I dumped the mare's water buckets and got in the truck and tried to compose myself so I could drive. I blew my nose a few times and took a drink of water. As I was just about to pull out, my phone rang. It was Bob Zochowski, Dad's lawyer, who said that Dad was, "Tweaking his will to avoid probate." I wondered why he was doing that now. What does he mean by tweaking? What's probate? Did it involve Yvonne? I thought of that asshole surgeon telling dad a couple of years ago, "You need to get your things in order." I still wanted to punch that guy, as if that would make him a liar.

I wondered if Dad had gotten a prognosis on how long he had left. I wanted to know what it was too. I told myself that I would get through this with God's help.

I cleared my throat and told Bob that I had just buried my mother's ashes. He said he was sorry and he just had a few simple questions. I answered them and hung up. All that worrying and all he needed was my updated contact information.

I headed next to Spur of the Moment Ranch in Nicolet State Park in Mountain, Wisconsin. We used to summer on Shawano Lake with my grandparents when I was little. All I remember of that time was water skiing though. I thought it was a lot smaller than it is. The further north I drove, the prettier the scenery got, with rolling green hills and the old red barns of dairy country.

Spur of the Moment was near a lake with a lot of summer cottages built around it, much like Shawano lake was. The camp was immaculate. There were nice small log cabins to rent and the horses had good sized sand paddocks. There were two other couples in my camping area. Neither were there with horses. One couple was in a huge RV and had two four-wheelers, kayaks and an old black lab named Duke with them.

The owner was very nice and gave me a trail map and magazine about the area. Reading it, I found out that the Chequamegon-Nicolette National Forest, where I was camping, was 1.5 million acres and there were 2,000 lakes! I thought what a lucky pick I'd made.

I marked on the wall calendar WI #38. September had a lot of notes on it already. Emily would turn 19 on the thirteenth and Brad would turn 25 on the twenty-second. Same date as Bob's—was he going to be 64 or 66? I remembered Emily getting upset when she realized that her father's birth year was wrong on her birth certificate. My wedding anniversary is on the 9th, it would be 25 years. Technically I was still married, which annoyed me to no end. And on the 18th I would have been on the road for one whole year.

Before I fell asleep I started reading the only other novel I had, Divergent. I didn't know why I'd bought it, nor The Book Thief, for that matter. This one was about a bizarre future society with a strange caste system. The backcover summary said it was told through the eyes of a 16-year-old girl who had chosen to change her caste from the predictable & selfless caste to the one that was courageous & dangerous. When she changes castes, she had to leave her family behind since the castes didn't mix. This sounded like my life now. And now that I thought about it, didn't that little girl in The Book Thief lose her mother in the first chapter? Had my subconscious picked out those books; is it that smart?

I rode Dreamy, with boots on all four feet, and she was awesome. We covered about ten miles in two and a half hours if my calculations were correct. I'd been looking for the ice cream store that I'd been given directions to, but couldn't find it. But I found a bar and I tied her to a tree and got a beer instead. As I drank from the bottle I looked to where Dreamy patiently stood just waiting for me to return. Whatever did I do to deserve such a perfect horse?

When I got back I let her and Wildflower eat grass for 45 minutes then put them in their pens. They stood at the rails and just stared at the grass, ignoring their hay. Wildflower was a muddy mess again; she must have done her usual rolling tantrum while we'd been away. Poor thing, she gets so scared when she's alone.

I stopped by the camp owner's paddocks to take some pictures of their herd for a painting. There was one huge black draft kind of horse they used for pulling a carriage and two tiny horses used for driving a cart. There were four donkeys and a bunch of Cornish hens. All of them were in the same paddock. It was a very cute combination of critters. The shot I liked the best had all three horses standing close together and it looked like a clustered still life to me, similar to one that I'd done of three pears for the Yale competition in college. My professor had commented on my painting as he passed my easel. "They look like mafia pears," he laughed. I won that competition.

There was thunder and lightning as it poured for most of the night. In the morning, I got seven bales of hay delivered by the owners, who then told me that another storm was coming in. So, I covered the new hay with a tarp and went to the trailer to work on the Wisconsin painting. I finished it in a couple of hours.

It was still pouring in the late morning. The prospect of sitting in the trailer all day finding something to do without internet, cell or a painting to do somehow didn't bother me. Usually rainy day camping made me anxious or depressed, but I felt good. I noticed that I wasn't anxious and I had no tension anywhere in my body. I had a strong sense that God was standing close by. I felt secure.

I pulled out my atlas and studied the Los Angeles area, considering where to look for a place to live. I noticed this didn't make me anxious either. When I'd lived there I'd had no sense of the surrounding towns, and was way too confused on the LA highways. I'd stayed in my little cocoon of a town most of the time. I had felt like I was losing my mind, or I was getting Alzheimer's and couldn't concentrate or finish anything.

It was the stress of living with Bob, I now knew. I felt an urgent need to save Teddy, who was still living with him. He was being stoic; he hadn't complained much, but I was sure this was why he failed another semester. I prayed, God watch over my son.

It was getting dark and the thunder was loud. I found Jessie shaking in the gooseneck. He was terrified of thunder and refused to go out. He curled up in a tight ball next to me on the dinette seat.

I went over my route and located a Wal-Mart on route to my next camp. Liza was meeting back up with me Saturday and I needed extra groceries. She drank special sparkling water and wine and I needed to get that stuff too. I thought how food was just fuel to me most of the time. How could siblings end up with such different attitudes about food? About so many things, actually.

It was still pouring so I finished my book. It was about facing your worst fears and overcoming them through exposure therapy, similar to Teddy's therapy. And how to become brave and selfless, which are the same thing I think. There was a love story tucked in there, which I found a distraction so I skimmed most of it. I closed the book and said out loud, "This book is about me."

I'd never thought of SHLEP as exposure therapy, but it sort of was. The theory is that after being exposed your fear many times, your panic reaction stops. Your amygdala eventually stops overreacting and sending out the adrenaline that gives you the feeling of panic. I think your frontal lobe gets stronger in controlling the amygdala. Or maybe it's the connection between them gets stronger; I know that it works for Teddy.

I remembered the list I used to read to Teddy when he was panicking:

- Fear is just a thought
- Thoughts can't kill you
- Thoughts don't predict the future

That last one used to seem so elementary to me;

obviously no one can predict the future. But now I thought how this might be why my worry over my kids' welfare was such a big source of anxiety and fear for me. Just because I thought Bob was going to be emotionally abusive with them didn't mean that they would be damaged by it. Maybe they didn't internalize unwarranted criticism like I did.

There was another spectacular storm as I slept that night—lightning, thunder, pouring rain. I got so much water in the trailer; it was leaking from the ceiling AC/heat vent and the fan that had the plastic cover duct taped over it. Jessie stayed cuddled next to me all night, trembling from the thunder; on my other side was Nalla. I pulled down the heavier shades on the windows by the bed so the lightning flashes wouldn't wake us up.

In the morning, the sky was crystal blue with snow white clouds swiftly gliding across it. I hoped it would stay that way for my drive. I hated hauling in the rain.

I talked with a couple in a ginormous/fancy RV before I pulled out of camp. They asked for my blog address so I gave them my cards. He asked me why I'd started this trip and I told him I left an abusive marriage and was trying to find myself again.

He replied, "It's amazing how little time it takes a schmuck to do a lot of damage."

I felt my shoulders relax; I hadn't noticed they were even tense before. I thought, affirmation is powerful stuff.

It was an uneventful haul to Minnesota. I got settled into my site at the Outback Ranch and saddled up Dreamy. We headed up the mountain, crossed a dirt road and entered onto the state park trails. The cool air in the forest smelled like what I thought heaven must smell like. Like dirt and pine needles on the ground smelled after it rained. I dropped Dreamy's reins and reached toward the glorious blue sky that was peeking through the tree canopy. I said my thank-you prayer, which had gotten a little longer lately. Then I asked God to use me to shine his glory, peace and joy onto others, especially to Liza, who was on her way to this camp. Dreamy continued walking down the hill, obediently following my seat and leg cues. I patted her neck and thanked her for being such a good girl while I prayed. I squeezed my legs and we picked up the pace. Dreamy was blowing hard on the steep and rolling hills and acting like it was too tough a ride for her. I felt bad about it and after an hour and a half I stopped at a small empty campground, got off and let her rest and graze for a bit. When I got back on, she charged down the hill towards home, she wasn't tired at all!

Both horses had gotten very buddy sour. When Wildflower balked at going out, I just got stronger with my cues, but when Dreamy did the same thing, I'd think she was lame or I was riding her too hard. Horses are herd animals and feel vulnerable to attack when they are alone, so being buddy sour is common. Sometimes a horse will get dangerous if you try to separate him from his "herd," but mine never did anything terrible. Dreamy never made me feel scared when she got frisky on the way home to her buddy, and I loved riding her when she was like that. Horse people call this impulsion and it's an amazing energy to experience in the saddle. Why did I hate it when Wildflower did this; why didn't I feel safe then? "Yer horse is a bully," Frankie had said; I didn't trust her. I had to get over thinking she was Bob, she was just a scared orphaned horse.

Liza had arrived by taxi while I was out riding. She was sitting in a camp chair in the shade of a huge tree, reading a book when I rode in. Jessie lay at her feet. I rode over to her, hopped off Dreamy and gave her a longer than normal hug. I was going to be a better sister this time.

"I'm so glad you came back!" I said.

She grinned, "It's so beautiful here! I had no idea

Minnesota was like this."

"Me neither!"

That night we joined two couples that were a few sites away. They had a roaring campfire going. They'd brought a hollow log they'd been saving for such an occasion; they stuffed it with a string of old Christmas tree lights and put it in the fire. The copper wire produced green and blue flames that exploded out the top like a volcano. It created so much heat that we all moved our chairs back a ways.

They asked about the e cigarettes that Liza and I were puffing on and we told them that we'd used them to quit smoking and were now hooked on them. I told them how earlier that day my e cigarette fell out of my back pocket and into the pit when I was using the porta potty. I was so upset about possibly losing it that I'd stuck my hand in to retrieved it. I then worried about how to sanitize it and my hand. They just stared at me with their mouths open for a few seconds and then burst out laughing.

We told them about Mom dying. I told them about losing Tucker. One of the women, Lori, had a 24-year-old Type 1 diabetic son who was a tri-athlete and we talked about how difficult it is mothering a teenaged diabetic son that thinks he's immortal. She had gone through many of the same fears and failures I had with Teddy. She had also gotten up in the middle of the night to see if her son was still breathing. It was the first time I'd ever been able to talk about this with another woman and I found it comforting.

We moved on to electrical shorts in the trailer. Lori told a story of when she'd plugged in her blow dryer to their trailer's outside plug while she was soaking wet and got zapped. She was a great storyteller and we all roared with laughter, picturing the scene. It was comforting to know that other more experienced campers had the same troubles I'd had and that I could now laugh at the stuff I'd cried about before.

We laughed for hours. I laughed so hard that tears

were dripping down my cheeks. I hadn't laughed so much in such a long time and it felt exhilarating. I'd never experienced anything quite like this and I realized that storytelling and laughing at our mistakes was what was so great about campfires.

The trail map was very hard to read so I downloaded it off the camp's website, messed with it in Photoshop and printed out one I could read a little better. The trails were well marked with numbers on the trees at every junction. They even had "caution steep" signs. One trail on the map was named The Man from Snowy River, referencing the best horse stunt scene ever done for a movie that I'd watched back in the Kentucky cabin.

In the morning, Liza fed the horses and Jessie, then made a pot of coffee. She gave me a huge smile with her "Good Morning" as I watched from my cozy sleeping bag while she put on her new boots and left with Jessie to go hiking. Wow, I thought, she was a morning bundle of energy now. I wonder what had changed her so dramatically.

I got up and poured a cup of coffee for myself and sat thinking about Liza. I didn't understand my sister; sometimes it felt like I didn't know her at all, how she felt or what was going on in her mind. It had always been like that. I knew she'd suffered greatly after her divorce but didn't know if she had resolved the trauma of remembering her childhood sexual abuse or not.

She'd never brought up my blocking her calls and emails last summer. She hadn't discussed her therapy. She didn't seem angry at me now. She hadn't gone on any big shopping sprees or pried about my divorce or the kids or given me advice when I hadn't asked for it or insinuated that I had an issue with money, or any of the other hurtful things she had done in the past few years.

When mom was dying, Liza had seemed almost professional and I was impressed with how she rose to the occasion, something I had trouble doing. That showed she was healing. When we were in New England I thought she was getting depressed again. And she'd said some strange things, like that "wanting to be my housewife" comment. I assumed she'd seen her therapist when she went back home and was on her meds. If I knew what troubled her, maybe I wouldn't take her ups and downs so personally.

I'd never pried and I hated it when people did it to me. Even if you answer, I don't want to talk about it, that's saying something's wrong. If someone wants to share, they will. I didn't want to share much lately, I'd already said all I had to say about my worries and concerns; repeating it didn't help me, so maybe Liza dealt with her stuff in the same way? I wondered if all our therapy made us different than most siblings were; we'd talked about our problems in our sessions and not with other people. With so much mental illness in our family, it seemed better that way. Crazy people say hurtful things and your family knows all your weaknesses to target. Words are powerful weapons in the wrong hands. And sensitive people, can interpret them in a myriad of ways depending on how we feel about ourselves.

I thought about the words that Bob used that hurt me the most; What's the matter with you? Taken out of context it doesn't sound that bad, no truly insulting name calling or profanity. Yet it hurt me as much as his profane pocket dial had. It hurt more than "You're unstable." A strong self-esteem would confidently answer that question with "Nothing is wrong with me." But I now knew that wasn't the case for me when I'd met Bob. What I'd taken to be my strength—success, beauty and talents—was just a superficial image that I'd crafted in an effort to get praise. To make myself feel worthy. What I wanted and desperately needed was someone to love me.

Would you ever say, "What's the matter with you?" to someone that you loved? I finally realized the truth—Bob never loved me. "I love you," was his biggest lie of all and I'd believed him.

I started the Minnesota painting of my horses romping on their hillside paddock, then saddled and booted Wildflower. It was a gorgeous sunny day again. I headed up on the yellow section of trails towards the Man from Snowy River trail.

Wildflower had gotten more compliant lately, giving me her head with just a little lift of the rein. I wondered if my calm was transferring to her. Or my stronger confidence made her feel safer. Horses are very tuned in with human emotion, so it had to be one of those things. We saw a herd of deer running through the woods and she didn't react at all. I thought how I hadn't been fair to compare her to Dreamy all the time. She was half her age and a different breed. And she had a typical alpha mentality of being on the lookout for danger all the time, kind of like me. I was glad I'd kept her. She's a great horse.

Liza and I started a Scrabble game on the picnic table and decided not to keep score, which made the game much more fun for me. I preferred to make real words, not the weird ones that competitive scrabble players came up with like "qi." It got cold after the sun went down so we quit and went inside. Liza cooked some burgers and we sat down to eat together. I thought about how eating a meal with someone was much more enjoyable than eating alone. I looked at her and smiled. We talked about our plans for the next few states.

Liza said, "I want to leave New Jersey for good."

"I don't blame you. It's depressing, too congested, too many people and cars."

She said, "It would be nice to live together, don't you think?"

"Yeah, it would." I said, "But you know, I have to go back to California first. Once Emily graduates and Teddy's independent, then I can do it."

I was sick of going solo, on SHLEP and in real life. It

wasn't courageous; it was lonely. Sometimes you have to be alone to get introspective and think about what's important in life without too much outside noise. To search your soul. Like when you think you've gone crazy or you'd rather just put a bullet in your head, you gotta get honest and dig till it hurts or nothing's gonna change.

I was a little worried what Dad's inevitable death, living in the congested Los Angeles area and the divorce would do with my PTSD, though. It hadn't bothered me in some time now; maybe it was gone.

The land flattened out as we drove west. The colors in the fields hinted that winter was coming, beautiful earthy tones of yellows, browns mixed in with some greens. Some of the fields were growing sunflowers and soybeans, but most of the crops were corn. The roads were stick straight, smooth and flat. The only hills were overpasses over railroad tracks, for transporting the crops to market. There were big groupings of silos on all the farms that we passed and I wondered how that all worked. Round bales lined the highways from where they were harvesting the grass along the highways as well. They must be getting ready for a hard winter I thought.

We finally pulled into Sheyanne Oaks Horse Camp in Leonard, North Dakota. The camp was set up in a grid instead of meandering trails like most places are. All the sites were pull-through so you didn't have to back your rig to get out. There were small 10x10 uncovered pipe stalls lining the two long sides of camp. There were about 10 other rigs there and 20 horses, a few of which I noted were blanketed. It was mid-September. Must get pretty cold at night, I thought.

The weather sucked. It rained all day. It was cold and the wind made it feel worse. Some hardy campers were huddled around a campfire all afternoon laughing it up. Liza and I stayed in the trailer trying to keep warm. The low was predicted to be 39 at night and I was anxious about my horses not having enough of a winter coat to stay warm, especially cooped up in their tiny unprotected pens. I gave them a huge pile of hay and big tubs of water and hoped for the best. I posted on Facebook about my concerns and got a lot of advice, ranging from "Put them in the trailer" to "Make a shelter with a tarp," to "Give them lots of hay and water" to "Go buy some blankets." I should have known by then not to post questions like that; everyone had a different opinion.

Kind of like asking childcare questions. Let them cry it out to have them sleep in your bed, the latter of which was the philosophy I'd subscribed to. Boy, did Bob hate that. He slept on the sofa or guest room bed most of the time anyway, he never got up when they cried—why did he care so much about it anyway? Dr. Sears was my baby guru: healthy self-esteem was my primary concern, I guess 'cuz I had none.

Jack saw my post and called me. He said not to worry, just give them a lot of hay. I knew he would say that, but it was reassuring to hear his voice again telling me so. We talked about me leaving my mares with him in October for a couple of years. It would be so hard for me to separate from them, but they would be happy at his ranch and I wouldn't go broke paying L.A. board and hay prices. It would give me more time to concentrate on my children's needs, to paint and write the book I was hoping to do. I told myself that it would just be temporary and I wasn't getting "rid" of my horses.

The horses were frisky in the morning, which is typical when it gets cold. There were empty beer cases flying around the campground left over from the partying group. No one emerged from the other trailers until 9 or 10. One woman was walking around with shorts on and I got cold just looking at her. I found my long underwear and put it on under my jeans. Many of the other campers were wearing camouflage-hunting suits. My big filthy white down jacket didn't exactly blend in.

I'd been thinking that it would be good to have a house all ready to move into when I got back to California and decided that Emily and Teddy should pick it out. I could care less what it looked like. As long as I could afford it and it was relatively safe, I was fine. They would own the decision; a location or too small a room couldn't be an excuse not to move in. It would be a good learning experience for them; they'd been given very few opportunities to practical life skills so far.

I texted Emily and Teddy that I wanted them to find a house to rent for us all by October. I lined them up with a realtor in Pasadena that I found on Trulia and told her I wanted a three-year lease. Emily was excited and sent me links for a few rentals in the area, and Liza and I looked at the listings.

Liza said, "Oh my God, look at the rent!"

"I know!" I said. "That's what I've been so anxious about. Teddy's flunked out so many times, he's got at least three more years till he graduates now. It'll be just for three years. I figure the rent and tuition will run me $300,000 and I'll take it out of my IRA. Besides, the divorce might take that long too; I need to take the reins on it."

I said, "It'll be worth it. I'm considering it like an investment in their emotional stability and our future."

Liza looked at me in disbelief, but I knew this was the right thing to do, the only way I would ever be able to live with myself again. I held her gaze with confidence and a determination I hadn't felt in a very long time.

By 2:00 it was as warm as it was going to get and I got on Wildflower and ponied Dreamy out onto the trails. Liza found a trail map with better resolution in the laundry room and gave it to me. I wanted to explore the land where the sheep grazed. The trail was basically a big loop with smaller trails branching off. Someone on Facebook told me to expect a lot of gates. They weren't the kind of gates you could open from the saddle. This was a pain since I was ponying. We went through one gate without much of a hassle but I avoided going through any more after that and just stayed within that area.

We came upon a very tall squeaky windmill with an

enormous round metal water trough. There were bras hanging off the lower rungs of the windmill, which reminded me of the bra trees I'd seen when riding on ski lifts in Vail and Whistler. Why would a woman do that, I wondered. Wildflower wouldn't even approach the water trough but of course Dreamy walked right up to it and drank deeply. Slowly, Wildflower edged up and took a sip. I cracked up.

I knew I could get disoriented in the hills so I tried like heck to memorize which way we went and what we'd passed, not just so I didn't get lost but as a mental exercise. My sense of direction was coming back to me and I wanted to keep working on it.

On Wednesday, Liza said she wanted to ride. I had thought about how I'd handle it if she'd say this, so I was prepared. I said, "No, that's not a good idea." I felt badly but I had been clear with her before she came. It was in her and Dreamy's best interests.

Liza looked a little hurt, and I felt a little bad, but that was it. She woke up the next day and said her busted ribs were bothering her again so she didn't want to ride anyway. We had breakfast and she took off with Jessie for a very long walk in the sheep pasture where I'd ridden the day before.

I ordered some hay, and it was dropped off by the trailer. The bales were much bigger and heavier than I was used to and it was hard to get them into the truck bed without unhitching the trailer. A guy came over and effortlessly threw them all in. It still kind of pissed me off that God made women so dang weak.

His jacket said Dead Horse Ranch on it and I had to ask about the unusual name. He told me he'd bought a horse on a payment plan and the horse died the first month after he took him home. He still had to make all the payments and his buddies teased him about paying for a dead horse. So, he named his ranch after the story. He said, "I can laugh about it now, but it wasn't funny at the time." He then told me that he had proposed to his wife with a horse instead of a ring.

Wow! How could a horse loving girl possibly say no? It made me think of my own engagement, which was not nearly as romantic or thoughtful. I had given Bob an ultimatum to "shit or get off the pot" and had given him a deadline of Valentine's Day 1989. He pulled through with an unmounted diamond on the specified date, which thrilled me at the time.

Did he ever actually say the words, "Will you marry me?"? No, definitely not. I think it was, "Here, I got this at the diamond center." He'd called earlier in the day asking if the stone had to be pink. I'd said no, the pink part wasn't a deal breaker. What a horrible way to start a marriage.

I checked the weather on my phone. The cold snap we were experiencing was hitting our upcoming camps in Wyoming, Montana & South Dakota with snow. I loved how pretty snow was but I didn't want to haul or camp in it. I hoped it would melt in the next couple of days.

I got busy with my million chores of getting ready to leave. Two guys sitting at a campfire nearby shouted over at me, "You're working so hard I had to sit down and have a drink." They all cracked up. Eventually Liza came outside and asked if she could help. I was finished already. The guys laughed again and so did I. I was so done with all this physical labor.

Liza and I huddled in the warm trailer to go over the next few states again. I lay the atlas on the dinette table. I wanted her to be more involved in the haul by at least helping navigate while I was driving. We had a three-day haul to the next campground. The western states were huge. We'd be crossing the Rockies in Montana on the way to our destination camp that was near Darby. It was not nearly as high as Loveland Pass in Colorado where I'd crossed last year, thank God. I told Liza that I was unsure about getting in and out of the Montana campground because the website said it was for small trailers. She looked concerned. I said I'd called the ranger there and he told me I'd be okay.

It was a perfectly flat-as-a-pancake drive to our next overnight at Halstead's Circle H Stables in Brookings, South Dakota. The landscape was like a patchwork quilt of subtle fall colors. The mares got settled into large stalls in a sturdy old barn with straw bedding, a first for me. It was nice and cozy in there. Outside there was a fierce freezing wind.

Emily's 19th birthday was coming up. I was going to send her money and a card but when I called to get her dorm address, she said she'd rather get a painting. I was surprised and flattered. She told me she was going to Disneyland to celebrate with her friends. I thought it was adorable that she still loved Disneyland so much.

I chose a photo that Jack had taken of Emily's retired mare, Tiara, in the pasture with the herd, some of them lying down in the sun for a nap. Tiara was looking at the camera. The tree line behind them was ablaze in fall colors. It was a gorgeous shot; Jack was good. I spent the afternoon working on it.

When I came out of the trailer Liza was talking with a perky college aged girl with a sweet little quarter horse, Two Bit. She was a nursing student at the University there and Two Bit was her first horse. Her Dad came by later on and she introduced us. He did mechanical work for this barn in exchange for his first horse. He'd come to use the heated garage they had there, to work on an old truck he'd just bought so that he could haul a horse trailer. He wanted to be able to haul and go trail riding with his daughter. He was a single Dad and his daughter was obviously his top priority. What an awesome guy, I thought. Too bad dad and I weren't younger, I thought. And I thought of him in his office marking his wall map with my locations. "Do it before you're too old," he'd said, and I smiled.

The girl's father had a compressor and added air to all

my tires for me. He asked me why I was doing my trip and I gave him a short version of my story. He then told me that he got divorced two years ago. He was good looking and had an easy smile. I could see myself with a man like this. He told me that he had been Type 1 diabetic since a child. He said he was not able to get a Commercial Driver's License for truck driving years ago due to being diabetic. I got a little outraged; wasn't that discrimination?

I remembered suggesting to Teddy that the Peace Corp would be an interesting experience. He'd said they don't take diabetics and I'd protested.

"Think about it, Mom, me in a remote jungle, refrigerated insulin."

It still pissed me off.

I had trouble sleeping, and that was unusual for me. I kept thinking about moving in with Emily and Teddy and was getting giddy. I woke up the next morning from a dream and told Liza about it.

"I was standing with my horses by a canal with a towpath running alongside it. Like they have in Bucks Country near where mom lived. Along came a horse-drawn, old-fashioned open carriage. Mom was seated in the back seat of the carriage, looking very comfy all wrapped up in blankets. She looked so beautiful and had a big smile on her face. Someone standing behind me said, 'Everyone has a different way of getting here.'"

In her therapist's voice, Liza said, "What do you think that means?"

I said, "I think mom just arrived in heaven." I felt at peace. She was finally happy, forever. Heaven makes up for all the pain in your life; it's the ultimate destination. I really was looking forward to it someday.

The following day was Emily's birthday and I thought about how she had miraculously, despite our dysfunctional marriage and all our mistakes, grown up to be so confident and wholesome. She had a profoundly deep-for-her-age faith in God, even though we'd quit going to church when she was eleven. She was a talented artist, she had a pitch perfect singing voice and she was tall lean and beautiful. She hadn't rebelled in any of the self-destructive ways that I had as a teenager. She was an A student. She had a tight circle of nice friends that didn't smoke or do drugs, and neither did she. I felt blessed to be her mother. Whatever did I do to deserve her?

While I was getting ready to leave, I introduced myself to a couple walking by. The woman had just moved there and was checking on her horse who she said had not fared well in the haul and was colicky. She introduced the man with her to me as her ex-husband. I couldn't hide my surprise and said "Oh, and you're still friendly, how nice." I couldn't picture Bob and I ever being friendly or going to the barn together.

She said "Not just friendly, but reconciled. We're getting married again."

I was floored and didn't know what to say. There was an awkward silence and then the guy said they had some friends who had gotten remarried too. I just stared at them. What would it take for Bob and me to do that? Was that possible? It sure would be a relief to drop our stagnant divorce. But I knew, that could, would, should never happen. Whatever was wrong with both of us might be okay alone or with someone else, but together was like mixing up a Molotov cocktail.

Finally, I found some words and wished them luck.

On our way out of Billings I stopped for gas. I went into the shop to pay and pick up some milk. The cashier was a nice looking man and he was vacuuming, something I'd never seen Bob do. He said, "Don't tell my wife I know how to do this." I chuckled. Why did men always try to get out of housework? It still puzzled me why Bob had flatly refused to bring his fucking dish to the sink for that marriage counseling exercise. Two more good looking country guys walked in to pay for their gas.

They sure did grow them pretty in Billings.

Three separate times in my brief stay in Billings, the same conversation took place: After seeing my plates, someone asked me what I was doing so far from California. I'd tell them I was trying to ride in all 48 states, to which they'd reply, "I bet you have met a lot of nice people!"

It made me think about the people I'd met along the way and how they'd been key to restoring my faith in humanity. And my faith in God. And resilience. That they cared about other people too. They made me feel special and worthwhile even though I was broken and transient. They helped me without being asked to.

We pulled into our next overnight, Diamond A Cattle in Pukwana, South Dakota, as they were just finishing up a barrel racing event. Late that afternoon I finished Emily's painting and started the North Dakota painting. The mares were frisky and running around in the big arena. Interestingly Dreamy was doing a little bit of pushing herself now; I saw her kick at Wildflower a couple of times. It made me smile. It was about time she stood up for herself.

When it got dark, I opened the door to let Jessie in. I was startled by the incredible display of stars in the sky. I grabbed my glasses and put on a jacket and went outside to enjoy the show. I saw three shooting stars! I hadn't seen one in over thirty years. It was so clear that I could see the Milky Way too. I loved staring at that night sky; it was overwhelming how many stars were visible and I felt tiny in comparison to the universe. I might be tiny, but I was a part of it again.

Chapter 12

I wrapped up Emily's painting and arranged to have the owners mail it for me. Then we headed out to Broken Arrow Horse Camp in Custer, South Dakota.

The last part of the drive to Custer was a long climb up the mountain but all the roads in were good. The snow had melted except for patches in the grass and trees.

The website directions said to look for their blue sign at the turn but there was no blue sign. And we never saw the llamas we were supposed to pass either. It cracked me up the directions people gave. GPS usually didn't work in rural areas, and I wondered why the heck couldn't they map the rural roads correctly? Didn't they have satellite pictures for heaven's sake?

It was only 37 degrees when we got there. The owner, Larry, was extremely nice and asked about all my "accoutraments" hanging off my belt. I showed him my hoof pick/knife with the wooden handle that I loved and always had on me, my carrot bag for rest stops to check for colic signs, my iPhone and my TENS unit controller. He had back trouble too and wanted to know all about my TENS unit.

Larry gave me forms to fill out for my brand inspection papers, yet another horse document I would need for the Western states. He happened to be qualified to sign them for me. Wow, that was easier than I thought it would be!

We were at 5,500 feet and the horses were a little tired from three straight days of hauling and the higher altitude. I'd had a small headache since I'd gotten there, probably from the altitude.

I woke up at 4:00 am. We'd crossed another time zone line and my internal clock was messed up. I stayed in bed writing till 6:30 when it finally started getting light outside. It was 34 degrees when I stepped out of the trailer. Brrr. It warmed up later, at least it felt warmer when you were in the sun. Liza went hiking with Jessie. She told me that she loved walking in the woods with him and all this exercise and fresh air helped her a lot with her depression. I was so glad she was finding some relief.

I rode Wildflower and ponied Dreamy on the brown trail. It was a one and a half hour ride, flat, easy and with few rocks along the way. They were huffing and puffing even at a walk. I stopped half way to let them graze and I took some photos of them for a possible painting. We were in a long prairie in the middle of the woods. I could see part of the mountain range in the distance at the end of the clearing. I didn't see any one else the entire time we were out.

There were huge stacks of left over parts of trees from logging that they called slash. Sue had told me that the forest had gotten too dense and they were thinning it, especially the diseased trees that were killed by some bark beetle. There were piles all over the place, some 20' tall. We saw a few deer, but Wildflower just took note of them and didn't react at all.

In the afternoon, I unhitched the trailer for the first time in a while and we went to the Crazy Horse Memorial. Native Americans were carving Crazy Horse on his horse out of a mountain. The face was beautifully done, and its size was so impressive. Mount Rushmore's four heads would fit in the space of Crazy Horse's head. Crazy Horse is depicted pointing straight ahead toward his tribal lands, which was basically the entire mountain range. It was sculpted on three sides, not just a one-sided relief like Mount Rushmore was. They were funding this project without Federal money, on principle I think, so it's progress was very slow. We stopped in the town of Custer on the way back. It was kind of disappointing, as most tourist towns are, but I took photos of all the painted buffalos that lined the main street.

The next day was a gorgeous sunny, warm and blustery

day and I had two wonderful rides. First I took Dreamy up 6,000 feet to a place called Heaven. We rode through a small herd of cows on the way up. At the summit, there was a 360-degree view of the Black Hills. The beautiful mountains stretched as far as the eye could see, rise after rise. Dreamy was perfect as usual. She didn't seem too affected by the altitude; Charni had told me that horses acclimate much faster than people do. We trotted most of the way and it took us a little over two hours. When I got back, Liza was just returning from a hike with Jessie. I asked Jessie if he wanted to go for a ride with me. He was so tired he didn't even pick up his head.

I then took off on Wildflower to Three Ponds. I took a wrong turn and we wandered off course for an hour or more. I swear that horse knew when I was lost and got mad about it. By the time we got to Three Ponds, she was very annoyed. I tied her to a tree to try and get some photos. She spent the entire time circling the tree, crunching over dead branches and big rocks and getting completely tangled in the pine branches. I untied her and let her graze but she still had her knickers in a bunch. As I tried to put her bridle back on, she would not stand still and stepped on the reins which snapped the headstall leather. I got so mad and tied her to another tree, where she resumed her temper tantrum, as I jerry rigged the leather pieces back together with a shoelace from my saddlebag. It was the headstall that the Judy in Maryland had given to me and I was pissed about it. We had already been out longer than I had planned. When I spotted a dirt road nearby, I decided to follow it back to camp. I asked her for collection and trotted the whole way back. She was compliant but kept hollowing her back when I relaxed the reins. Buck Brannaman said you need to ask a thousand times on some horses. Kind of like kids, I thought.

I got a copy of an email from the California realtor arranging a day of rental house showings for Emily and Teddy. I couldn't wait to get back to them.

I checked my calendar and today was the date I pulled

out of California a year ago. I'd ridden in 41 states so far. I posted the milestone on Facebook. My friend Chris commented, "It's amazing what a year can do."

Yes, but more amazing is what God could do with your mess when you let Him in.

Larry had said his friend's camp in the Big Horns had closed on the 12th due to the snow. The impressive mountain range loomed in front of us for hours as we headed towards them. They looked so high I got a bit anxious about driving over them. Our next camp, Ten Broek RV Park inTen Sleep, Wyoming was on the opposite side in the flat.

The drive through the pass was so beautiful it left us speechless. Most of the snow had melted and the road had been well designed with no crazy steep grades. The view coming down into Ten Sleep was not to be believed. The road switch-backed through incredibly tall cliffs on both sides. No wonder it was such a popular rock-climbing destination. The river, on our left, was raging over boulders on its way down the gorge. I wished Liza could drive the rig so I could have gotten a better look at it all. We agreed that this was definitely the most gorgeous place in the world. The land eventually flattened out and the river followed us more lazily to the tiny town of Ten Sleep.

The owners, Bonnie and her husband were very friendly, just as I'd been told by folks on the Horse Camping Facebook page. They offered to ride with me, using their stock trailer to head back up into the mountains. There was only one other horse camper there, a couple that was stuck there while the wife was getting diagnosed and treated by a local doctor for a sudden illness. The rest of the campers were rock climbers and a few construction workers, who were in RV's and the small cabins.

The camp was on Highway 16, the same road that brought us through the mountain pass, so there was traffic noise from vehicles passing by. The road was being widened and the construction noise was annoying. I also heard some strange water noises that turned out to be a water treatment pond on the other side of the football field right next to us. Adjacent to the football field was an old rodeo arena. The campground was well kept and completely shaded with tall trees. The town of Ten Sleep was just a block away and was two short blocks long. There was a bank, a pub, an ice cream store, a real estate agent and a coffee house. What else could you ask for?

Camping next to us in a little pop up camper was a young French Canadian couple with their adorable three month-old daughter. They were rock climbers. The baby was in one of those Jolly Jumpers hanging from their awning brace. Dad told me that he was a fine artist and gave me his website address. Seeing my license plates, they told me that they wanted to go to Bishop, California to climb there. I told them to be sure and drive up to the tiny mountain town of Aspendell, a 20 minute drive up the mountain to 4,000'. My riding buddy, Jan, had a house there and I had visited there a couple of times. It was a really cool area. I thought how I'd probably never get to go there again now that Jan thought I was a Jesus freak.

The next morning, Bonnie knocked on my door asking if I wanted to go for a ride. I unhitched the truck and hitched her stock trailer to it, booted and saddled Wildflower. Dreamy pitched a fit in her pen as we loaded our horses. Liza and Jessie hopped in the back seat. Liza wanted to go for a hike. I drove up the pass I had hauled down the day before coming into Ten Sleep. We parked near a National Forest Campground and told Liza that we'd be back in a few hours. Jessie followed her wagging his tail.

Bonnie led me up through a pine forest, a few meadows with meandering creeks running through them and up to a pristine lake at 10,000'. There were mountains in every direction. It was the most beautiful place I'd ever seen. It wasn't an easy ride but Wildflower did great. She had no trouble navigating the rocks, mud and occasional snow. Bonnie and I had a nice easy conversation as we rode. She said that they'd be celebrating their 50th wedding anniversary soon. I told her that was something to be proud of. They had a great grandchild already too. They'd lived in Ten Sleep for twenty years and loved their life there. Bonnie told me that real estate prices were going up and it was getting harder to find land because most of it was now owned by the government. Local ranchers leased their grazing rights from the feds. I wondered why the government owned all that grassland, but didn't ask. I asked how bad the winters were there. She said they had a short mild winter that was pretty dry and they didn't get too much snow down in town. I really wanted to live there some day.

On the way back, Bonnie pointed out a lot of elk droppings, but we never saw any elk nor moose. It was bow hunting season so they were hiding. Bonnie and I passed a few hunters' camps. One had a beautiful canvas tent shaped like a small house with a chimney. Bonnie said that it was free to camp anywhere you wanted to. I asked her if she ever saw horse campers. She said, "Not any more. Most of the hunters these days drive their gear in with pick-up trucks or on four wheelers. But you could do it on horseback if you wanted to. I used to see them up here all the time."

We all met back at the truck and Liza and I said at the exact same time, "You wouldn't believe what I saw, this place is awesome!" Then we laughed. Liza told us that she'd gone over to the National Forest camp to ask the camp host about where to hike. He warned her about the moose and said, "If your dog goes after a moose, the moose will turn and charge your dog, who will retreat to you, so the moose will end up charging straight towards you!" That had sounded scary, so she'd kept Jessie on his leash the entire hike.

That night, Liza and I walked over to the "saloon" for

dinner. We wanted to get more of a feel for this town that we'd both fallen in love with. To live in a town where you could access that kind of wilderness with just a twenty-minute drive would be heaven. We showed each other the pictures we'd taken on our phones. As we were eating we overheard a conversation going on at another table where two couples and two adolescent kids sat.

"Well, I never got a DUI before I came here!"

Some crude language was thrown in and further complaints about getting pulled over for DUI's. The kids were just sitting there listening to all this. I felt bad for the kids and mad at the parents, Liza just shook her head in disgust.

The next morning was cooler and sprinkling a little bit. Bonnie, Liza, Jessie & I trailered to a different trailhead. I brought Dreamy this time and Liza hiked with Jessie again.

This was an even tougher ride, but just as spectacular. At times, we were in a dense pine forest that smelled heavenly. We climbed up to 10,000' again. We picked our way around rocks, waded through streams, crossed meadows and rode past mountain lakes. At one point we crossed some snow, which Dreamy had never seen before. She didn't take one bad step with some crazy footing challenges, jumping streams, stepping between big rocks into mud, and heading down steep hills.

Liza described the waterfalls that she'd seen on her hike. She said that Jessie got a good workout and he'd conked out back at camp afterwards. "There were many chipmunks that needed chasing." I laughed, I was so glad that Liza was experiencing this place and found it as magical as I did.

The H in SHLEP was definitively answered, my forever home was going to be in Wyoming, after the next three years in Pasadena were over with. My children wouldn't need me around after that.

I spent the rest of the day in camp. I bought some weed free hay from Bonnie for my upcoming Western states that required this certification, and loaded it in the truck bed. I did a little prep work for my next painting and chatted with a few other campers there. That night I realized that I'd forgotten to book an overnight for the next day. I also realized my horse health certificates expired the next day as well. I called Bonnie's vet to see if he could come out and take care of my paperwork in the morning, but it went to voice mail, so I left a message.

We went to the saloon in town for supper again. We found out that Dirty Sally's, the ice cream parlor, was for sale, and so was the saloon. I asked our waitress if she knew why so much real estate was up for sale there. She said that oil drilling and fracking was going to be starting soon and some old timers didn't want to be there for that and were getting out of town.

I didn't know what fracking was and neither did Liza so we looked it up on Google. It didn't sound good.

Liza said that she wanted to get rid of her New Jersey apartment and explore the North West and maybe move there. She spent quite a bit of time learning about RV's from a guy camping near us. He was somewhat of a self-proclaimed RV expert and answer her many questions. He helped her figure out what kind of RV she should get for what she planned to do. I think he was kind of sweet on her too. I was watching a metamorphosis take place in my sister.

The vet (who also happened to be the local pastor) called me back that night but my phone must have been on silent. I got his message in the morning saying that he could be there at 11:00 pm. Wow, I thought, that was impressive. I called him back and he said that he was on his way to do "cow work" but could come by in the afternoon. Neither Liza nor I minded staying an extra day.

Over coffee, Liza told me that she'd had a strange dream.

"You had a very, very tall, handsome boyfriend. We were all standing around Mom who was lying in a bed like she was at Peggy's House. She looked very frail, like when she was dying. Your tall boyfriend reached to shake her hand and pulled her out of her bed and she fell to the floor."

My immediate response was, "It was God taking her to heaven!"

Liza said, "That's kind of a rough touch, no?"

I got a call back from the owner of our next overnight. She was on a cruise in Alaska but she said that there were people working at her ranch and that there was room for me there. She said Montana was very tough about livestock paperwork so it was good I was not trying to leave without my papers being updated.

We went to the cafe in town for lattes and breakfast burritos, which were awesome. We walked the side streets of town, looking at the houses and trying to get a feel for what it'd be like living there. I thought about getting a place there and renting it out for a few years before I was ready to move. But I really couldn't buy anything until my divorce was settled; all our community property assets were supposedly frozen until then. I wondered how long I was expected to comply with this financial limbo. One of the first things I was doing when I got back to California was having a heart to heart with my lawyer. I was beginning to think that he just didn't want my case for some reason, and that was why he hadn't done anything. Or maybe Bob had paid him off. I probably needed to switch lawyers.

My kids texted me that they'd found a three-bedroom they liked and sent me the online listing for it. I spent the rest of the day filling out application forms for the owners. I was getting excited thinking about having a stationary home again. I kept looking at the photos of the house and imagined living in it with Teddy and Emily.

Driving through the rest of Wyoming on a country highway was disappointing, it was flat and dry. It got pretty again once we entered Montana.

Along the way, Liza called Dad. After she hung up she said, "He sounds really bad."

"Maybe he's on pain meds?"

Liza said, "He asked us to both come to Florida."

I asked, "Right now? When?"

"I'm not sure."

I called Dad when we arrived so I could speak to him personally, but he didn't answer so I left a message. I fretted over what to do. We were less than 300 miles from Jack's place. We could drive there the next day, drop the horses and trailer and continue on to Boise Airport to catch a flight to Florida on Tuesday. I was unsure of the urgency and got very anxious. It wasn't like Dad to request a visit. If Dad wanted us there, we would go; SHLEP could wait. My kids could move into the rental without me being there for a while. That wasn't how I planned it but even though I was anxious, I had a strong sense of peace, that it was all somehow in God's hands, that we would all be okay.

I still had my concerns about going to the Montana camp in Darby. It was primitive, there were no trail maps and no running water "nearby." I called the ranger again and he told me that the water was being shut off for the winter. And even though he said the camp could handle my sized rig, I couldn't get the website's description of "for small trailers only" out of my head.

As I was going to bed I started worrying about Dad again. I really wished I knew how close he was to dying, so I could figure out which way to head in the morning; Challis, ID or Darby, MT? I was okay with aborting SHLEP. I had achieved everything I set out to do now that I had pinned Ten Sleep, Wyoming as my place to settle once my kids were independent. I had a strong connection with God and knew that he was watching over me. The self-doubt and incessant worry that had tripped me up so badly a year ago had dramatically diminished.

In the morning, I texted Brad happy birthday. He was now 24. I thought how it was also Bob's birthday.

Liza finally got in touch with Yvonne, who told Liza, "It's not an urgent situation. You don't need to come."

Liza asked why he'd asked us to come. Did he just miss us? Was he lonely?

Yvonne finally said, "He's not going to die any time soon."

After she hung up, I said, "Do you believe her? I don't trust her."

Liza shrugged and tilted her head as she took a drag on her e-cigarette.

Honestly, I thought, the thought of aborting the trip was appealing. There were several times along this journey where I'd wanted to abort because of fear, insecurity or physical pain. But, this time was different. I thought I was actually finished, my goal was achieved even though I hadn't technically ridden in all 48 states yet. I felt whole again.

We decided to believe Yvonne and set the GPS for Darby, Montana.

Darby's altitude was around 4,500'. Higher elevations really appealed to me. The air was cleaner and fresher and all the scents seemed more pure and intense. The scenery at Lake Como, in Rock Creek National Forest, rivaled Wyoming. Camp was at the end of a manmade lake that looked an awful lot like the Italian Lake Como it was named after. Liza commented that it looked like one of those cheesy travel posters, just too beautiful to be real. The surreal jagged-topped mountains rose severely right out of the sides of the lake. The lake was seven miles long and at our end there was a long stone dam with a sandy beach on one side and a boat launch on the other. It was shallow at the boat launch side and Jessie had a blast running through the water. Back at our campsite he commenced digging to China and was filthy once again.

We couldn't see the lake from our campsite, but it was just a short walk through the woods to get there. I'd parked under large pine trees so there was plenty of shade. Most sites were pull through, which I had no trouble getting into, so I wasn't sure why the website had said that it was only suitable for small trailers. Maybe the pull through's were new and they hadn't updated their website?

The weed free hay bales had special two toned baling twine to identify it as such. The border crossing Ag stop had been closed but a ranger might still ask to see it. I set up the electric fence, put the horses in it and threw them some of the new hay.

We had picked up a free real estate magazine at our rest stop in Wisdom, which a sign said had a population of 100. Liza was browsing through the magazine as I finished my Wyoming painting at our picnic table. Liza kept oohing and ahhing. She said that Montana's land prices were very reasonable. She reiterated that she was serious about getting a RV and spending the next two years on the road. "I was so depressed when I went home. I love this mobile lifestyle. It makes me get outside and motivates me to exercise, which in turn, makes me feel so much better. I love meeting new people at camps, walking in the woods and seeing the scenery."

"Wow," I said, "you've really caught the travel bug."

"Yes, I have. I want to spend more time out west and get a feel for what it would be like to live there."

I'd never heard my sister sound so passionate.

She again brought up the idea that we might live together, and I felt even more positive about it.

That night I made my fourth campfire. I found a half-burned log at a nearby slash pile and threw it in on top of the branches I'd gathered and lit it. It caught on fire quickly. Liza went to bed early and I sat by the fire for a long time. Jessie was at my feet snoring. It felt so peaceful there.

I'd go on two rides the next day, one on each horse

because I only had one ride day there. I had shortened Montana's stay to make up for the day I lost waiting to do my health papers back in Wyoming. No one had even asked to see my horse papers. Not a single Montana crossing weight station had been open and there was no ranger in camp to ask for them either. Nor had anyone come by to inspect my special weed free hay either.

I worried about Dad and if he was in pain or not. If Yvonne was taking good care of him. I wondered how much longer he had on this awful road of dying. I thought about all the treatments he'd subjected himself to and if he still thought it had been worth it. I didn't. The sky was black with sparkling stars peeking down through the trees and eventually the fire died. I kicked some dirt on it and went to bed.

I woke up during the night at 3:00 am. I lay in bed cuddling with Jessie. At 5:00 I finally crawled out of my sleeping bag and got up. I tried to quietly make coffee without waking Liza.

Eventually the sun came up and I touched up Wildflower's feet with my rasp that was now dull. I got Wildflower saddled and booted. Once in the saddle, my mind cleared of my anxiety about Dad's health. It was still so mysterious how riding stopped my worry, anger and back pain. It somehow freed me, it made me concentrate on the present moment and enjoy it. It made me thankful for everything as it was. I got a beautiful shot of Wildflower on the beach with the spectacular backdrop of the lake and mountains.

We rode over one of the streams that fed the lake. It came tumbling down off the hillside over big boulders. Eventually we got to the other end of the lake and to my delight there was a waterfall there!

Back at the trailer, I had a peanut butter and jelly sandwich and saddled up Dreamy. We left camp out the back way and ended up on the other side of the lake, the non-horse side, but since those camp areas were closed I didn't think it mattered. I wandered down a trail that led out of the back side of camp through the woods heading in the direction of the people beach side of the lake. We crossed a nearby stream that I didn't know was there, making a mental note that it would be a good place for watering the horses if my tank ran out. It had gotten quite warm, it was probably in the 80's by then. The trail turned into a paved path. Once in a while pavement was actually good for horse's legs, it helps reduce swelling. Eventually it turned into a dirt path again that crossed over some big rock slide areas. Dreamy was stumbling a little, but I thought it was just her normal "buddy sour going out stumble." Jessie was with us and he seemed totally pooped out by then, so we turned around. Dreamy wasn't stumbling at all coming home so I'd been right.

Our plan was to leave in the morning, overnight in northern Idaho, then haul to Washington where Liza would leave me again in Seattle. She would fly to Florida to go see Dad.

I ran out of horse water overnight, so I tried filling their bucket by lugging teapots from the living quarters sink out to them. It took a lot of trips since they drank it as soon as I poured it. I gave up on this and walked them to that stream I'd crossed on Dreamy the day before. I loaded them up and pulled out of our site at 9:30. Five states to go, I was counting down to the end, ready to wrap it all up.

The last turn out of the horse area was about 90 degrees. There were big boulders and large trees lining the narrow dirt road. I realized then that this must have been what they were referring to on their website about being "suitable for small trailers." I was preoccupied with not hitting a tree on the right side of the trailer and was just about to release a sigh of relief that I had made it, when I felt a big bump.

I glanced in my left-hand mirror and said, "Oh shit!"

The trailer tires were ON TOP of a 2-1/2' high boulder stationed at the corner! The trailer crashed down smashing the back corner on the boulder. Amazingly the tires didn't blow. I put it in park and got out to assess the damage.

The boulder had ripped off everything in its path on the underside of the trailer including the septic valves, pvc pipes, the aluminum protective trim covering the generator conduit and of course the conduit itself was shredded. It all lay on the ground in my path. The back "c" frame corner (the same part that had been replaced a year ago in California) was visibly out of whack and the corner was crunched like a soda can.

I opened the windows at the horses' heads and they seemed fine. All the doors still opened. The support "T" beams under the floor had dog-eared corners now but the axles didn't appear damaged but I couldn't really tell; I'd never actually inspected them before so I wasn't sure. A ranger pulled up out of nowhere and helped me break off the remaining aluminum strips that were dangling and told me where there was a feed & tack store in the next town. He said one of the employees might know where to go to get a horse trailer repaired.

I crept to the feed store with my flashers on. I was terrified the trailer floor or box was compromised. Liza called a neighboring camper she'd met, who told her that we could board the horses at the fairgrounds if we needed to. I got to the feed store and they gave me the name of a trailer repair shop in town and I proceeded there at 15 mph.

The owner of S&S Body Shop inspected the trailer. He said that the floor wasn't compromised and that it was travel worthy. He said that he wouldn't be able to touch it for at least two weeks.

I mulled over my options and talked with Liza. We were standing by the truck with the atlas opened and lying on the seat. Liza didn't offer any opinion, saying that it was my decision. If it was safe for the horses, we could continue to Washington, but we'd have no electricity or toilet. If anything happened to my horses I'd never forgive myself. I was only 150 miles from Jack's ranch in Challis, Idaho.

I looked at Liza and said, "I quit." I'd never said that ever. It was such a relief.

She said, "I don't blame you."

We got to Challis in a few hours, and Jack's hand, Keith, was there. He was surprised to see me and said that Jack was in Oregon. He helped me unload hay and feed and put the mares into a corral with an adjoining private pasture. I unhitched the trailer in the school bus turn around on the dirt road and left it there.

We drove back to town to a B&B I'd stayed at years ago when visiting Tiara. No one was there but the door was wide open and there was a note pinned to the door frame with the owner's cell number on it. I called the number and left a message. We sat in the picket fence trimmed yard playing with a few kittens that were scampering in and out of the house. Liza got on the internet and figured out that Salt Lake City was on my way back to California and booked a ticket to Florida. She called Dad to let him know that she was coming.

A couple of hours later the B&B owner called back and said that she was at base camp for an outfitting trip her husband was guiding. She said she'd be back late and told me which room to settle into and that I could take my dog and cat in with me.

As soon as I hung up, I got a call from the Pasadena house owner, the one I was trying to rent. She wanted to get a feel for who I was before renting her home to me. After a long chat and asking me a million questions she said I had the place! I was on cloud 9! She told me I could move in next week.

Liza and I brought our bags up to the room. It was so pretty and comfy with old pine furniture and a huge fluffy quilt on the bed. We had our own bathroom with an old cast iron tub. We both felt too dirty to even be in the room so we shed our clothes and cleaned up. We drove to a pizza parlor and had supper.

I was trying to shift gears from camping and all the planning and physical work and driving and being dirty and doing without and sweating and living in a trailer, and spectacular riding and meeting wonderful people, to planning and creating a loving civilized home for my children and me. I was so grateful for the loving care that God had provided me during SHLEP. I felt like a whole relatively normal person again. Thank you, thank you, thank you. What a wild ride it had been. It was finally over.

The next 36 hours were a whirlwind of activity and didn't give me a moment to get upset about what I was about to do. We packed up all my clothes, bedding, pots and pans, the printer, my art supplies and paintings and files into large black trash bags that I threw in the truck bed.

I then walked down to the pasture to kiss my mares good-bye. I thanked them for taking such good care of me for the past year and told them that I hoped they enjoyed this well-deserved vacation on 100 acres of grass with a herd of horses. I burrowed my face into their manes and told them that I loved them so much, that I would see them soon. That I would miss them with all my heart.

That day, I pulled the busted up trailer to Bisch's RV in Idaho Falls. I went over the long list of broken things on the trailer with Riley, the service manager, while Liza looked at new RV's with a salesman. Man, she's really serious, I thought. Riley pointed out unusual wear on my tires and said that the axle might be damaged.

Liza, Jessie, Nalla and I stayed in a pet friendly Motel 6 in Idaho Falls that night. I cried into my pillow until I fell asleep. I missed my horses already. I thought of mom singing that song when we moved to New Jersey in 1960. She was pregnant with my brother and so unhappy about moving.

"California here I come, right back where I started from..."

Chapter 13

The next day I dropped Liza at the Salt Lake City airport. She promised to call me once she got to Dad's. We hugged and she said, "Thank you so much. I had a great time."

I said, "Thank you for all your help. I'm really glad you had a good time. I prayed hard before you joined back up with me. I asked God to use me as his vessel to reach and heal you."

"Well, it worked!" she said. She kissed Jessie good-bye and walked into the terminal. Jessie started whining.

On October 1, I arrived in Pasadena. I moved all my black plastic bags of clothes and things from the trailer into the garage then went to the mattress store to pick up a real bed. Teddy came by a couple of hours later and helped me carry it inside. I could not have done it myself, so I was very grateful he showed up. And it was great to see him, to hear his voice again and get a hug! He didn't stick around very long though. That was the last I saw him for some time.

I had been in the house for a week alone. Emily came Thursday night after going to the Dodger's game with Bob. He still had enough money for those $12,000 seats.

Emily thanked me for coming home and said she was really happy she had a home again. I said, me too. We shared a champagne toast together in the living room. She asked when the handyman was coming to fix her door latch, which led to me complaining a about the house owner coming around so often and worrying about how Jessie behaved with her small children running around. Emily got mad about my complaining and said that I was "judging" the owners. This was not the first time I'd heard this speech from her. She started crying.

As she talked, I began to understand that this was coming from all the years she had listened to me complain about Bob. It didn't matter to her that I had valid complaints because she didn't believe that his behavior towards me was abusive. She didn't know the whole story and it wouldn't help for me to tell her. So, I said nothing and apologized and said I would try not to judge.

She then asked, "Do you think Dad makes sense?" I said no and I told her about a session with Dr Lasarow, Teddy, Bob and me years ago and his opinion that no one could understand Bob.

She said, "You should ask Dad about using Brad's car or your old X-5, they're just sitting at the plant now."

"I have my truck. I don't want his car honey."

She said, "Poor Dad. He's losing his company."

I thought how I'd been hearing this fictitious sob story for 25 years, so I didn't respond. She said, "He's lost everything, but he still annoys me."

I had to be silent, mustering up everything in me not to respond. It was okay for her to say it, but not me. I remember when she'd acted annoyed with me. I remembered my own annoyance with Mom and I wondered if Emily had repressed anger. This thought made me very sad.

Two weeks later, Teddy came by to visit. In the beginning, I thought it might take him some time since he might feel guilty about leaving his Dad all alone. I thought that the peace here would draw him in. But, sadly, that was not happening. It appeared to me that he had chosen not to move in. It was crushing for me to accept this and I felt rejected.

Liza was still in Florida and went with Dad to the doctor where he was told he had "a few weeks left, one to two months if he was lucky."

Liza reported to me that Marty came to the house and ranted on and on to Dad, "You will fucking hate Hospice, John! And fucking Kathy, don't listen to her!" She said that Marty was a raving lunatic and couldn't repeat all the horrible thing that he said to Dad about me. I thought how Dad had told us that he wanted his ashes scattered at sea from Marty's boat.

Liza was with Dad for two weeks. Then she bought an RV and set out for New Jersey on a roundabout route. She said she loved it! Who would have ever thought my sister would be so adventurous?

I had spent three weeks basically alone in the house. I had seen a handful of old friends, but most of the time I was alone. Being alone was not new to me, but it was more pronounced because I was now living in a city and my PTSD jumpiness was more of a problem. I didn't have my horses with me either. I was fighting the feeling that there was something wrong with me that I was alone. I felt adrift without a horse.

I booked flights to go to Florida for a week and had Teddy & Emily join me there for a weekend. A few days before my trip, Dad called and asked me not to come. He said it was chaotic there; there had been a wind storm and the patio chairs had blown into the pool. I was confused and hurt. I remembered Mom talking about the chaos in the morning at the nursing home.

I talked to Dad a couple more times over the next day and he repeated this story, adding "You don't get along with Yvonne." I felt rejected all over again. I cancelled the trip. What a waste of money!

A couple of days later Dad called and asked me if I had cancelled my flights; he wanted me to come now. My first impulse was to not get sucked in, to say no. He might change his mind again and I'd get hurt all over again.

But I booked another flight anyway and came for three days without the children. Dad was now in a wheelchair and only awake about six hours a day. About half that time was spent "cleaning him up" as Yvonne called it, in the privacy of his bedroom, and her trying to get him to eat something. He rarely spoke and when he did, I had a hard time understanding him. Gone was his exuberance and mischievous smile. His whole being was a shadow of what he'd been six months ago.

One afternoon I sat down on Dad's bed and tried to talk

to him about getting hospice care to come in. I explained what they do and how it had helped mom with the physical pain. That he could go to a facility or they could come to his home. He said it sounded like a good idea and he'd like that.

And then he said, "That's assuming that I am dying. I could get better you know."

I asked him who told him this. He didn't answer me. It had to have been Yvonne. That was cruel and evil, I thought. He should be facing death and finding God.

Teddy took care of my animals while I was in Florida. He was still there when I returned. He had finally moved in and I was ecstatic! Teddy didn't seem damaged by his last two years without me; in fact, he seemed very mature and level headed. I loved being with him when he was home. I morphed back into my Mommy role right away. I enjoyed making breakfast for him and watching TV on the sofa with him at night. He made fires for us in the fireplace and this was my wonderful cozy new life. Jessie loved him too. He finally had a rough and tumble boy to wrestle with.

I'd spoken to Dad only once since I visited him. He could barely talk. Every time I called, Yvonne said that he was asleep. Dad's friend, Eddie, called me and said the situation there was "urgent," that Dad was incoherent and having trouble breathing and why wasn't hospice there yet? Eddie and another friend had been visiting Dad daily and Yvonne had been giving them a hard time about coming into the house.

Eddie said, "You have to do something now!"

I called Dad's doctor; he called Dad's house and spoke to Pauline, the weekend caregiver, who told him that Dad needed hospice now and that Yvonne had been dismissing this need all together. Yvonne then grabbed the phone away from her and told the doctor, "Mr. Burns is just fine."

Dr Millstein wasn't fooled and called the hospice company and told them to come to Dad's house immediately. I booked the next flight out of LAX, which was at 7 in the morning.

The hospice nurse arrived and Pauline let her in. The nurse did an assessment and called me saying that Dad was in need of 24/7 nursing immediately, there were open wounds and he couldn't breathe. Dr Millstein called me and said that Dad was in kidney and liver failure. I called Liza who had stopped for the night in northern Florida. She'd called Dad, and Yvonne had told her that Dad was just fine and she should stop for the night to sleep.

Dad died just after midnight. Pauline and the hospice nurse were the only ones there. I got the call as I was packing my bag.

Pauline waited at the house for the funeral home to pick up Dad's body. While I was talking to her on the phone, Yvonne showed back up at Dad's front door and Pauline handed the phone to her. I told her how angry I was that she hadn't called me when Dad declined, she snottily said, "You could have called."

I screamed, "I have been calling! Why did you lie to me? Why didn't you mention any changes in his condition! My Dad died without any of his children there! He was our father!! He was my hero! What are you doing there anyway?"

She said she was getting my phone number to call me.

"Seriously? Do you think I'm a fucking idiot? Get the fuck out of the house right now!"

I arrived in Jupiter the next morning. I cried most of the flight and continued sobbing in the cab. The kind cab driver was playing Christian rock and I asked him to turn it up. He asked me if I was okay. I said no. At the Admiral Cove's guardhouse the guard offered his condolences and told me I may not be able to get into the house, that a locksmith had been there last night.

Liza said that whenever there is money involved, a death stirs up true ugliness. My Dad was living in a house owned by a trust that Bobbi, his deceased wife, had set up that allowed him to live out his life there. After he died, the house reverted to her daughter, Caroline, my step sister. The contents went to his estate, to his children. In the house were all Dad's financial records and personal things. It would be months before we were finally allowed in.

If I had been stronger maybe I could have overcome Yvonne. I'd been torn by Dad's wishes—his words to me that he loved her—that I now knew were mixed up by Yvonne's deceit and because he was so weakened by the cancer, the chemo and his fear of dying. He chose her. He had always been such a good judge of character. And she was obviously a bad person.

I was confused by it all. He wanted to die at home and he did. But it could have been made much more comfortable with hospice care and with someone who really loved him. It killed me to think of him suffering, unable to pick up the phone and call me, to tell me to come and take over. I was racked with guilt and sorrow.

I spoke with Pauline on the phone again and she told me about Dad's last hours. I asked her to speak at Dad's service.

Dad's service was on November 15th, which was coincidentally my Mom's birthday. Teddy and Emily flew in. The service was packed. Neither Marty nor Yvonne was there, which was no big surprise to Liza or me. An Irish Catholic priest spoke eloquently and then Pauline got up. I was glad that Pauline was the one with Dad when he died. She seemed like a good person.

"I was with Mr. Burns the night he passed. I prayed with him and sang Gospel songs to him. As I sang, he mouthed the words to the songs. No sound came out; he couldn't speak anymore, but he didn't stop trying. He passed as we sang this song together."

Pauline's strong voice belted out "How Great Thou Art."

I got a shiver up my spine and started sobbing as I realized that God had brought Pauline to Dad's death bed. Dad was singing with Pauline! He believed! Pauline's faith was rock solid, much stronger than mine and God worked through her. I felt Teddy's strong arm on my back. I wanted faith like Pauline.

I felt awful for quite a while. The mountains of bank forms and life insurance forms and bills and death certificates cluttered my Pasadena bedroom for both my parent's estates and my brother's trust. I missed my horses and riding. I went through my first Christmas without parents. Nothing was going on with the divorce. My life was far from normal. There was still too much stress and I was overwhelmed with anxiety, but I had no panic attacks, so I thought that was a good sign.

Liza stayed in Florida at an RV park in Stuart. One night friends dragged her to a Karaoke bar and she met Ron. They fell in love. She moved her RV to his backyard and moved in with him. They got engaged. I had mixed emotions: I was skeptical about how fast it seemed to be moving and sad because it seemed my last chapter would be solo after all. But I was happy for her; she deserves to be loved. God has a plan.

I was at home recovering from surgery for my sciatic pain when permission was finally granted to enter Dad's home. Liza was escorted in with a cop and my step-sister's attorney, as if we were criminals. Everything of any value, including the camera bag of cash, was gone. The cop told Liza that there was nothing we could do.

Brad was stateside over Christmas. We sat out in the bright sun alone one afternoon. We talked about how family is the most important thing in life. I asked, "Do you remember me back in Illinois, do you have any memories from then?"

"Yes, you were so much fun! And I was so proud you were my mom—big business woman and all that."

I'd thought that none of them remembered the old me, that they only remembered the dishrag part, and I was having trouble proving I was any better than that now too. But Brad remembered and it validated me so I thanked him. He flew back to Spain and graduated in the spring but said he wasn't coming home.

I went to see Lydia. The first thing she said was that she didn't recognize me. She said I look so different, she could see it in my face. My first session was basically catching her up to speed on what I had been through the past 16 months since I last saw her. I paid her for the year that she saw me without charging me and it felt good. Lydia, who also does divorce mediation, gave me the name of another divorce lawyer. I continued seeing Lydia and she said that it was more important that I be with Dreamy than that I pay her, so I made arrangements for Dreamy to be hauled down. I asked Lydia why SHLEP hadn't worked. She said that it had; she thought I was much better, but that the divorce conflict was blocking my final resolution.

I made an appointment with Ellen Driscoll, the lawyer Lydia had recommended. Ellen was compassionate and fascinated with my SHELP story. In our first meeting, she brought up the possibility of Bob trying to cash in on any money I might make from a book or movie, something I hadn't even considered before. Now, when Bob stalled or missed deadlines, my attorney did something about it. She was always quick to respond to my calls and emails too. But as legal work started getting done, $20,000 retainer checks were requested. Between that, tuition and my $3,400 a month rent I was bleeding money. I thanked Dad every time I wrote a big check.

I started re-doing all my state paintings on 18" x 24" canvases in oils. I was invited to exhibit them at a group show that spring, my very first art show. I started writing my book, which was much harder than I thought it would be. Reliving my marriage memories put me right back there and I quit several times.

In May, Dreamy arrived skinny and lame. Wildflower had pushed her away from the hay all winter and I got mad at Jack for not doing something about it. Within a couple of months Dreamy gained the weight back. She continued to have soundness issues on and off for the next couple of years; progressively worsening arthritis in her crooked leg seemed to be her biggest issue. I rode her when she was good and there was a magical energy field where our bodies touched. My iPod played "God Songs" and I still got chills up and down my body.

Emily took me to church again. I sat next to her in the high school theater of Monrovia High School as a vocalist sang, "Holy Spirit you are welcome here, come flood this place and fill the atmosphere. Your glory God is what our hearts long for, to be overcome with your presence, Lord!" Chills ran through my body and I was hooked. I found the pastor just as inspirational.

I joined a small group to study the book of James, where I learned how a Christian lives their lives according to God's plan. Our group served dinner one night at Hoving Home, a women's Christian rehab home in Pasadena. I asked how long they were expected to study the Bible every day and the guide told me, "Eight hours a day." Eating dinner with the women, I heard invincible strength their voices and saw true joy in their faces. The stories from their past were tragic and desperate. Their transformations were awe inspiring to me. When I was asked what I thought about our visit at our next small group meeting, I said, "I want faith like theirs. I think I need to read the Bible more." I started reading it in the mornings before the sun rose, curled up in a chair with a cup of coffee.

One night when Emily was at home, I apologized the right way, with no excuses. "Emily, I'm sorry for all the pain I caused you; please forgive me."

She started to cry, "Do you know how long I've waited to hear this?"

I grabbed her shoulders. "I'm sorry that I didn't do it

right the first time, I didn't know how to then. I made excuses and that's not a real apology. Thank you for taking me to church. You saved me, you know."

"Do you know how much this means to me? Do you know how long I've been praying for you to find God? All I ever wanted was that you'd love God as much as I did. That's why I wanted you to come home so badly."

I was crying now too, but these were tears of joy and it felt good. I wrapped my arms around her as I silently prayed, God, bless this amazing young woman. Thank you for letting me be her mother.

Ellen was now dealing with Bob's third lawyer. This one was a Beverly Hills divorce attorney to the stars, Mr. Leeds. Ellen said that he was more professional to deal with than the previous ones and that the divorce would now start moving along. She contacted the Chicago lawyer who'd written our prenup and found he was now "elderly" and his files had been destroyed in a flood.

Our depositions took two full days and were very stressful. Bob's was first. I'd never been to a deposition before. I was told not to speak, but could give Ellen notes or request a break to speak to her in private. It was held in Beverly Hills at Bob's attorney's office and there was a court reporter there. Ellen asked Bob questions that were often to be answered with yes or no or a date. The deposition took four hours and the subject was our date of separation. A few months back, he'd come up with a separation date of 2003 but then changed it to 2006.

Ellen effectively destroyed Bob's credibility on the date of separation. Bob and his attorney called about six breaks to go speak privately and Bob needed questions restated frequently. His attorney reprimanded him and seemed exasperated with him on occasion.

He contradicted almost everything he said within

minutes of saying it. He denied that signatures were his; there was at least a half hour devoted to his signature, which is more like a scribble.

My deposition went well and Bob accepted my date of separation.

Three years and eleven months after I'd filed for divorce, I sat in an LA courtroom.

We'd been there for hours already listening to the ramblings of Bob and his attorney. We were arguing over the legal definition of the word "terminate."

The judge said, "Mr. Roettig, if you decide to pursue this legal argument, it will end up in the California Supreme court and will take at least another year to get a ruling. It will cost you both at least another $100,000 in attorney fees. I suggest you come up with a compromising offer to settle this case."

He was going to kill me with this divorce. The continued chaos and conflict made me feel like a trapped victim all over again. I was ready to just walk away from it all. I quit!

I heard the judge say, "Mr. Roettig, are you making an offer?"

Bob said, "Yes."

"Then repeat it as an offer, to Mrs. Roettig."

I snapped to attention. Ellen looked at me sternly, reminding me not to speak.

Bob looked at me and stammered his offer.

I proclaimed, "I accept!"

Ellen grabbed me by the arm, "Reconsider, Kathy, it's not nearly enough!"

I knew she was right, but I wasn't going to pass up the opportunity to end it now, if that was possible.

I asked her, "Could I be divorced today?"

She deflated and said, "Yes."

I looked at the judge and he concurred. I looked at Bob,

the man I had once loved with all my heart, the father of my children.

I said, "I accept."

I was now Kathy Burns again! I wasn't prepared for the physical euphoria that over took my body and carried me out of the courtroom. It felt as if it was God himself. It's over, it was finally over. My divorce was finalized on July 29, 2016.

Several times during my three years in Pasadena, Emily said to me, "Mom, you just can't move to Wyoming; it's too far away and I want you to be a part of my children's lives." Emily didn't even have a boyfriend, but if she wanted me to be there for her future family, I did too. So, I started looking for horse property in southern California.

In late 2016, a new friend, Marcy, called me and asked, "You wanna go visit Tehachapi for the weekend?

On July 8, 2017, I pulled onto my property in the Tehachapi Mountains of California with Wildflower and Tiara in the trailer. Liza was by Dreamy's pen; she said, "Dreamy is so excited!" I smiled back at her.

I'd hauled through the night to avoid the desert heat and was happy to cut the truck's engine. Jessie jumped out of the back seat and ran to her. I saw Ron out in the meadow, putting up the new pasture fence. He looked up and waved. I've never known anyone that works as hard as that man does. Dreamy was joyfully galloping circles and bucking, tossing her head and whinnying as the two in the trailer called back to her and stomped on the floor.

As I opened the trailer's back doors, I looked at my left hand where I'd recently had "Jesus" tattooed and whispered, "Thank you for getting us home safely today. And thank you for blessing me beyond my wildest dreams."

I believe God wants me to tell this story. He fixed me when I was broken. This is His story and I pray that I have told it well.

God can fix you no matter how broken you think you are. God loves all his children; He is always by your side. Turn to Him, trust Him and watch to see what He will do. You will be amazed.

Made in the USA
Columbia, SC
25 July 2019